The

Graphic Designer's Guide

to Portfolio Design

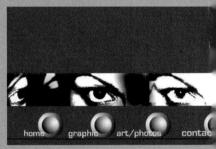

The
Graphic Designer's Guide
to Portfolio Design

SECOND EDITION

Debbie Rose Myers

WILEY

JOHN WILEY & SONS, INC.

Library of Congress Cataloging-in-Publication Data:

Myers, Debbie Rose.
   The graphic designer's guide to portfolio design / Debbie Rose Myers. — 2nd ed.
      p. cm.
   Includes index.
   ISBN 978-0-470-18476-9 (pbk.)
 1. Art portfolios--Design. 2. Design services—Marketing. 3. Graphic arts—Vocational guidance. 4. Computer graphics. I. Title.
   NC1001.M94 2009
   741.6068'8—dc22

                          2008011008

Printed in the United States of America

10 9 8 7 6 5 4 3

contents

Computers? In art? I remember telling my boyfriend (later to become my husband) Glenn that computers would *never* be used in art. As I watched him carry those long boxes of computer punch cards to class

each week, I chuckled, secure in the knowledge that artists had no need for computers. How wrong I was!

Back when I studied graphic design and art in college, you learned how to prepare art for printing with materials such as Rubylith and stat cameras. Rubylith was a thin, semitransparent acetate material that was used to block out areas of color. I remember spending hours cutting CMYK (cyan, magenta, yellow, and key) color separations with an X-ACTO knife. Type involved an even crazier process. You would go to a gigantic drawer filled with type of various sizes and styles and pick the sheets of type closest to the sizes you needed, because, unlike today, type came in only a few sizes. Then you would use Popsicle sticks to laboriously rub (or set) the type in place on the page. Stat cameras gave you the ability to "resize" your type through the photographic reproduction method. You would first photograph the type, then enlarge it and paste it down on the final boards. My tools of choice in those days were the T

square, the triangle, and my trusty nonphoto blue pencil, used to draw lines and grids for the type. Naturally, it took forever to build a layout. Who knew that only ten years later, I would be teaching computerized page layout to a whole new generation of art majors!

Why a book on digital portfolios? Once upon a time, it was enough to have a great set of boards to demonstrate your design ability. You went to an interview, talked about your credentials, opened your portfolio, discussed your work, and if all went well, you were offered a job. Today, though, things are a little different.

- You go to job-specific Web sites, enter your credentials, and begin searching for a job that matches your requirements.
- You design a Web site, post it at a place established specifically for your profession, send out announcements, and wait for job offers.
- You are asked to submit a CD of your work before you are even invited in for an interview.

I teach at a college that is always on the cutting edge of design trends. Students are instructed in industry-specific software. But I have learned one thing in my 30 years of teaching: design majors are true right-brained thinkers. You say, "programming language," and they say, "bye-bye"!

Here's how this book on digital portfolios came about. Over the years, I have spent much time trying to find ways to introduce complex computer programs to creative majors in order to enable them to embrace the newest technologies. This book, then, is for all my students—past, present, and future—and is designed to allay their fears, answer their questions, and ultimately empower them to succeed.

I know it takes time, energy, and patience to create a digital portfolio that will get you the job of your dreams. If you're just starting out, you have many multimedia programs to evaluate. You want one that meets your needs but doesn't take a lifetime to master. You want proven interface design techniques that are easy to understand and utilize. You want to know what problems you may encounter and how to solve them. Or maybe you're already at the next level—you know all about the popular programs but want to learn more about interface metaphors. Whatever your level—novice, intermediate, or professional—this book will help you learn how to create a successful digital portfolio.

What's New in This Edition?

This second edition presents interviews with leaders in the graphic design and advertising industries at the end of every chapter. They will offer you their many years of wisdom and practical experience regarding the interview process. Their answers are funny and real, and they offer sound advice on successful interviewing. I know you will enjoy their insights.

Also new in this edition is the "designer's challenge"—one or more project assignments that appear at the end of every chapter. So often students come to me and say that they're stuck and don't know what to make next. These projects will not only challenge your unique design talents but also enhance your portfolio.

If You Are a First-Time Reader

Chapters 1 through 5 of this book will give you some perspective on the digital portfolio. Think of it as the whys and wherefores of interface design. You'll learn what should be included in a good portfolio and see a discussion of what stays and what goes. If you need to generate new pieces for your "port," you'll find ways to jump-start your creativity.

Once you have some projects, Chapters 5 through 8 will help you organize them into a cohesive system. There are chapters that discuss CD-ROM design versus Web design. You will learn about all the most popular multimedia programs and find many tips and tricks to make your time on the computer more productive.

If you are already a design professional, familiar with the software, Chapters 5, 6, and 9 will show you new ways to utilize your knowledge, including various techniques for designing efficient yet creative maneuverability features for your multimedia port.

If you're struggling with type and color, head directly to Chapter 8, which presents a detailed discussion of type issues, not just in design but also on the computer. Confused about what typefaces work best on the Internet? You'll find answers on that topic in Chapter 7 as well.

If you're worried about technical problems, don't miss Chapter 13, which examines what can go wrong in every phase of your portfolio development.

Do you know how to write a résumé, an artist's statement, or a cover letter? Have you taken a job interview lately? Do you know what questions the interviewer is prohibited by law from asking? Chapters 3 and 14 offer examples of résumés and techniques for taking a successful interview.

This book focuses both on the ever-changing world of technology and on the enduring principles and techniques of interface design, which do not change over time. It is my hope that you will find this book both supportive and enlightening—and that it will be the key to your success.

Debbie Rose Myers

acknowledgments

This book would not have been possible without the support and inspiration of many people, and I would like to take a moment to acknowledge these wonderful friends and colleagues.

Throughout this book, you will see art by many of my most talented students. I thank them all! I especially want to express gratitude to Julie Ruiz, Ryan Skinner, Sigrun Eggertsdottir, and Etni Estrella for their insights and art.

In particular, special thanks go to the many fine folks who agreed to be interviewed for this book: Christine David, Stephan Donche, Steph Doyle, Tom Kane, Nancy Karamarkos, Jamie Kluetz, Andrea Lubell, Blaise Nauyokas, Dani Nordin, Barry Rosenberg, Rick Tuckerman, and Roberto de Vicq de Cumptich.

Kyle Fisk, associate professor, Sinclair Community College, and Donna Teel, assistant professor, computer graphics design, University of Mary Hardin-Baylor, also deserve special thanks. They helped me to track down some of the best student design projects in recent years. Thanks, too, to Kim Metzger, from Pina Zangaro, who provided the images of today's best-looking designer portfolios.

Many of my colleagues, who are industry professionals as well, graciously allowed me to feature their artwork in this book: M. Kathleen Colussy, Christine David, Randy Gossman, Paul Kane, and Linda Weeks. Howard T. Katz, Catherine Ramey, and Mark LaRiviere also provided the wonderful artist's statements you will read in Chapter 4. The compelling and dazzling art contributed by these fabulous friends has truly enriched the book.

I am most grateful for the encouragement I received from Margaret Cummins, senior editor, Lauren Poplawski, editorial assistant, and Jacqueline Beach, senior production editor, at John Wiley & Sons. They knew when to support me and when to just let me do my thing.

And deepest thanks to my beloved husband, Glenn, who always knew when to hug me, when to leave me alone with my laptop computer, and when to bring me lots of chocolates!

The
Graphic Designer's Guide
to Portfolio Design

Fort Lauderdale, Florida
Graphic Design - B.S.
October 2005 to December 200
Dean's List - Winter 2005, Spring
Honors List - Summer 2006, Fall,

Buffalo State College
Buffalo, New York
Communication Arts
January 2004 to May 2005

Kent State University
Kent, Ohio
Interior Design
August 2002 to December 2003

education

3D Modeling

1

The Portfolio Process— Start to Finish

OBJECTIVE:
TO USE MY CREATIVE KNOWLEDGE AN
A GRAPHIC DESIGNER IN THE ADVERT

"Can you start on Wednesday?" The words floated across the table. I paused for a moment before answering. "I believe I can free up the remainder of the week." (Not that I had had anything lined up.) The dean of

education handed me a completed teaching schedule, shook my hand, and said, "The meetings are all day Wednesday. You start teaching on the following Monday. I'll need all of your syllabi by next week." I nodded and mumbled, "No problem." As I stood up, the dean spoke once more. "We're taking a chance on you, so don't let us down." Taking a slow breath so as not to hyperventilate, I said, "I'll do my best." I picked up my portfolio, walked out of the office, and headed back to my car.

This certainly wasn't my first job interview. I had completed the interviewing process many times before. What made this interview so nerve-racking was that I wanted the job so desperately. The expression "Never let them see you sweat" came to my mind as the adrenaline

finally gave out. Then it hit me: "I'm teaching college!" I hurried to the nearest phone to call home. I couldn't wait to break the news about my new position.

So why was I offered that job? Was it my interview skills? My attire? My positive attitude? Nope! It was my portfolio—plain and simple. I had brought to the interview a portfolio of design projects that I had completed in college plus a number of projects that I had created in my freelance business. Those pieces, together with my ability to discuss the portfolio projects and what they represented, were what got me the job.

Building a portfolio and interviewing for jobs is possibly the most intense process you will ever undertake as you begin or advance your career. Your portfolio must reflect the very best of what you can contribute to a

above Preparation is the key to a successful portfolio.

right Be prepared to discuss your art. You will be asked to explain why you created a piece in a certain way. Your ability to articulate an answer can influence how you are perceived as an artist and web designer.

potential employer as an artist/designer. And the pivotal moment in your interview process begins as the employer slowly opens your portfolio, allowing it to reveal the best of what you have to offer.

You Need a Portfolio

As you arrive for your job interview, you notice that another applicant is leaving. And when your interview concludes and you are departing, you see that yet another applicant is waiting. Assume that each of these three candidates has equal qualifications for this job, a similar college degree, and an excellent interview. How does the company make a decision?

No doubt about it, the competition is tough in today's job market. So you cannot just say you are an extraordinary designer: you must provide proof of your qualifications. That's the purpose of your portfolio: it demonstrates your skills and abilities. Instead of just talking during a job interview about what you have done or can do, you can show samples of your work. Your professional portfolio showcases your talents. In this way, a well-designed portfolio can help you stand out from the other candidates. It gives you the edge.

It was once thought that only fine artists, graphic designers, architects, and fashion designers needed a

portfolio to get a job. Not anymore. Today, portfolios are used to secure jobs in many different areas. Teachers, interior designers, multimedia and Web designers, engineers, and journalists can all use a professional portfolio to advance their careers. A portfolio for each of these professionals will be unique to his or her field of specialization; however, the overall purpose is to present a unified body of work that represents what the candidate can offer. Thus, regardless of your design background, you can develop a portfolio that highlights your accomplishments and shows off your talent. Portfolios are especially necessary for people seeking a new job, changing career fields, or negotiating for a promotion or raise.

It's one thing to say, "I have great organizational skills," but when you can back up that statement with examples, you're demonstrating that you can do the job. It's the difference between saying, "I can do it . . . really!" and showing you can—the difference between talk and action.

Obviously, you need to feel comfortable in the job environment, and the company must have confidence in you as well. A job almost always requires a match of personalities—yours and the potential employer's. I once took an interview at a community college. I had made the initial cut from 175 applicants to the final 5 who would be interviewed. The unusual thing about this particular interview was that about 20 minutes into

Jonathan Daiello's design skills are clearly apparent; hence, this piece would be an excellent way to showcase his ability to design logos.

the session, I began to notice a pattern to the questioning: certain individuals on the interviewing committee would ask certain questions. It really surprised them when I turned to the next person, smiled, and said, "I believe the next question is yours." They were slightly taken aback, then started laughing. That interview, scheduled for 45 minutes, was really good and ended up lasting almost two hours! Only a few days later, I was offered the job.

If you look up the definition of *portfolio* in a dictionary, you'll probably read something like "a portable collection of paper and artifacts that demonstrates one's experience and skills." That's pretty vague, considering that these materials can be made up of almost anything—artwork, writing samples, award certificates, even performance reviews. Other samples might include customer-satisfaction surveys or graphs that chart improvements in products or services based on your contributions. The point is, the artifacts you include in your portfolio should always be chosen carefully to highlight your most relevant skills and achievements.

A Portfolio Must Stand Alone

Suppose for a moment that you are not allowed to remain in the room while a potential employer is viewing your portfolio. Will he or she be able to understand the pieces it contains or your participation in those projects? Think of what it's like to watch a silent movie—no sound. You have to interpret what you see using only the images.

Looking at your "port" is like watching that silent movie. The body of work has to stand alone. The point is, once you have selected what to include in your portfolio, organize the pieces in a logical manner. You may decide to arrange your work by strengths or chronologically. Whichever way you choose, document your involvement with each project. For instance, if you include a brochure from a training program, make sure the interviewer can tell whether you designed the brochure, attended the class, or organized the event. Add a simple caption to clarify your connection to the piece.

This project, which I created to promote a study-related trip, demonstrates that portfolio opportunities are always available. Don't hesitate to volunteer your services as a designer.

Start Building Your Portfolio

The hardest part about building a portfolio is deciding where to begin. You know that you must include your best art in the port, but just how do you go about organizing the presentation? You may have several dozen pieces of your work or just a few. As you begin to develop your portfolio, you must first think about which pieces are worthy of inclusion. Your design background and history will most certainly influence this process. If you are still in college, your portfolio will more than likely contain a collection of projects that reflect the classes you have completed. In contrast, a professional in the field will exhibit a different set of layouts based, at least in part, on completed client jobs. Consider the following situations for which it makes sense to develop or enhance a portfolio.

Brian Anderson creates a wonderful set of direct-mail pieces. When seen together in a portfolio, they make an unmistakable statement about his abilities.

You Are a Professional in a Related Field

You have been working in advertising but want to move into the area of graphic design. You are a fine artist who illustrates or paints, and you have a number of finished pieces but don't feel that they best reflect your current design sensibilities. In the case of the advertiser or the fine artist, consider taking one of your design projects, illustrations, or other art pieces and creating a layout that shows off the work; in other words, demonstrate the application of the piece. A good illustration will look even better as an editorial spread. A clever advertisement will look even more professional when it is presented as an "actual" ad in a magazine.

Perhaps you have worked in a related field but want to change the direction of your career. In this case, consider displaying early versions of any client-based projects. You may have lots of sketches for ideas that were eliminated in the course of choosing the final concept. I have a number of pieces I created that were never selected. They allow the viewer to see how the project progressed, from its beginnings to the final solution. Don't feel you have to hide the final piece if it wasn't the one you would have selected. (I have frequently felt that many of my initial concepts were actually better than the ones the client eventually chose.) The very fact that

you have worked with a client may be enough to convey the impression that you're a "seasoned" employee.

Or perhaps, as part of your job, you were a member of several design-related work groups. Why not display the art developed by the group, then clearly define your involvement with the project? Including these concept designs in the portfolio shows your range of design abilities and the thought process involved, and it freshens up the look of your port. In addition, it demonstrates that you can work effectively in a group environment.

Demonstrate expertise and technical skills. Demonstrate that you are a problem solver. Employers want to know not only what work experience you have had but what skills you gained. Explain your involvement with a project and how you contributed to its overall success. You want to be able to demonstrate that you are a top-notch designer who is both creative and self-disciplined.

You Are Still a College Student

Much of the design work you complete in college or a technical school can be considered for inclusion in your portfolio. You may, for example, have recently finished a series of design-based classes in which your professors challenged you to prepare a variety of creative pieces to the design criteria they established. Take a good look at these projects. Many of them demonstrate your style of design. And because student portfolios tend to be general in nature, be especially aware of projects that show your area of expertise. If you are an excellent illustrator or photographer, make sure your portfolio reflects that special talent. (Selecting appropriate projects is discussed further in Chapter 2.)

You Are Searching for New Ways to Develop Artwork

Artwork prepared while you complete your basic studies is important, but you might also want to consider these additional options for generating art projects:

- Joining an art organization or a design group in your area
- Participating in industry organizations, such as the American Advertising Federation or the Society of Illustrators
- Applying for an internship
- Entering a community-based contest

Each of these venues provides an excellent opportunity to show what you can do. And the best part is that you could end up with a printed piece that demonstrates real-world experience. The point is, don't be afraid to show off.

This colorful résumé, designed by Soraya Saltiel, is a part of a complete self-promotional package that includes business cards and envelopes.

Newsletters can be created free of charge for a local organization. A newsletter such as this, created by Nicole Weik, is a great way to develop pieces for your portfolio and (who knows?) maybe get a freelance job or two.

You Participate in a Summer Program or Attend a Special Workshop

Special seminars in design are offered in most major cities throughout the year. And companies such as Adobe and Quark regularly offer free demonstrations of their best-selling software. Firms that specialize in training frequently hold one-day workshops in design-related areas. Workshops such as these look great on your résumé. They show that you are going to work hard to stay current in your field of specialization.

College summer travel or study-abroad programs offer more opportunities to generate art that can enhance your résumé and portfolio. For example, as part of my master of fine arts program, I studied Native American culture and art for two summers in Santa Fe, New Mexico. During those months, I attended week-long workshops and created a number of artistic pieces, many of which were incorporated into my portfolio. I highly recommend that you explore any opportunity to advance your design skills.

Was this thrilling editorial spread, created by Lina Hererra, completed in college or in the field? A truly professional piece gives no hint of its origin; it simply shows off your artistic skills and abilities. This one is very unique.

You Design for Family and Friends

Never miss an opportunity to generate artwork that you might be able to include in your portfolio. Perhaps your aunt is starting her own business. Offer to design her business card and stationery package. Maybe she could use some interior design advice for her new building or home office. And designing a professional-looking Web site would most certainly make you her favorite relative. Likewise, your friends (especially the noncreative types) will appreciate your designing creative résumés for them. And why not create original holiday or birthday cards? In short, keep your eyes open for project opportunities that will help you build up a body of work. At a weekend art festival, I once met an artist who created the most wonderful watercolors. I ended up talking her into allowing me to create her monthly national newsletter. You never know where the next design opportunity will come from.

You Take Advantage of Freelance Opportunities

Don't overlook the chance to take on some freelance work. Most design schools feature a freelance bulletin board where local companies post their need for design assistance. Check out this board on a regular basis, then contact any company of interest and offer your services. The prospect of approaching potential clients may sound a little intimidating while you're still a student, but the rewards are many. You'll generate some artwork and earn a little cash as well. If you are unsure about what to charge, there are a number of ways to research the going rates. Books such as *Artist's & Graphic Designer's Market 2007*, edited by Mary Cox; *Starting Your Career as a Freelance Illustrator or Graphic Designer*, by Michael Fleishman (2001); and *Pricing Photography: The Complete Guide to Assignment & Stock Prices*, by Michael Heron and David MacTavish (2002), will help you determine your costs and profits.

You Advance Your Design Skills Using the Barter System

In addition to freelancing, another viable way of marketing your design expertise is via the barter system. The benefits here are twofold: you get some valuable design experience as well as some (nonmonetary) compensation. I once had a student who went to local restaurants and offered to redesign their menus. In return, he received gift cards for food from the establishments. He not only generated some great art but also got to sample some terrific food. What a deal!

You Design for Yourself

If you don't already have a personal identity package, design one. Start by designing a distinctive logo that truly represents you. Then use that logo to create your own business card, résumé, and stationery. You might also design an invoice for billing freelance clients. Additionally, you might create a self-promotional package. Use any design strategy you can think of to create memorable pieces.

You Compile Examples of Improvements You've Made to Bad Design

You've seen them: those horrible ads in the back of magazines and newspapers. Find a particularly bad one and create a series of interpretations to improve on it. All types of design majors can use a comparable strategy. Bad design is everywhere! If you're an interior designer, find a less-than-effective interior space and show how good design can improve the environment. Likewise, industrial designers can demonstrate how home appliances, children's toys, and computers can be more effectively designed. And there is nothing so compelling as making upgrades and improvements to a really horrible Web site.

Tailor the Portfolio to Your Area of Specialization

The second step in the portfolio creation process is the most important: deciding which type of job you're interested in. Each of the design disciplines contains many different areas of specialization, and you will need to tailor your portfolio to the job you want. For example, let's consider some of the job possibilities in the field of graphic design:

- Layout or production artists
- Assistant art directors
- Broadcast graphic artists
- Mock-up artists
- Spot illustrators
- Web page or multimedia designers
- Prepress specialists
- Presentation artists
- Storyboard illustrators
- Senior designers
- Art directors or assistant art directors
- Corporate design managers
- Freelance artists
- Creative directors

Creating a mock editorial magazine spread is a great way to challenge yourself. This spread, by Jacqueline Thrailkill, reminds us that regardless of your background, you can develop pieces worth including in your portfolio.

This beautiful calendar, created by Kristalyn L. Burns, not only showcases her ability to illustrate but also demonstrates that she understands how the illustration will look in print.

This corporate identification package, created by Megan Fore, illustrates her consistent use of color, type, and design elements.

Similarly, the field of advertising offers a vast variety of job opportunities, including the following:
- Advertising and promotion managers
- Marketing and sales managers
- Account executives and supervisors
- Public relations managers and specialists
- Purchasing agents
- Market research analysts
- Art directors
- Graphic designers
- Lobbyists (for industry trade organizations, unions, or public-interest groups)
- Media and research specialists
- Editors
- Writers and authors
- Advertising sales agents
- Demonstrators and product promoters

Although every design portfolio will look different depending on the field, the basic objective is always the same: to create a portfolio that demonstrates your unique ability.

Identify Your Strengths

In order to develop a portfolio that highlights your accomplishments and shows off your skills, you must blend two different concepts. First, your portfolio must give a snapshot of your creative talents and imagination. Second, and more important, your port must represent your ability to communicate design concepts and ideas. As such, your portfolio must be an effective tool for promoting yourself. So, regardless of the job you're applying for—designer, illustrator, or photographer—include in your portfolio only those samples that match that particular job. Beautifully designed greeting cards will make no impression if the job calls for a logo designer. Remember, you can always add samples of other work you have created in the back of your portfolio. Label those pieces and include them in a separate section. Or you can create a second portfolio just to show how versatile you are. I actually have two portfolios. I move pieces in and out depending on the type of job I am applying for.

Throughout this book, you will find all types of techniques to assist you in your job search, including the creation of traditional paper résumés, interactive CDs and DVDs, and even Web sites. Just remember, there are still more ways to find jobs, some of which are very twenty-first century. E-mail, blogs, job search–specific sites, video résumés, and online networking sites are just as important as your portfolio. These new methods for finding jobs are discussed as well in the upcoming pages.

The most important thing to remember when creating a portfolio is to ensure that your work always represents your best efforts. Never include a weak piece in your port even if it demonstrates the skills that a particular job requires. A friend once told me that a designer will always be judged by the weakest pieces in the portfolio. If you're not sure what to include, ask for advice. Consult with professionals and professors. Allow them to critique your work. It may make you a little uncomfortable, but it will help you to focus on your strengths. Also, as you gain experience, don't forget to replace older design work in your port with newer, fresher designs; and, whenever possible, use professional work.

Make eye contact and demonstrate your confidence. You would be amazed how many people cannot look you in the eye! Practice in front of a mirror if necessary, but do be ready when the time comes.

Decide Whether to Diversify or Focus Your Portfolio

There are a number of differing viewpoints about whether your portfolio should be diversified or focused. Many companies feel that you should diversify and show a wide range of pieces. On the other hand, I have spoken with many art directors who believe that the portfolio should highlight a well-defined style by displaying art created within that narrow range. The problem with a narrowly focused port is that it can exclude you from a number of different jobs. A port that focuses exclusively on, say, corporate identification work may not get you an interview in a company that's looking for someone to design packages. Or a graphic designer who creates art with an urban approach might be passed over

I created this poster to promote a class in Web design. It demonstrates that portfolio opportunities are always available. Don't hesitate to volunteer your design services. It will help you develop new port pieces.

These playful brochures, by the talented Aron Fine, demonstrate a very highly developed sense of color.

Ilse Simon creates an inspired cover for her annual report. Soft corkboard and grommets are used to give a very tactile edge to her piece for a building company.

by a design firm that caters to a corporate clientele. Simply put, a diversified portfolio opens you up to a wider range of job opportunities.

So do you diversify or focus your portfolio? The answer is . . . it depends. If the description of a particular job appears to ask for specific skills, you should tailor your work to the position you are applying for. However, if you are just starting out, it is better to have a portfolio that showcases the many different types and styles of work you can offer as a designer.

Some companies recommend taking a commonsense approach. Every potential employer has an idea of what should be in a portfolio, and most agree that the pieces in a portfolio should be selected to demonstrate what the designer wants to say about himself or herself. If possible, have a couple of extra pieces on hand. Perhaps the best advice is to research each company and determine what it might be looking for in a designer. Then rotate your design work into and out of your portfolio as the job indicates.

This much is clear: your portfolio should present the best examples of your designs and concepts. The pieces you ultimately choose for your portfolio will stand as an indication of your ability to organize, conceptualize, and present. Whatever artwork you decide to include, make sure that each piece represents the best of what you offer as a designer. Keep the goal in mind: you want a potential employer to decide that he or she must hire you in order to gain access to your unique design abilities and skills!

Be Prepared

Once you have created a portfolio, always keep it at the ready. You never know when an opportunity to interview for a new job (or a promotion) will arise. And when opportunity does knock, you will be ready to answer the inevitable question about your qualifications by opening your port and demonstrating those qualifications. "I've created a set of projects that would really contribute to your company. Here, let me show them to you." This book will help you stay prepared.

An Interview with James Kluetz

James Kluetz is the vice president and creative director for Pinpoint Communications as well as the creative director of Brand Tango. Mr. Kluetz graduated from the Fashion Institute of Technology in New York. You can find out more about Mr. Kluetz and his work at www.brandtango.com.

1 What qualities do you look for in an applicant?

Typically nowadays, before we meet the person, we meet the portfolio . . . . Before I meet someone I meet their electronic portfolio . . . so the electronic port helps me to weed out the people who will not be able to succeed in this company. We are a very busy agency . . . so you need to do something extra to drive us to your site. . . . When I get those files, I want some context for what I'm looking at. How was a piece conceived? What was the budget allocated for the design? What were the influences on the design? What is that little extra something in the work?

At the very least, label your work and give me a short explanation of the purpose of the piece . . . .

If we do decide to call the person in, that person needs to be prepared to talk about the piece . . . even though the piece may not have been actually printed in the real world. I am also looking for a sophisticated design vocabulary during the interview . . . I want to see a sketchbook that clearly shows how you get to the piece . . . . Where is the strategic thinking that goes into it?

2 In your opinion, what makes a successful interview?

There's a fork in the road when you graduate . . . . You can either do basic design work, or you can really become a true creative and move fully into the design realm . . . .

So first you have to get your foot in the door! *[laughs]* It's all about the whole collective team, so you will need to demonstrate how you will fit into this particular community . . . . Once you get the interview, be confident. Make eye contact . . . and take some time to make a thoughtful arrangement of the art in your port . . . Lead with the strongest piece up front and again at the back . . . . And once again, gain the ability to discuss your work . . . . I am looking for someone who is well-spoken and talks about their designs in the context of business.

Understand paper, printing techniques, embossing . . . . Understand the mechanical aspects—type usage . . . widows, kerning.

You should always have questions for the interviewer, so research the company. Find out about the awards we've won . . . . Be prepared to say things like "I really liked some of the projects I saw at your Web site, and here's why . . . ."

This should be fun, and you should represent yourself as someone who wants to be part of the personality of the agency. Your sense of humor should come through during the interview.

3 Has the Internet had an effect on your interview process?

Absolutely! I want you to find a way to stand out from every other designer applying for the job. So create a unique self-promotional piece that will drive me to your Web site . . . a small booklet with intriguing type that

teases me to visit your site . . . . Lay out a cool résumé. Send me your PDF files on a small CD and attach it to an extreme key chain design.

4 What are the five best things job candidates say that impress you during an interview? What are the five worst?

Best

- Be able to comment on my agency's artwork.
- Be able to talk about typography. (I want to understand your taste level.)
- The emerging trends in the industry as a whole.
- Be able to explain your career goals.
- Be able to describe your understanding of the position you are applying for.
- Have questions.

Worst

- Not be[ing] able to say why you created something.
- "I'm not good under pressure."
- No ability to discuss a piece.
- No sense of humor . . . This is supposed to be fun . . . so relax . . . .

5 What are skills that really help all artists succeed regardless of their specialty?

- Typography.
- Cultural knowledge of the world.
- The ability to spend some time conceptualizing a project.

- Passion.
- The ability to question and refine your own work.
- The quest to get better.

6 What advice would you offer to designers looking to impress you with the presentation of their work?

- Use multiple levels of presentation.
- Understand that people are busy and you need to find a way to distinguish yourself from the rest . . . . We will prescreen, so how can you get yourself to the top?

- Follow up.
- Try and then try again.
- Determination.
- Conceptualizing your approach to the job.
- The ability to market yourself.

challenge

Designer's Challenge

Can you produce a consistent set of magazine pages that have a similar look and feel?

Create a four-page editorial spread using highly stylized images or your own illustrations. The designs should exhibit a sophisticated collection of colors and fonts. Don't forget to add elements such as an author, page numbers, magazine name, and month.

Cynthia Grynspan invents a great solution for this designer's challenge. Her editorial is engaging and shows a marvelous color set.

Planning Your Portfolio

If the portfolio functions as an evaluation tool for identifying the best applicant for a given position, then the way it is designed and arranged serves to demonstrate the designer's organizational skills. The initial layout and overall display of the work in your portfolio should be the focus of your first attempts at its creation. You want to make it as easy as possible for a prospective employer to examine your work. To help you in that effort, this chapter begins with a discussion of the planning process for the portfolio and concludes with an examination of layout styles for the portfolio. (Note that this book is written to include many different design disciplines, so the concepts presented here often span the arts.)

It is best to start considering your portfolio as soon as you determine that you will need one. For many of you, that will be when you enter college or technical school. Developing the portfolio as you advance your education gives you the best opportunity to create top-quality pieces. Think about it this way: with each class

assignment, you create a new piece to satisfy the requirements of that class. Thus, in time, you can build up a body of art. These pieces become the basis of your first developmental portfolio. Although this is an exciting process, at times it can also be overwhelming. Sometimes it seems as if there is simply too much to organize and no easy way to carry out the work. Don't worry about where to start; just jump right in.

How do you recognize when you have professional-quality work? What should stay? What should go? What should the portfolio reflect? Answering these questions will enable you to develop a strong, creative set of visual solutions. A good rule of thumb is never to include a piece of art in your portfolio unless you are prepared to discuss it in detail.

To assist in the design process, consider these three rationales:

1. Concept
2. Content
3. Follow-through

Let's examine each of them in turn.

Concept

Regardless of your creative background, you can develop a portfolio that highlights your accomplishments and shows off your skills. The first step is to define the objectives for each of the pieces that you will include. Ask yourself questions such as these: What was the overall purpose of the art or design? Why did you pick the particular colors and the layout of the piece that you used? Were you targeting a particular age or gender? The following is a sampling of the types of questions that might be asked about the accompanying magazine advertisement, which is to be included in a graphic design portfolio:

- What kind of company or organization would request such an ad?
- What was the ad's purpose?
- Who was the ad's target audience?
- What was the page size (full page, half page, quarter page, etc.)?
- What images were included, and where did they come from?
- What was the ad's message?
- Where does the client want the ad to be run?

Content

What do you want to say about yourself as a designer? Do you specialize in specific areas of design, or are you a generalist? Do you have a well-defined style? The work you select for your portfolio will speak volumes about your art and design skills. Here are some guidelines to help you get started identifying content.

Don't Throw Away Good Ideas

Too often, students come to my port class and inform me that they don't have any pieces good enough to fea-

GRAPHIC DESIGN TOOL #39

Late nights, brainstorming, and your eyes are slowly closing while trying to meet the deadline. It's too bad we don't sell this tool in particular though. We do have everything else you need when it comes to being informed about *your* design world. Subscribe today. create.com

CREATE magazine

Can you answer questions about this ad, designed by Giovanni De Paz? Think about the use of type and color and be prepared to explain your answers.

ture in their portfolio. In fact, that's not the case. Most of their projects incorporate some wonderful concepts that just didn't quite work out. In some cases, the correct image wasn't available to support the project. Maybe the 3-D piece was constructed poorly, or they simply ran out of time and had to hurry the piece. You need to learn to recognize when a project contains a good idea, even if the result is not all that you had hoped. And when you find yourself in such a situation, redesign and refine the piece. A good idea is always a good idea worth developing. Building a portfolio doesn't mean you have to start completely from scratch. If you have doubts about the quality of a project, seek other opinions. Professors, industry professionals, and friends can often offer a valuable fresh perspective.

Chapter 1 discussed some of the many other ways in which people no longer in school might create pieces for a portfolio. Freelance jobs, workshops, redeveloping related art into new pieces, and designing for family and friends all are ways to generate portfolio pieces. For the working professional, the portfolio process is exactly the same. Look for ways to utilize existing art. Keep in mind, your portfolio exhibits the growth of your talent as a graphic designer.

Keep Every Successful Piece

Don't just keep every successful piece; keep every unsuccessful piece as well. Do not discard even preliminary sketches. You never know when inspiration will hit and you'll think of a better solution or a new way to handle the project. Your portfolio is more than just a case filled with work; it is a collection of work gathered over time that reflects your visual approach to design.

Identify Your Format

Before you assemble all of your design work, you must decide on a display format. How you organize and present your concepts speaks volumes about you as a designer.

A versatile portfolio case is one that can hold a lot of work yet is easy to manipulate during an interview.

Your portfolio display case can be traditional, elaborate, or even wild in the extreme. Whether you display work on loose boards or on CDs, keep in mind that the presentation must not overshadow the work. Its purpose is to enhance the design examples. Let's begin by taking a look at the traditional method of display—the portfolio case.

The Portfolio Case: Functionality versus Appearance

As you begin assembling your work, you must think about the available presentation methods. One of the most popular display methods is the traditional portfolio book or case. A variety of sizes and styles can be found in art supply stores and at numerous Web sites. A typical portfolio case consists of a bound set of pages with a coiled edge, although some cases feature a ring binder and sheet protectors, which allow you to add and remove pages as necessary. Work is then slipped into the sleeves. Traditionally, black pages have been the color of choice, although gray and white pages are sometimes used to display work as well.

Some portfolios feature a permanently bound case without the inside spiral binding. As with most cases, you simply insert your artwork into the sleeves. The difference is that the portfolio has a finite number of pages, which may be a problem if you wish to display a large number of pieces. However, these types of cases tend to be a bit sturdier than others, and you don't run the risk of your pages getting mangled from constant changing.

When deciding on a case, look for one that allows the pages to turn easily. The portfolio should be easy for you to handle. Look for a quality case with comfortable handles. The case should be big enough to give your art some "breathing room." Buy one that is at least a couple of inches larger than the biggest piece you intend to showcase. Most artists choose 11×14 inches or 18×24 inches. (Chapter 4 presents a more in-depth discussion of portfolio case sizes.) And if you can afford it, buy a case with a nice cover. Leather (or simulated leather) makes the most professional-looking presentation, although recently I've seen some high-tech metal cases that look pretty sharp. A good case will help protect your work and keep it in a logical sequence.

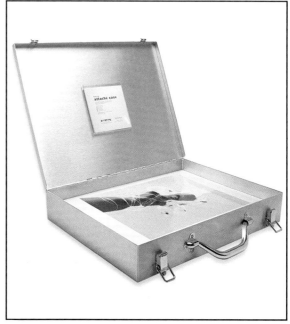

These stylish aluminum cases, designed by the Pina Zangaro company, are used to showcase larger-format pieces. (Photo: Courtesy of Kim Metzger.)

Notice the cardholders on both the outside and inside of the case. Use them as an extra design opportunity by inserting cards with your name and logo. (Photo: Courtesy of Kim Metzger.)

Frayed and ripped cases, pages that fail to turn properly, and torn sleeves make a poor showing and imply that you do not care about your work. The care you take in displaying your work says a lot about how you feel about yourself as an artist.

Another important criterion for deciding on the right case is to keep in mind that you may have to open the case on someone's desk. So don't buy one that is cumbersome or difficult to work with. You don't want to fumble around with it during the interview. You may find that a letter-size case is more convenient to carry and can more easily be used to present smaller works such as logos, business cards, and postcards.

In contrast, if you are a fine artist and your work is too large for a traditional portfolio case, you may choose to display it in an altogether different manner. Since much of your work may be large, you might choose a case that allows for slide displays as well as several small works. Yet another option is a colored box, which might be plain or embellished. This innovative style of case can easily accommodate loose pieces and 3-D works.

Many artists feel that more than one type of case may be necessary. They bring both small and large portfolios to a job interview. In short, the size of the portfolio case you select should be dictated by the size of the pieces you'll be displaying.

The Digital Portfolio

Digital portfolios have become very popular in recent years. They are small, easy to carry, and can be left with the potential employer as a reminder of your skills and abilities. They allow you to take your work to the employer in a small, easily transported format.

The digital portfolio is another way for you to showcase your best work. It allows you to include all of the items mentioned above, housed in a compact presentation. Digital portfolios are generally created and "burned" (or saved) onto CDs. The CD-based port can be duplicated for a relatively low cost and provide you a way to leave your port for the employer to review at a later date. You'll learn more about digital ports and see some terrific examples in Chapter 4.

If you really want to set yourself apart from the crowd, you might want to use a different kind of portfolio that will display your work in a creative and original way. You want a concept portfolio. A concept portfolio thematically ties together both the art and the presentation. This unique system, usually created from scratch, allows you the freedom to fully display your creative vision. What you are trying to achieve is an entire identity system that begins from the moment you present the portfolio to the prospective employer. A concept portfolio goes far beyond the traditional port. It may feature a case created from thin sheets of steel bolted together with small rivets or introduce unusual colors to offset the art. A series of dazzling layouts may be applied to show off the contents. Whatever methods are employed, the concept portfolio will not look like any others.

As you can probably tell, deciding to use a concept portfolio usually involves taking some risks. So before you go full speed ahead, sketch some ideas and try them out on your artistic friends or professionals in the field. Make sure you get the response you desire. A comment like "Oh, man, that's weird" is not necessarily what you want to hear. Make sure the portfolio does not overwhelm the work it displays. Described below are two examples of well-designed, single-theme concept portfolios, by Ryan Skinner and Julie Ruiz, shown at a portfolio review sponsored by

Julie is not afraid to embrace the portfolio interview day experience. She dressed up in a 1950s waitress outfit and gave out lunch boxes with her work. She got five job offers that day!

the Art Institute of Fort Lauderdale. Every quarter, the Art Institute invites employers from area design firms to come and view the work of its graduates. A large room at a convention center is rented so that all design majors can display their work. For graduates, the goal is to find a way to make their work stand out from the rest. Ryan and Julie show us two examples of the best of the concept portfolio.

Julie created an identity system for her portfolio that went far beyond the boards and presentation case. She assembled a concept portfolio that was a study in blue. Julie began by choosing the name of her graphic design company: Blue Box Graphix. Then she began to think about an overall strategy for presenting her work. Julie decided to invoke the nostalgia for the 1950s as the overall theme. One of the first items she created was a promotional piece that could be given out at portfolio reviews. This consisted of a metal lunch box with her logo on the front. Inside was a digital portfolio, a "bologna sandwich" CD. A bag of potato chips was relabeled with the Blue Box Graphix logo. A small juice container with blue-colored juice

Julie Ruiz turns to the 1950s for inspiration. Her self-promotional piece is not only sharp but fun as well.

continues

Here are two examples of Julie's work. She shows tremendous versatility in her designs. As you can see, Julie not only creates graphic design work but also illustrates beautifully.

was included to complete the fifties look. Julie mounted her résumé, based on the same theme, on silver board along with a matching business card. The accompanying illustrations show some examples of Julie's work.

Julie's presentation boards were spray-painted with silver glitter and clear coat so that they resembled a sparkly bowling ball from the 1950s. The sketchbook received silver airbrush treatment to match the other colors of the design. A miniature bowling ball attached with a tiny chain was added to connect the sketchbook to the rest of the work, and a red-and-white checkered tablecloth was selected to extend the retro style. At the portfolio review, Julie completed the concept by dressing as a waitress from

the 1950s. Each visitor to her table received a "bologna sandwich" CD.

Julie offered this concept portfolio advice: "Everything must mean something. Each thing you create must represent design in all aspects. Don't just slap a logo on a layout; leave an impression on people. Send a self-promotional piece. Don't be afraid to talk about yourself. Be a creative person all around. Think creatively about everything that goes beyond the norm—it's all about details."

Today, Julie Ruiz is a talented designer who creates promotional pieces for VH1. She's one of the designers featured in Communication Arts Design Annual 45 for her outstanding design work.

Ryan Skinner is driven by concepts. He began to develop his initial ideas by writing a comic book story about an action hero, a champion of graphic design who would attack and kill problems and create new ideas. Instead of a gun, Ryan's hero would use his weapon of choice: a T square. Ryan developed different versions and formed new ideas, and kept showing his ideas to his teachers to get fresh feedback. As the concept evolved, Ryan researched the additional support elements, such as paper that would be the right color. In his words: "I believe that most conceptual things are right there and are the easiest to understand. Look for the obvious and tailor it to your needs. Talk to everyone about your ideas."

Ryan's extensive research led him to call his company Design & Conquer. "I wanted to design a think-tank company with an army motif. This army would shoot down design problems. Bombs would be the creativity. . . . I spent a lot of time online and brainstormed with a friend. Eventually, we came up with the company name. We took every idea and wrote it down."

Ryan's final portfolio used a flip-book system. His self-promotion consisted of a CD case that had the company logo on the front and a flip-out printed booklet of his work. Ryan purchased an army helmet, put the

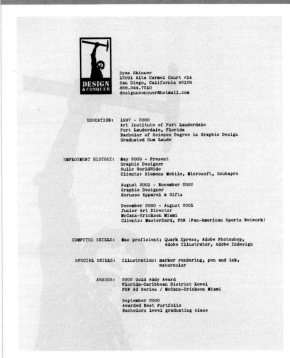

This résumé, designed by Ryan Skinner, advances his "action hero" theme. He chose a type that is deliberately rough-and-tumble. It gives an army feeling. The theme is carried through to the entire promotional package.

logo on it, and placed it on the table. Little green soldiers were scattered everywhere on the table. On the day of the portfolio review, Ryan wore a business suit. He distributed his foldout book, résumé, and business card.

Here is Ryan's advice: "Don't wait until the last moment. . . . I look back and wish I could have done more. I could have worked a lot harder. . . . Be passionate about your work. See what's going on now in the design world; see what ideas are out there. Live and breathe it. Redesign everything in sight. Professionalism is huge. Know the industry-standard programs. Know what clients want—that they have seen many other designers such as yourself. Don't be arrogant, but do be confident. And don't be afraid to try the newest ways to find jobs. I was hired from the Web site I posted on the Internet." An employer saw Ryan's online work and invited him in for an interview.

He arrived at the interview with his portfolio and all of his self-promotional pieces. "The company liked the look, printed the pieces, and showed them around the office. The flip-out book got me the job! Your rough book is very important!"

Today, Ryan Skinner is a creative designer who specializes in collateral material designed to support the overall identity of a company and its advertising campaign (such as pens, mugs, wall and desk calendars, postcards, mailers, or small gift packages). You can see some of his work here.

As you can see, the army theme is evident in Ryan's self-promotional book of art. The cover has "CLASSIFIED" stamped on it for effect, and the paper is a gray-green army-inspired choice.

Humbert Fleitas has designed a CD package that not only holds his digital portfolio but also uses a consistent color system that pulls the entire package together.

Here is a well-thought-out display that shows the resourcefulness and vision of the artist, Soo Bin Chu. The work is displayed using both traditional (boards and bottles) and sophisticated (computer) methods.

The Web-based Portfolio

Why put your portfolio on the Web? One word: marketing. A Web-based design portfolio offers numerous opportunities to have your work seen. Potential employers think highly of Internet portfolios for four main reasons. First and most important, your portfolio is easily available to recruiters anytime, from anywhere in the world. Second, a Web-based port uses flexible new media that enables its contents to be changed whenever a new piece needs to be added. Third, it demonstrates that you really do understand how to use the Internet and Web-based software technologies. A Web site can include animations, film clips of you in action, and voice-overs. Fourth, a Web portfolio can have e-mail links that give the potential employer a way to reach you immediately. You'll learn more about Web-based portfolio design in Chapters 5 and 9.

Follow-through

Planning your portfolio means thinking about the end result even when you're at the beginning of the process. Ask professionals in your field for specific feedback on

In this wonderful ad, produced by Brian Anderson, the tree generates an exciting texture that really supports the message.

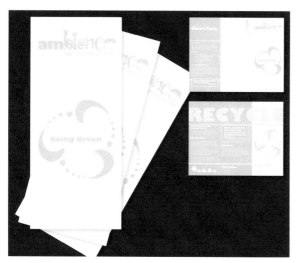

Amanda Grieve creates an attractive folder that demonstrates that even a one-color printed design can be beautiful as well as functional. (Amanda Grieve, graduate, Sinclair Community College.)

your portfolio. Don't know anyone in the field? Ask your artist friends before you assemble the final port. Check for "portfolio days" at area colleges. Frequently, you can attend seminars at which industry professionals will be on hand to offer thoughts about your work and suggest solutions to problems with it.

Research all prospective employers. Look them up at the library or on the Internet. What type of service or product do they offer? How can your services be of benefit to them? If you are to market yourself and your portfolio effectively, you must know the company's history and philosophy in advance. The more you know, the better you will be at appropriately answering the questions you'll be asked.

Be prepared to discuss your work. During an interview, you will be asked about specific pieces. Your greatest challenge is to prove that you have the skills and experience to do the job. Never answer a question with a shrug and an "I don't know," and don't make excuses about the art. The employer will think you have no conceptual skills. Rehearse if you have to, but be ready with answers. And always be positive with your responses. If possible, explain how you can achieve results for the employer.

Career Development Checklist

OK, so you think you're ready to begin the process of building a portfolio, but are you really? Do you know what you're good at? Do you know what kind of job you want? It's time for a bit of self-analysis. This section contains a list of questions and some possible answers to assist you in your career development phase. In business, this process is known as the SWOT technique (for strengths, weaknesses, opportunities, and threats). A SWOT analysis focuses on both the internal and external environments that affect your ability to make a good career decision and will help you learn more about what you want in terms of a job and a career. A SWOT table generally looks like this:

INTERNAL	STRENGTHS	WEAKNESSES
EXTERNAL	OPPORTUNITIES	THREATS

Using the SWOT Table

Write down your answers to the following questions. Don't be modest, but do be realistic. Put yourself inside the head of a potential employer as you consider how you will come across during an interview.

Strengths
- What are you skilled at?
- What do you do best?
- Who needs what you have?
- What do other people see as your strengths?

Every time you see an ad for a job in your field, ask yourself, "How do I compare to the competition? Why should this company hire me over everyone else?" When you can answer these questions, you will be well on your way to getting a great job.

Weaknesses
- Which of your job-related skills need improving?
- What are your negative personal characteristics?
- What types of tasks do you find difficult to perform?

A weakness might be that you don't always do enough research before making a decision. Or you may get impatient with yourself or others. Ask yourself if these

Here are some ideas for projects that you might want to include in your design portfolio:

TYPE OF PIECE	PROGRESS	DATE COMPLETED

1. Corporate identity materials for a company
- Logo (black-and-white or color) _____
- Letterhead (logo, address, phone, fax, e-mail, Web site) _____
- Envelope (logo, address) _____
- Additional pieces such as uniforms, shipping labels _____
- Graphic standards manual _____

2. Folder or brochure
- Trifold? Gatefold? _____
- Pocket inserts _____

3. Annual report—*Must:*
- Meet legal requirements for an annual report _____
- Be at least 25 pages, plus cover _____
- Demonstrate continuity of design and concept _____
- Have a corporate "voice" _____
- Demonstrate brand image _____

4. Poster
- Ideas: concert, gallery opening, new movie coming soon _____

5. Ad series
- Product or service _____

6. Self-promotional materials
- Résumé, business card, letterhead stationery _____
- A self-promotional piece _____
- A CD with your portfolio _____

7. 3-D design
- Food, perfume, toys _____

8. Web design—*Must include:*
- Home page _____
- Objectives page _____
- Résumé page _____
- Gallery page _____
- Contact Me page _____

9. Magazine cover page and table of contents
- Four-page editorial spread _____

10. Twenty photo images that show your "designer's eye"
- Digital or traditional _____
- Presented in a bound book or contact sheet _____

11. Digital CD portfolio—*Must include:*
- Home page _____
- Objectives page _____

TYPE OF PIECE	PROGRESS	DATE COMPLETED

11. Digital CD portfolio *continued*

- Résumé page _____
- Gallery page _____
- Contact Me page _____

12. Rough book of your concepts

Additional Pieces to Consider

You may wish to consider specializing in a particular area or choose from any of the following:

1. Advertising

Advertising campaigns, including:

- Print ads: _____
- Broadcast: radio or TV _____
- Support collateral for your campaigns: _____
- Postcards, mailers, pens, pencils, fortune cookies with your business card, gift bags filled with small examples of your work— in short, any material that will help the potential employer remember you _____

2. Graphic design

- Direct mail _____
- Out of home (signage, bus wraparounds) _____
- POP (point-of-purchase) displays—those neat promotions that you see in the front of the supermarket, such as "Back to school" or "Holiday decorations" _____
- Corporate promotional pieces _____
- Multipage documents _____
- Newsletters _____
- Information graphics (charts, illustrations) _____

3. Additional editorials

- Magazine cover, table of contents _____
- Multipage spreads _____
- Newspapers _____
- Books _____

4. New media

- Web sites _____
- Interactive CDs _____
- Banners _____
- Presentations _____

5. Illustration/photography

- Posters _____
- Ads _____
- Books _____
- Editorial _____
- Magazine layout _____

are characteristics that you see in yourself or that others see in you. Try to be as realistic and honest as you can. Recognize that there are some changes you can make immediately, whereas other changes may require some practice and help from others to implement.

Opportunities

- Do you have a clear idea about what you want to do for a living?
- Do you know what size company you want to work for?
- What is the likelihood of job growth in your area?
- Are you aware of any interesting trends in your field?
- Does your knowledge of technology give you a competitive edge? How?
- Would additional education help you get the job you want?
- Would relocating enhance your job prospects?

Opportunities help you to define goals. For example, what do you want to be doing in three or five years' time? Are there related career fields you might wish to explore?

Threats

- What is the likelihood that your field will be downsizing?
- Are you in a dead-end company or field?
- Do you need to change the nature of what you do in order to stay employed?
- Have you been doing the same thing for too long?
- Are there competitors out there with better skills? Who are the competitors, and what are their skills?
- What obstacles do you face to improving your knowledge of the field?

- Are the required specifications for your job changing?
- Are technological advances threatening your design position?

Decisions, decisions, decisions! Making a career decision is not as simple as choosing where to go for lunch. You must really involve yourself in the process. Conducting a realistic SWOT analysis should enable you to see the big picture a little more clearly. If you need further help, talk to your family and friends, or contact a former professor or boss. They may offer some insights to help your quest. If your school or college has a career advisory office, make an appointment to consult with someone there.

I always say it's important to know where you are going before you try to get there. To that end, pages 24–25 is an example of a graphic designer's portfolio checklist. Be aware that each medium or genre has very different requirements. Therefore, it is to your advantage to verify the required minimums for your discipline. Many of you may already have a checklist from your student days. If not, develop one of your own to help you decide what you need in order to produce a winning portfolio.

Layout and Design Evaluation Sheet

Look at each piece in your portfolio. What do you think of it? Use the following evaluation list as a guide to help you better understand and evaluate your work.

DESIGN ELEMENT	AVERAGE	GOOD	EXCELLENT
Is the project visually exciting?	Does it need type?	Does the type support the message? Do the images support the intent of the piece?	Does color enhance the design?
Does it use the principles of design effectively?	Is there a consistent presentation?	Is the design original?	Do all images and type choices improve the final design?
Does it communicate the artist's intent?	Is there just too much of everything?	Are the attempts focused and rational?	Does it demonstrate an advanced knowledge of design?
Is it good design?	Should it be included in the port?	Could it be improved?	Is it "the best," and should it appear first?

An Interview with Barry Rosenberg, Creative Consultant

Barry Rosenberg is far from your run-of-the-mill consultant. Barry is both creative and resourceful. His company specializes in providing complete advertising agency services, including planning and placement of print and broadcast media. His company has provided services for such diverse clients as Leo Burnett (Chicago) and N. W. Ayer (Los Angeles).

Barry grew up in Los Angeles and graduated with honors from the Art Center College of Design (BFA in advertising design, minor in packaging and film).

His awards (too many to list in full here) include:

- *CLIO International, Award for Excellence in Creativity*
- *West Coast Art Directors, Creative Excellence, Gold and Silver*
- *AIA, Excellence in Business Advertising, Gold*
- *Champion Paper, Excellence in Design*
- *Microtek Electronics*
- *Georgia-Pacific, Excellence in Design*
- *Potlatch Corporation, Excellence in Design*

Barry can be reached at brmktdesign@earthlink.net.

1 What qualities do you look for in an applicant?

Someone who is passionate about design and visual and verbal communication. Someone who is able and willing to solve all kinds of problems. Not just nice aesthetics but effective communication. Someone who can pick up a pencil and show me their ideas. Someone who is conceptually oriented as well as exceptionally capable. Someone who looks and observes everything and has an opinion about it!

Honesty and straightforwardness. And finally . . . *great work*! Work that I can touch, see, and feel, from pencil roughs to tight comps to finished produced pieces.

Motivation and desire to do the *best* work possible.

2 In your opinion, what makes a successful interview?

Honesty! Honest confidence and a straightforward attitude. No BS!

3 Has the Internet had an effect on your interview process?

No.

4 What are the five best things job candidates say that impress you during an interview? What are the five worst?

Best
- I love your work and I'd really like to work for you.
- I'll work nights and weekends.
- I'll do whatever you want.
- I'll run errands and make coffee.
- And I'll do it all for free!

Worst
- I love your work and I'd really like to work for you.
- I'll work nights and weekends.
- I'll do whatever you want.
- I'll run errands and make coffee.
- And I'll do it all for free!

Kidding aside . . . it is a very individual thing. I basically want to know how much they care about what they are doing. And who they have been, are, and want to be.

Aside from capability, I am looking for honesty and sincerity. Worst? When they try to hard to *sell* me. No BS.

5 **What are skills that really help all artists succeed regardless of their specialty?**

Problem-solving ability. The ability to come up with solutions that are fresh and new and most importantly . . . *innovative*, yet appropriate to the situation. The ability to sketch these ideas on a piece of tracing paper with a pencil . . . to do pencil roughs that are understandable. Must be able to communicate verbally. Most importantly, conceptual abilities, imagination, experimentation, and exploration.

6 **What advice would you offer to designers looking to impress you with the presentation of their work?**

I want to see the *work*! I want to know what the problem was. I want to see the thought process that solved the problem, and I want to see the final/finished piece. A slide show or computer-generated display should only be part of the presentation. Take into consideration my time . . . not more than a dozen pieces. And . . . the problem is to convince me to hire you. The solution is the design of your presentation. Remember, you are the most important part of your presentation. Dress appropriately, show up on time, and know your stuff. Good luck.

challenge

Designer's Challenge 1

A primary objective of your portfolio is to demonstrate to potential employers how much you've invested in your job search. Thus, your career becomes a collection of skills and talents rather than a series of job titles. My experience tells me that an organized and professionally designed portfolio could be just the thing that sets you apart from the other applicants.

Here's an exercise to help you better organize your thoughts. Ask yourself the following questions; then write a descriptive introduction for each of the pieces in your portfolio.

- *What is each piece about?*
- *How does it represent the client, assignment, or whatever prompted you to create the piece?*
- *Why did you include it in your portfolio?*
- *What is it about the piece you are most proud of?*

Designer's Challenge 2

Can you tell a story without words?

Create a poster that visually illustrates the evolution of an object through time without using words. Think about objects such as the wheel, reading glasses, or toys. Where would a poster like this be seen? What might be the sponsoring organization?

TELEVOX

Tatiana Malinine exhibits a fantastic solution to the evolution poster. Notice that you can see the evolution of the television from its earliest use to today's contemporary look.

3

The Traditional Portfolio

The Résumé, Cover Letter, and Business Card

You have created a body of art, and now you must determine the best way to showcase it. As explained in Chapter 2, most artists choose either the traditional or digital method, but, in recent years, many artists are using both.

Although digital portfolios have received a lot of attention of late, most employers (and artists) agree that the traditional method is the best overall visual approach, as it allows you to display your work in a structured way. You decide what constitutes your best work. You decide on the display approach, and it all begins with your résumé.

Writing an attention-getting résumé does not necessarily mean you should follow "the rules." Talk to almost anyone who has a résumé, and you'll hear many differing opinions about what constitutes the perfect one, but it's all relative. Résumés need not have a specific number of pages or follow a specific format. Every résumé should represent the individual. It should articulate your job needs and offer the reasons why you should be given a specific job.

The upcoming pages present tons of ideas and tips, but the bottom line is that you will see the basic principles of writing a successful résumé and preparing an effective cover letter and business card. The focus of this chapter is on the written aspects of the traditional portfolio.

What Goes into the Written Part of Your Portfolio?

As stated previously, your design portfolio helps to establish your skills and experience through the quality of your work. It enables the employer to make the connections between your interests and abilities and those of the company. Your portfolio is a collection of projects and achievements that help to define you as a person—your skills, interests, activities, and ability and willingness to commit to the employer. Clearly, then, it should highlight your strengths and areas of expertise.

What you include in your portfolio will, of course, depend on your background and work-related experience. If you are a recent graduate of a college or technical school, your portfolio will primarily be made up of projects completed as a student, and your degree major will determine the appearance of the projects.

Every portfolio should have a unique look and feel. In addition to reflecting your special skills and talents as a designer, it should also demonstrate to the potential employer the range of your abilities. All that said, regardless of what else you may choose to showcase in your port, there are a number of items that you should always include.

- Résumé
- Awards
- Professional memberships
- Letters of recommendation
- Cover letter
- Business card
- Significant samples of your work
- Artist's statement
- Portfolio case

The overall look of your résumé conveys as much about your design sensibilities as the information you choose to include.

Although not considered traditional in nature, the digital version of the portfolio (whether posted on the Internet or burned to a CD) is rapidly gaining in popularity in the design world. You will learn more about the creation of a digital portfolio in Chapters 5 and 6.

The Résumé

Your résumé is the document that itemizes for the employer the reasons why he or she should hire you. It establishes your knowledge of your profession and gives the employer a good overview of your background. Moreover, the résumé sets forth your goals and highlights your accomplishments. Thus, the résumé should reflect your experience and establish your credentials. (Note: In Chapter 5, we will take a closer look at the digital résumé.)

Organization is the key to a well-designed résumé, so to create a successful résumé, you must first decide on the format. There are two different formats for you to consider: chronological and functional. The following subsections explain the factors that determine which of these formats you should select.

The Chronological Résumé

Without question the most widely used format, the chronological résumé lists your work experience as history—specifically, in reverse-date form, followed by job titles and responsibilities. Thus, your latest employment is shown first, and the list continues in reverse order until you have included all your previous relevant positions. The chronological résumé makes it easy for the company to see your experience and background in your area of specialization. It is especially effective for accomplished designers with a strong work history.

The problem with chronological résumés, however, is that they tend to focus the reader's attention on what you have done rather than on what you can do. If you are just starting out, you may not have a great deal of industry-related experience, and this format will make that more obvious. So unless you can demonstrate increasing levels of responsibility in a series of jobs, it's probably best to opt for the functional résumé, described next.

The Functional Résumé

In the functional résumé format, you can describe your skills and talents. Instead of listing your experience in chronological order, you can organize your experience according to your areas of specialization. It is particularly useful for college students who have minimal "real-world" experience. Career changers who wish to enter a different field will also benefit from this format. Likewise, if there are gaps in your work history—say, for child rearing or furthering your education—the functional résumé is a good format to consider. Check out the functional résumés in this chapter.

The functional résumé is not, however, as popular as the chronological résumé. One reason is that it is more difficult to write, because it requires a skillful reorganization of information. Another reason is that it makes it more difficult for the employer to determine your con-

A complex résumé will benefit from a "Summary of Qualifications" section, which clearly highlights the applicant's accomplishments.

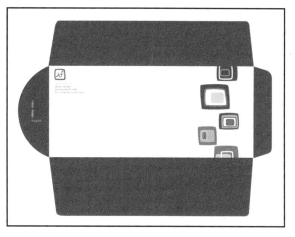

There should be no doubt in your mind that this is the résumé and business envelope of a designer! It's fun, playful, yet conveys all the information necessary to give the artist's background. It's a little piece of art in itself.

tributions to previous employers. That said, a functional résumé can be very effective in showing your skills in job-related areas. Let's say you have worked in retail. Chances are you were responsible for dealing with customers, organizing merchandise, training or mentoring personnel, and handling purchase problems. These are all skills that an employer will value and want to discuss during an interview.

Parts of the Résumé
Contact Information

A well-designed résumé always begins with basic information about the applicant. Your name and address are important to the employer. (Believe it or not, I've seen beautifully designed résumés on which the designer forgot to include his or her name.) You want the employer to be able to reach you, so don't forget to include your home telephone number and a cell number if you have one; and if you have an e-mail address or perhaps even a Web site, indicate those as well.

The point is, make sure the company has an obvious way to reach you. As soon as you can, buy an answering machine and check it on a regular basis. I have a friend who lost a job because he didn't respond to a telephone message fast enough. The company was in a hurry to reach him, and, in the two days it took him to respond,

the company hired another applicant. In short, time is of the essence. If you add an e-mail address to your résumé, then, by all means, check your messages frequently. If you have multiple e-mail accounts, consider having all your messages forwarded to one central e-mail server where you can see all incoming messages at a glance. You might be amazed at the number of job applicants who forget to check for e-mail messages on a regular basis during this most critical time!

Where should your name appear on the résumé? It depends on the résumé's design style, but generally your name and address should appear at the center top of the page, although some prefer to place this all-important information to the right or left, for a slightly different look. This style of design usually works best with résumés that feature a lot of information. You might even consider a very unconventional approach, such as tilting the address on its side or even arranging it at a 90-degree angle.

Of course, résumés can be much more creative in their design approach. A well-designed, innovative layout helps to balance a résumé that is light on content. Take a look at the accompanying examples. These cleverly designed résumés feature a variety of artistic themes. Notice that there are all sorts of unique compositions; design motifs such as logos, lines, bullets, and

The colors and layout of your résumé offer a preview of your design style. Don't be afraid to have some fun!

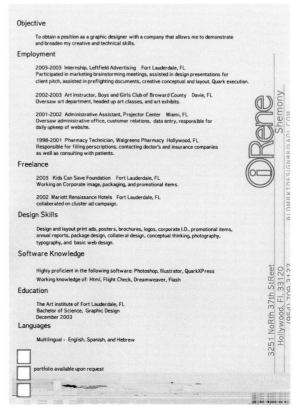

Clearly define your goals when writing the objectives section of your résumé.

watermarks provide additional appeal. All of these innovative ideas help the potential employer to remember you as a serious designer.

It is important to think about color (of both the paper and the ink) when designing your résumé. Color is an eye-catcher and can set you apart from the competition, but it can cause problems as well. Suppose you are asked to fax your résumé. Will the color paper you use cause your résumé to come out illegible at the other end? Just because you like science fiction doesn't mean you should create a résumé in "alien green" with an "alien typeface." I encourage everyone to try faxing the newly created résumé to a friend to ensure that it emerges cleanly on the other side.

How long should your résumé be? Experts differ. When I was a college graduate, the popular length for a résumé was one page. The theory was that any résumé longer than one page would immediately be thrown into the proverbial circular file. The average length of most résumés today is about two pages, but it all depends on your background and level of expertise. My résumé is now four pages long, but I have many years of experience in my area of specialization. If your résumé is longer than two pages, it is important to highlight your key qualifications for the job. This is usually accomplished by creating a list of career credentials. There are many ways to name this part of the résumé. On mine, I use the title "Summary of Qualifications." Alternative titles are "Highlights of Qualifications" or "Objectives." Take a look at some of the many examples in this chapter for some inspiration.

If you are just graduating or perhaps are going through a career change, you may not have a great deal to include on the résumé. In this case, highlight your important qualifications, achievements, and background. Suggest reasons why you will make a terrific employee. And don't forget, a résumé that is interesting or beautiful (especially in the different design professions) counts for a lot. A good rule of thumb for establishing the length of the résumé is to balance economy with appropriate depth and detail.

The Objective or Summary Section

You want to grab the potential employer's attention. One way to accomplish this is with a philosophy statement or a career mission statement that sets the tone for what is to come. Bullet your accomplishments. Highlight your objectives. Tell the employer what you can do or what you are looking for in a job. This gives the employer an understanding of how you can best fit into the company's structure.

If you are developing a longer résumé, the objective or summary section is important. Without it, you force the employer to read the entire résumé to figure out if you are suitable for the company (assuming he or she will read the whole thing!). When a prospective employer finishes reading your key accomplishments, you want him or her to run immediately for the phone to invite you in for an interview!

Employment History

Your employment history usually comes after the summary section (unless you believe that your education is your best qualification for the job). This section of the résumé traditionally lists your past employment in reverse chronological order, as already noted. Most companies prefer to see dates of employment.

Your employment history should be more than a listing of job titles and descriptions. It should emphasize your skills and experience. It answers the question, Why will you be valuable to the company? Use this section to highlight how you have made a positive impact in your previous jobs. To achieve this, you must use action and skills verbs. Incorporate as many of these "can-do" verbs as possible, but don't go overboard. In the sidebar, you'll find many such verbs to get you started. But you can find even more in a good thesaurus; and the Internet offers numerous resources. Here are some examples of how to use action verbs effectively to describe your skills and experience:

- Established educational workshops.
- Developed budget requirements.
- Participated in all department meetings.
- Facilitated new tracking system.
- Organized and maintained client files.

• Take Action

Positive and powerful action verbs tell your story effectively. They describe your skills and accomplishments in a succinct and persuasive manner. Used wisely (that is, accurately and with restraint), action verbs make potential employers take notice. Here are more than a few top-quality verbs for you to incorporate into your résumé.

accelerated	addressed	advocated	answered	attracted	built
accomplished	adjusted	aided	anticipated	audited	calculated
achieved	administered	aligned	appointed	authorized	canvassed
acquired	adopted	allocated	appraised	automated	capitalized
acted	advanced	altered	approached	awarded	captured
adapted	advertised	amended	approved	balanced	carried out
added	advised	analyzed	arbitrated	bargained	cataloged
			arranged	beat	centralized
			ascertained	began	chaired
			assembled	borrowed	challenged
			assessed	bought	changed
			assigned	briefed	channeled
			assisted	broadened	charted
			attained	budgeted	checked

continues

chose
circulated
clarified
classified
cleared
closed
coached
coauthored
collaborated
collected
combined
commanded
commissioned
committed
communicated
compared
compiled
completed
complied
composed
computed
conceived
conceptualized
concluded
condensed
conducted
conferred
conserved
consolidated
constructed
consulted
contracted
contrasted
contributed
contrived
controlled
converted
convinced
cooperated
coordinated
corrected

correlated
corresponded
counseled
counted
crafted
created
critiqued
cultivated
customized
cut
dealt
debugged
decentralized
decided
decreased
deferred
defined
delegated
demonstrated
described
designated
designed
determined
developed
devised
devoted
diagnosed
diagrammed
differentiated
directed
disclosed
discovered
dispatched
displayed
dissembled
distinguished
distributed
diversified
divested
documented
doubled

drafted
drew
earned
eased
edited
educated
effected
eliminated
employed
enabled
encouraged
endorsed
enforced
engaged
engineered
enhanced
enriched
equipped
established
evaluated
examined
exceeded
executed
expanded
expedited
explained
extended
extracted
extrapolated
fabricated
facilitated
familiarized
fashioned
fielded
figured
filed
financed
fixed
focused
followed up
forecast

formalized
formed
formulated
fortified
fostered
found
founded
framed
fulfilled
functioned
furnished
furthered
gained
gathered
gauged
gave
generated
governed
graded
granted
graphed
greeted
grouped
guided
handled
harmonized
hastened
headed
heightened
held
helped
highlighted
hired
hosted
housed
identified
illuminated
illustrated
imagined
immersed
implemented

improved
improvised
inaugurated
included
incorporated
increased
incurred
indoctrinated
induced
influenced
informed
initiated
innovated
inquired
inspected
inspired
installed
instigated
instilled
instituted
instructed
instrumental
insured
integrated
interfaced
interpreted
intervened
interviewed
introduced
invented
inventoried
investigated
invited
involved
joined
judged
labored
launched
learned
lectured
led

leveled
lightened
liquidated
lobbied
localized
located
logged
lowered
maintained
managed
mapped
marketed
mastered
matched
maximized
measured
mediated
merchandised
merged
met
minimized
mixed
mobilized
modeled
moderated
modernized
modified
monitored
motivated
moved
multiplied
named
narrated
navigated
negotiated
netted
neutralized
noticed
notified
nurtured
observed

obtained
offered
offset
opened
operated
operationalized
orchestrated
ordered
organized
oriented
originated
overhauled
oversaw
paid
painted
participated
passed
patterned
perceived
perfected
performed
permitted
persuaded
photographed
pinpointed
pioneered
placed
planned
played
pointed
positioned
practiced
prepared
presented
preserved
presided
prevented
priced
printed
prioritized
probed

processed
procured
produced
programmed
projected
promoted
prompted
proofed
proofread
proposed
proved
provided
publicized
published
purchased
pursued
pushed
qualified
quantified
quoted
raised
ranked
rated
read
realized
rearranged
reasoned
reassembled
recalled
received
recognized
recommended
recorded
recruited
rectified
reduced
referred
regulated
rehabilitated
reinforced
related

remodeled
rendered
renegotiated
renovated
reorganized
repaired
replaced
replenished
represented
researched
reserved
reshaped
resolved
responded
restated
restored
restructured
returned
revealed
reversed
reviewed
revised
revitalized
revived
rewrote
routed
safeguarded
salvaged
saved
scheduled
scouted
screened
searched
secured
segmented
selected
sent
separated
served
serviced
set up

settled
shaped
sharpened
shipped
shortened
showed
shrank
simplified
sketched
smoothed
sold
solved
sought
spearheaded
specialized
specified
speculated
spoke
spread
stabilized
staffed
staged
standardized
started
steered
stimulated
stopped
stored
straightened
strategized
streamlined
strengthened
stressed
structured

studied
submitted
substantiated
substituted
succeeded
suggested
summarized
superseded
supervised
supplied
supported
surpassed
surveyed
switched
synchronized
synthesized
systematized
tabulated
tackled
tailored
talked
targeted
taught
tended
terminated
tested
testified
tightened
timed
took
took over
traced
traded
trained

transacted
transcribed
transferred
transformed
translated
transported
traveled
treated
trimmed
tripled
troubleshot
uncovered
undertook
unearthed
unified
united
updated
upgraded
used
utilized
validated
valued
verified
viewed
visited
vitalized
volunteered
weighed
welcomed
widened
witnessed
won
worked
wrote

As you can see, this visual identity package has design elements that carry over from cover letter to résumé and business card. The various pieces all share the same selected fonts.

What kinds of jobs should you list? There are two schools of thought on this question. Some people believe that you should list only those jobs most relevant to the position you are seeking. Others say it is important to show that you have held down a position for a period of time even if it is out of field. I believe that it is best to play to your strengths. If you have worked in your field, that experience should always be included. If you are a recent graduate with little job-related experience, it is still important to show a steady employment record. Perhaps you have completed some freelance work for a client, friends, or family. Maybe you just finished an internship. These jobs are important and demonstrate your abilities, so be sure to include them.

Education

In this section of the résumé, you will list all of your education, in reverse chronological order (that is, the most recent degree back to the earliest), as you do for your job history. And if you have any certificates or advanced training, list them in this section as well, but be selective with this information. Include only data that will impress the company. If you are in college or are a recent college graduate, you need not indicate when you attended and graduated from high school.

If you are still in college but near graduation, include the degree and, in parentheses, the expected date of completion—for example, BA (expected 20XX). If you are a recent graduate, it is not necessary to include your grade point average unless it is high—3.4 or better. List selected coursework if you think doing so might help you secure the job.

A consistent arrangement is very important in this section. Set the degrees apart so they can easily be seen. Use boldface type for emphasis. Make it as easy as pos-

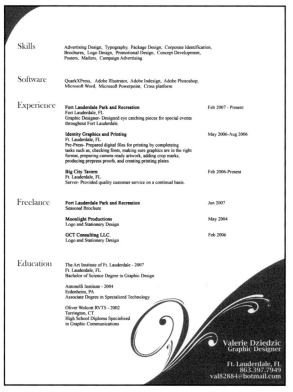

It's important to list in-house job-related experience, but don't forget to include any freelance work you have done as well.

Finding ways to distinguish yourself from other applicants is the key to your success. Shown here are a résumé and self-promotional giveaway with an unusual die cut around the edges. Sure, it's a bit more difficult to pull off, but the results are certain to get you noticed!

sible for the employer to focus on your qualifications. Here is an example:

University of Miami, Coral Gables, FL, 1995–1997
Degree: MFA; Major: Graphic Arts

Nova Southeastern University, Fort Lauderdale, FL, 1992–1994
Degree: EdS Computer Applications, Emerging Technologies

Florida State University, Tallahassee, FL, 1986–1987
Degree: MS Mass Communication; Major: Video Production/Advertising

University of Florida, Tallahassee, FL, 1982–1986
Degree: BEd; Major: Art; Minor: Mass Communication

If you didn't finish your college degree, don't try to hide this fact. Instead, begin with a phrase describing your major, then indicate the name of the school and the dates attended. List any continuing education courses you have completed that relate to the job you are applying for. This points to your expertise in the subject. If you have taken continuing education courses after completing a degree, list those as well.

Honors, Awards, and Certifications

What special skills set you apart from everyone else? Always highlight anything that demonstrates a unique set of talents. Perhaps you were invited to participate in an honors program for designers. If you received any special design awards, such as Best in Show, Best Up-and-Coming Designer, or Highest Academic Achievement, be sure to include this information. And mention any academic accomplishments, such as making the dean's list. If you think the résumé reader may not understand the nature of a particular award, be sure to include a brief explanation of its meaning and significance.

Professional Affiliations

Are you a member of any professional organizations? Professional groups such as the American Advertising Federation, the American Institute of Graphic Arts, the American Society of Media Photographers, or the

Society of Illustrators usually have student chapters available in your local area. Memberships in career-related clubs or honor societies indicate you are an involved designer, someone who takes an interest above and beyond his or her work. Be sure to list any affiliations that demonstrate leadership skills.

Additional Personal Information

One item frequently left out of the résumé is relevant personal information such as your hobbies and interests. Many employers like to see that you have a life beyond your job. Outside interests demonstrate that you are a well-rounded person with a natural curiosity about or passion for things other than work. This is especially important if it relates to your job interests as well. A graphic designer who enjoys painting and museums will look mighty good on paper. Keep it relatively simple, though. You want to have something interesting to talk about during the interview.

Technical Expertise and Computer Skills?

Most design jobs today require some degree of technical experience. It is important to highlight any skills you have, especially in related areas of design. List any software or operating systems with which you are proficient. But don't necessarily include version numbers. Since most software companies are constantly bringing out new versions, that can date your résumé very quickly and force you to keep redoing it.

Be sure to spell the names of the industry software you use correctly. One art director I interviewed for this book flatly stated, "I wouldn't hire a person who doesn't know how to spell the software he works on!" Take a few extra minutes and double-check the software manual or the company's Web site to see exactly how each name is spelled (For example: InDesign).

Military Service

If you have spent time in the military, you might want to put this information on the résumé. Military service that includes responsibilities related to your job search is especially valuable. If the job was technical in nature, provide a description and keep the military terminology to a minimum.

Dos and Don'ts of Résumé Design

Do

- Use a direct, active writing style. Begin sentences or phrases with action verbs.
- Pick a résumé format and be consistent.
- Make the résumé visually appealing. You don't want your résumé to look like everyone else's. (For an example of visually appealing stationery, take a look at the examples scattered throughout this chapter.)
- Write with short phrases rather than complete sentences. If you can say it in 5 words, don't use 20.
- Watch for errors in spelling and punctuation. Ask a qualified friend or colleague to read your résumé. I promise you, they will find mistakes that you missed!
- Spell the brand names of all industry software programs correctly.
- Highlight your accomplishments with positive action words.
- Utilize capital letters, underlining, bullets, or color to emphasize certain items. Be sure these techniques are used consistently.
- Tell the truth. Do not skip dates or titles on your résumé in an attempt to hide your background or lack of experience. If the employer finds out the real story, you might be fired.
- List sports you were involved in if you are (or were) a college student. Some employers actually seek out athletes because of their teamwork ability and leadership skills.
- Keep the company in mind. Ask yourself, "If I were the employer, would I interview this person?" If you can't answer yes, you're not finished writing your résumé.

Don't

- Use personal pronouns (*I, my, me*) in your résumé.
- Give any personal data regarding age, ethnicity, or race; height or weight; marital status; number of children; or health. It is against the law.
- Lay out your résumé in such a way that critical information breaks awkwardly at the bottom of a page.
- Include interests or affiliations that might be considered controversial.
- Cite your high school education unless you've had no additional schooling.

- Use abbreviations or acronyms.
- Include a snapshot of yourself.
- Use too many big words or the wrong words.
- Mention salary or vacation requirements.
- Give any negative information about yourself—for example, if you were ever in trouble with the law.

References or Letters of Recommendation

The popular thinking today is to include a line at the end of the résumé that states, "References furnished upon request." If you include such a line, be sure you have them handy to supply to the employer who asks for them. You may also wish to include the letters inside your portfolio.

Choose your references carefully. If you are currently working, consider asking a supervisor for a letter of recommendation that can be included with your résumé. (Just make sure he or she doesn't panic, thinking you are about to depart!) Select people who know and can describe your work as an employee, a student, or on a personal level (such as a religious contact). Include the name, title, address, and telephone number for each of your references. If needed, add a line or two establishing your relationship with this person. A letter of recommendation can describe your good character and offer reasons why you would make a valuable employee.

In general, include no more than two or three letters of recommendation. These powerful documents can give you the edge over your competition, but you don't want to overwhelm the potential employer with too much information.

If you can avoid it, do not use personal friends or family members as references. Simply put, they do not carry the same weight as a professional in your area of design. Former clients, former managers, or professors will offer the most credibility in your job quest. Seek their help, but make sure they will be comfortable recommending you and your qualifications. Give each reference a copy of your résumé so that he or she is knowledgeable about your history. Explain to all your references that they might be contacted and that you will expect them to respond in a timely manner. I once offered to act as a reference for a fellow professor. Unfortunately, I was unable to respond to an employer's

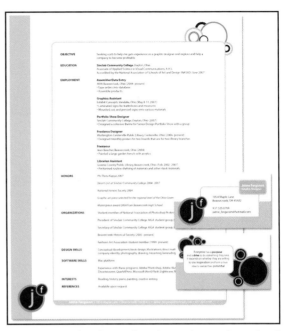

A good résumé lets the employer know what you have already accomplished as a designer. Here is a great example, designed by Jaime Ferguson. (Jaime Ferguson, graduate, Sinclair Community College.)

call for several days due to a conference schedule conflict. In that short time, the employer turned to another person for the position. Fortunately my colleague had additional references available.

Cover Letter

Your friend's birthday is tomorrow, and you decide that a book would be the perfect gift. You walk into your favorite bookstore, looking for an appropriate book, only to discover that every volume in the store is devoid of information. Each book has nothing but a plain white cover showing the title and the author. You see no synopsis, no review, no pictures, no information to help you choose.

To the potential employer, sorting through résumés resembles this scenario. After placing an ad for a designer in the paper or posting it online, the employer is soon deluged with résumés, and there are just too many similar applications to sort through. Obviously, it is important that your application get read, so how are you to differentiate yourself from everyone else applying for the job? One tried-and-true way to achieve this is with a cover letter. Your cover letter is, essentially, your sales pitch. In it, you have the opportunity to highlight your accomplishments and stress to the employer the primary reasons to hire you. A cover letter alone can't get you the job, of course, but it can open doors for the interview process. I assure you, if two people apply for the same job, and only you include a cover letter, you will be called first.

The goal of your cover letter is to, first, introduce yourself to the potential employer and, second, point out why you're the most qualified for the job. A cover letter is most effective when written for a specific employer or a specific job opening; that means you don't use a "boilerplate" letter to apply for every job. It also means you will have to do some research to learn as much as you can about the company, then use this research to tailor the contents of the cover letter for the job opening. The extra time this takes will pay off in the long run, since it will demonstrate your interest in the job and the company.

The cover letter generally has three sections:
1. Introduction
2. Body
3. Closing

We'll consider each of them in turn.

Introduction

In the first section of the cover letter, you introduce yourself and state the purpose of the letter. You indicate the position you are interested in and how you heard about the opening. If you learned about the job from another person, you might need to mention who referred you. Use this first paragraph as a lead-in to why you are the best-qualified candidate for the position.

If possible, address your cover letter to a specific person; do not use a generic opening such as "To whom it may concern." Be sure you spell the person's name correctly (if necessary, call the company to confirm this). Here are two examples of an opening paragraph:

Dear Mr. Ross,
I am seeking a position as a Web designer at Eastern Advertising. I am a hands-on, results-oriented person with

a comprehensive background in training, design, and development. My enclosed résumé details the specifics of my experience and accomplishments.

Dear Ms. West,
I am writing in response to your advertisement regarding the junior art director position in your organization. Please consider this letter as my formal application for the position. I am including my résumé, which presents my background, education, and experience.

Body

In the body of your letter, you tell the employer why you should get the job. Make the employer understand why your experience and background fit the company's needs and the job requirements. Don't make this part of the letter too long—two or three paragraphs are probably enough. Summarize your experience and give examples. If you have a "Summary of Qualifications" section in your résumé, you may use excerpts from it. But do not repeat what is on your résumé, except to expand on areas you think the employer might want to, or should, know. Here is an example of the body of the cover letter for a graphic designer:

I have more than five years of in-depth experience in graphic design, on both PCs and Macs, including installation and maintenance of state-of-the-art computer programs. I acted as the interim art director of the graphic design area at Eastern Advertising, where I hired and trained new employees in order to maintain continuity in support of current clients. I also installed additional computers to support growing company needs.

I created the company's first desktop publishing and computer graphics work-flow process, from initiation of client contact to fulfillment of final project. I originated advanced procedures to cover all aspects of production. In addition, I organized and implemented the company's first television production facility, including three-camera online studio production, as well as location shooting. I designed television graphics, incorporating storyboarding and television camera cards for new clients.

I am a versatile, energetic, and organized designer who has experience originating and implementing production-

sensitive layouts as well as defining budgetary needs for a project.

Closing

In your final paragraph, sum up your experience and express why your qualifications make you the best person for the job. Be very positive about yourself. Close your letter by clearly identifying what you will do next. Write an active statement, such as an offer to contact the employer within a specific period of time. Then do so. Your call shows serious interest, enthusiasm, and willingness to work—exactly what employers want to see. Here is an example of a closing paragraph:

Based on my job experience and educational qualifications, I am confident that I can contribute to the quality design work provided by Eastern Advertising. I will contact you in several days to discuss my credentials with you further and would appreciate the opportunity for a personal interview.

Yours very truly,
[your name]

Don't forget, all of the caveats described in the résumé section of this chapter apply here. Grammar counts. Spelling counts more! Always have someone you trust proofread your cover letter. Then get someone else to proof it as well. Invite them to criticize your word choice. This will help you make the cover letter as clear and effective as possible. All employers value your

This business card actually features an eye that you can see through when it's held up to the light. It was a lot of work to create, but the effect is awesome!

ability to communicate at a professional level. Use this first opportunity to write a cover letter that demonstrates how your background, education, and work experience can fit the employer's needs.

Business Card

The business card may be one of the most overlooked aspects of the designer's portfolio. Most designers spend countless hours creating the work that will be showcased in their port, yet they design their business card almost as an afterthought. This is a big mistake. Think of your business card as a miniature résumé. Contained within this small document is much of the information necessary to learn about you, locate you, and get you a job. Ideally, your business card should convey a sense of who you are and what you do as a designer.

Your business card should have a unique appearance. Take a look at the terrific examples in this chapter. Once

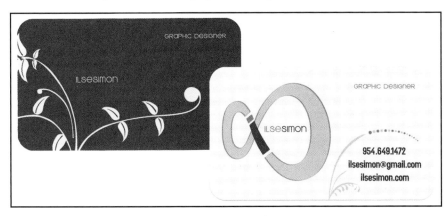

This card has a cohesive feeling. The small organic objects emphasize the design established in the main logo.

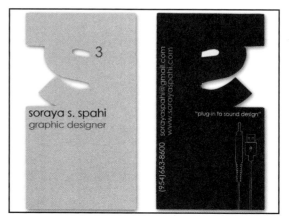

Here is a business card with a die cut. In order to save money, the artist produced each piece by hand to give out at portfolio review day.

Don't waste space! Here is a business card that effectively uses both sides. The card is playful yet conveys key contact information.

again, the idea is to distinguish yourself from the other applicants. Think about the person who will look at the card, and ask yourself, "Would I hire this person based on his or her card?" Let's consider some of the different types of business cards.

Types of Business Cards

Basic Cards

The basic business card is a simple, low-cost way to display your information. It is usually printed in black ink on plain white or cream card-stock paper. The basic card offers a clear and concise amount of information and uses a no-nonsense design approach.

Picture or Photo Cards

A business card can feature your personal logo or represent the design services you offer. It can frequently communicate your design skills faster than a portfolio. A second or even third color adds punch to the design and makes it still more memorable.

Tactile Cards

Many different materials can give a business card some extra pizzazz. Special papers can feature plastic, transparency, holographic effects, and even 3-D raised surfaces. Die cutting can be used to make cards that distinguish themselves with unusual shape and edges. Tactile cards are more expensive than traditional cards, but they can be an effective marketing tool.

One-of-a-Kind Cards

Want your business card to stand out from all the rest? Make your card one of a kind. Cards can be made of chocolate, metal, cheese. OK, well, maybe not cheese, but you can design cards that are truly unique. Your business card is your personal public relations representative. A clever card offers insight into your design capabilities. The sky's the limit.

Creating Your Business Card

Begin by selecting either a horizontal or vertical layout. The standard-size business card is generally 2 inches × 3.5 inches. This allows the card to be easily inserted into a wallet or revolving card holder. Keep critical information away from the edges of the card, so none of it gets cut off when the edges are trimmed. Here is some of what might be imprinted on your business card:

- Your name
- Your address

- Your phone, fax, and/or cell phone number
- Your e-mail address
- Your job title (if applicable)
- Your Web page (if you have one)
- Your logo (if applicable)
- Graphic elements

And don't forget to design the back of your business card. While the front of a card features a person's name and logo, the back can highlight some of his or her design services or specialties.

The business card is part of your complete business package. In graphic design, this is known as a visual identity system. What does that mean? It means that your business card should have the same look and feel as your cover letter and résumé. For example, if you have a logo or graphic on your résumé, include it on your business card as well. Take a moment to look at the ideas presented in this chapter to see how you can achieve your own results.

Likewise, use the same fonts from one piece to another. Use a type size large enough to be easily readable. (One of my students recently showed me a beautiful business card, but the type on it was so small that I needed a magnifying glass to read it!) Use paper color and texture, logos, and other decorative motifs consistently. And while we are on the subject of paper, don't be penny-wise and pound-foolish. Buy the nicest card stock you can afford.

Expanding Your Reach with Business Cards

Offering a business card is a sign of respect. When you first meet a potential employer, have your business card where you can reach it readily without having to fumble around looking for it. Then present the card to the individual with your name side up, so that it can be easily read.

The world is a much smaller place these days, and we all have opportunities to interact with people from many different cultures. There are a number of books and articles on the subject of international business etiquette. If you are considering an international position, it is essential that you review the etiquette of that country. In many Asian countries, for example, it is consid-

CD-ROM Business Cards

The newest, and possibly most high-tech, way to promote yourself is with a CD-ROM business card. All of your most important information—name, address, e-mail, and telephone and fax numbers—can be stored in digital form. In fact, you can store your entire digital portfolio on a CD. A tiny CD can present pictures, animated 3-D graphics, and interactive forms that will link the potential employer directly to your Web site. The mini-CD-ROM can hold between 30 and 50 megabytes of data—more than enough for most digital portfolios. This equals about five minutes of video or hundreds of images or thousands of pages of text.

The mini-CD works exactly the same as a full-size one. It can be used in almost all CD drives and carries the same data formats as regular circular CDs. In fact, you can create your own mini-CDs. All you need is a computer and a CD burner. If you have an older computer without a burner, local office supply stores in your area can create as many CDs as you require. This is a very cost-effective way to provide examples of your art in a unique format.

The benefits of creating a mini-CD-ROM are that it's:

- Easier and less expensive to mail
- Compact and convenient to carry

The only caveat: not every computer can read mini-CDs. Some of the newer Macintosh computers have trays that hold only full-size CDs.

ered a faux pas not to both offer and receive a business card. You are expected to take the business card and examine it for a short time as a show of respect.

But wherever you go, never leave home without a stack of business cards. You can hand out this powerful small document and market yourself to a possible employer anywhere. You never know when a job opportunity will arise. A great business card will help a potential employer remember you long after an initial meeting or interview is finished.

And, finally, do check your cards from time to time. Make sure they are clean, neat, and accurate.

Designing Your Self-promotional Package

As graphic designers, we brand products and services. Now it's time for you to brand yourself. In every creative professional's career, there comes a point when the need for some form of self-promotional material comes into play. This could be a personal logo, a business card, or a Web site. Almost every graphic designer or illustrator I've spoken with describes self-promotional design as a struggle. It's something that is frequently put off until the last moment. Still, a well-designed self-promotion reflects your design sensibilities as well as your most marketable skills and qualities. The material you develop will continue to speak volumes about you as a designer long after an interview has ended.

All the pieces in this wonderful promotional package are given away in a custom-embroidered pouch highlighted with a catch line about creativity. The student was fortunate to have a relative in the embroidery business, so the cost was minimal.

Start by Asking the Tough Questions

Before you can design the self-promotional (or self-promo) package, you must engage in a bit of self-examination. So who are you? And what do you want people to remember? Your sense of humor? Your ability to work under pressure? Questions such as these are the beginning of your development process. Start with some basic types of questions:

* What is my favorite color?
* What is my favorite song or type of music?
* What are my hobbies?
* Who is my favorite artist?
* What is my favorite art movement?
* Would I rather be indoors or outdoors?
* What is my favorite food or drink?
* What is my ideal vacation?

Now take each one of your answers and ask the next question: why? Does your favorite color remind you of a vacation you once took in the mountains? Think about the sights, smells, and sounds of your mountain adventure. Does something come to mind? Maybe it was the wildflowers or the pine needles. The flowers or trees might help you create a logo based around nature. The colors of that landscape could serve as the beginning of your color palette.

Here are a variety of business cards to jump-start your creativity. Notice that not a single one is printed on plain white cover stock. Also note the interesting edges that were produced.

This self-promotional package features a paper doll that represents the designer. Inside the package are a résumé, a business card, and a small CD. Also included are instructions for assembling the doll and even miniature scissors to complete the task.

Examine your love of sports. If baseball is your passion, perhaps a sports-themed promotional piece, such as a small baseball bat key chain or a yo-yo in the shape of a baseball with your name on it, could be designed.

As you ask each question and consider the "why" behind it, you will begin to frame a concept. This method of free association often leads to happy surprises. Your horoscope sign is Pisces, and this initial idea leads you to design a business card holder in the shape of a small fish.

So what type of self-promo piece should you create? Your digital portfolio can most certainly be used as a promotional tool, but you can develop support materials as well. For example, you might design a folder that contains your résumé, business card, digital portfolio CD, and some small printed examples of your work. One thing's for sure, your promotional piece should:

- Present yourself to others in an unusual way
- Make the recipient take action

Present Yourself to Others in an Unusual Way

As I was helping a student, John Masulonis, with his digital portfolio, we were listening to some copyright-free music and came upon some intriguing 1960s spy-inspired tunes. . . . The music really hit me, and I suggested that John might use the spy theme for all of his materials. About a week later, he showed up in my class with a business card holder in the shape of a small black attaché case. This was the beginning of his promotional theme. The digital port was created to look like a "secret" file, and his logo was reworked to look like a secret agent holding the black attaché case. At portfolio review, John even wore a black suit with a black tie to complete the theme.

Here is a promo package you won't soon forget! Everything included is coordinated with the artist's colors and designs. Even the mouse pad shows a section of the résumé.

Create a Self-promotional Piece That Reflects the Type of Work You Want to Do

Are you interested in package design? Create a clever business card holder. Do you have any hobbies, such as painting? Prepare a package that uses a small paint can and put all your promotional pieces inside it.

Use a Good Tagline or Pun as the Starting Point

You create taglines for products and services. Why not create one for yourself and use it on every piece of the promotion? A lightbulb paired with the tagline "Lighting up with creative designs" ties together a witty visual and written idea. I know it's hard to think of ways to accomplish this, but, I promise, your time and creativity will be rewarded.

Think Crafty

Scrapbook supplies can be turned into nifty little visual books of your work. Bead supplies can be worked into key chains with your business card attached. Small palette stands can hold miniature versions of your layouts. Bake cookies and decorate them with your logo to make a memorable (not to mention delicious!) impression. Create a calendar and use your artwork for each of

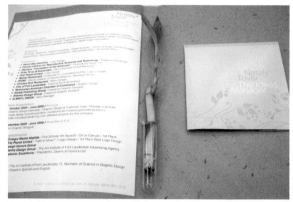

Nataly Tovar creates a beautiful organic promotional piece using recycled paper and a small bamboo plant.

the months. Here are several terrific Web sites to get those creative juices flowing:

Michaels: www.michaels.com/art/online/home
Pearl: www.pearlpaint.com
Oriental Trading: www.orientaltrading.com

Make the Recipient Take Action

A promotional piece is something that makes your recipient remember you as a possible employee. Good self-promotions stay on the recipient's desk. And if they happen to be useful—a pen, a small desk accessory—they won't be thrown away so easily, and your name will be there, reminding the potential employer that you're waiting to be hired!

What Should You Spend?

How much you should spend depends on your budget. For a small amount of money, you can make a big impression. If your budget permits, have some promotional materials created that feature your name prominently. Hats, golf balls, T-shirts, clocks, business supplies, tote bags—all with your name—can have maximum impact when they arrive at the potential employer's desk. Here are a few Web sites you can visit for inspiration:

Branders.com: www.branders.com
Pinnacle Promotions:
    www.pinnaclepromotions.com
Promo-Force: www.promo-force.com

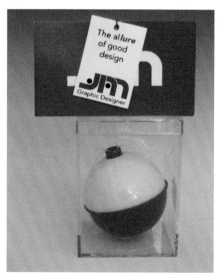

A passion for fishing turns into a great promotional piece with this clever pun. This package is both memorable and amusing.

No money? Don't let that stop you! Head to the nearest dollar store in your area and pick up some items that might make nice giveaways. You may just find the right item that can be turned into a low-cost promotional piece. That small wooden puzzle you find sitting on a shelf can be supercharged with a clever tagline, such as "Got a design puzzle to solve? Call me and I'll put everything together for your company!" A small pair of socks can provide the inspiration for a tagline such as "Need a designer? I'll knock your socks off!" (Just don't purchase anything you deem to be questionable in terms of taste.)

The last step in the design process is to try out your idea on friends, family, and coworkers. If the response is less than you had hoped for, seek another solution. If you have to explain the idea, it's probably not a good one. The best concepts are self-explanatory. Discovering your own unique theme for your self-promotional package requires you to really think about yourself in a way that is sometimes difficult. After all, you are examining yourself not just as an artist but as a person. Self-exam-

Matilda McIntyre finds a great way to display her business cards and résumé using a small artist's palette stand.

ination, when done thoughtfully, will enable you to learn more about yourself and create a wonderful giveaway as well.

Once you've finalized your self-promotional package, send it to anyone you think might be beneficial to your career.

An Interview with Dani Nordin

Dani Nordin is the founder and principal designer of "the zen kitchen," in Watertown, Massachusetts. She has more than ten years' experience designing award-winning work for small to large businesses and nonprofits. Her work has appeared in such publications as Rockport Publishers' LogoLounge 3 and Branded, by Début Publications. In addition to keeping the zen kitchen cooking, Dani is an accomplished writer on the subjects of green design, the design business, marketing, and ethically driven business. Her work has appeared in the Holistic Business Journal (www.holistic-business-journal.com); Boston Women's Business (www.bostonherald.com/business/womens/index.bg); and Creative Latitude (www.creativelatitude.com), an online community of creative professionals. She also maintains a business blog called "Notes from the zen kitchen" (http://zenkitchen.blogspot.com), in which she talks about her experiences as a business owner. To keep herself sane, Dani also spends time reading various books and magazines she's been meaning to find time for, journaling, meditating, doing yoga, and cooking—she even gets to throw the occasional dinner party! To learn more about the zen kitchen, visit http://tzk-design.com.

① What qualities do you look for in an applicant?

There are a number of things. The main thing is whether their personality, work, and values fit in with my studio. With our focus on green design and branding, it's important to find candidates who are passionate about the environment as well as those who have solid design skills. I like folks who are friendly, take direction well, and can describe their process on a project beyond "I used Illustrator to trace this image."

2 In your opinion, what makes a successful interview?

I like interviews to be relatively short and fairly informal; I don't want to see everything you've ever done, but I want a good sampling of the work you feel is strongest as well as good explanations of why you feel it's so strong. In terms of the samples themselves, I look for folks who have work that either fits in with the studio's current work or is complementary to it; for example, one woman I collaborate with has a very rough, handmade feel to her work, which is similar in feel, but entirely different in execution, from my own work.

3 Has the Internet had an effect on your interview process?

Absolutely! What I love about the Internet is that it gives me the ability to screen applicants before I have to actually interview them. One thing that young designers can sometimes overlook is that your Web site is almost like a pre-interview; how it is presented says a lot about you as a designer. It's that whole attention-to-detail bit.

4 What are the five best things job candidates say that impress you during an interview? What are the five worst?

Honestly, I really like folks who can share a bit about themselves in an interview—talk about their passions outside design. I like folks who can admit where they need to grow but also be up front about areas where they just completely rock. I'm impressed by candidates who are confident, but not cocky, and who are willing not only to work proactively with clients directly but to work with other designers/art directors.

Mostly in interviews, I'm trying to look beyond the obvious nervousness to see what's inside: Who is this person, and why does he want to work here? Is this a good fit, or is he just saying whatever he thinks I want to hear? If I start hearing overblown claims or hearing things like "I guess my only weakness is that I'm too much of a perfectionist," I start tuning out immediately. Be honest with yourself before and during the interview.

5 What are skills that really help all artists succeed regardless of their specialty?

Well, this is fairly specific to graphic design, but a good knowledge of prepress is *essential* to a good career; it saves you money, time, and headaches when you start sending stuff to press. Also, a good knowledge of basic business processes—contracts, average hourly rates, client/designer interaction. Work on your social skills—there's little that's more annoying than an antisocial designer. Also, a good sense of how to do production, especially programs like Quark and InDesign.

6 What advice would you offer to designers looking to impress you with the presentation of their work?

Learn how to talk about your work in terms of the business problem you were trying to solve and the results that the final piece got for your clients. Most folks who know how to do design will know that you used XYZ filter or you did the logo in Illustrator; they'll even probably know that you took X photo and digitally remastered it. Technique is assumed unless you're being directly asked about it; what I want to know is, How did your clients respond? How did their customers respond? My ability to talk about my work in a business-results context is one of the primary reasons my clients hire me, second only to the quality of the work.

Designer's Challenge 1

Create a children's book. Write a story that teaches a child one valuable lesson, and design a book that tells the story. Use your own images if possible. Explore various bindery systems.

Amanda Grieve demonstrates a beautiful solution to the designer's challenge. The piece features a strong layout and color that is appropriate to the age group. (Amanda Grieve, graduate, Sinclair Community College.)

Designer's Challenge 2

Design an effective self-promotional piece. It should reflect your talents, hobbies, or sense of humor. Remember, it doesn't have to cost a lot; it just has to reflect who you are as a designer and an artist.

Angela Paniza shows us that a terrific color set can hold all of your support pieces together to form a comprehensive package of work.

4

The Traditional Portfolio

Design and Art Projects

Chapter 3 was devoted to an in-depth discussion of the written components of your portfolio: the résumé, cover letter, and business card. It's time now to turn our attention to the visual components of your portfolio: the art and design

projects. These will help to focus the potential employer on your strengths as a creative designer, so it's important to choose thoughtfully and carefully. Each piece should establish your conceptual skills and problem-solving abilities. In addition, the pieces you include must demonstrate not only your talent but also your potential for growth.

Most employers agree that the design portfolio should be composed of about 10 to 20 pieces of recent, original work. These pieces should demonstrate your strength and experience in design as well as highlight skill areas of particular interest to you. In sum, you must use your portfolio to create a coherent, comprehensive message about yourself as a designer.

Before we go much further here, though, I want to stress that there really are no right or wrong pieces to

include in your port. That said, you should also be aware that the first piece viewed by the employer is the most critical: it sets the tone for what is to come. So a good rule of thumb is to select your finest piece of art as the first. It should be visually provoking and conceptually clear. And it must be perfect: no mistakes of any kind. Remember, you are setting the stage for the rest of the portfolio. Even a typo in some copy will give a negative impression.

Of course, the job for which you are applying will also influence the pieces you include in the portfolio. Although, in general, it is best to show a broad base of abilities and styles, resist the temptation to include pieces because you think you have to. If, for example, you are not an illustrator, don't include weak drawings

A small booklet of your work allows you to showcase your designs in a keepsake that will help potential employers remember you.

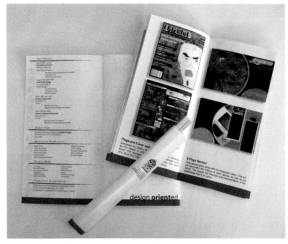

A good rule of thumb is to keep all support materials consistent. Here you can see that the artist carefully crafts both the design book and the résumé.

just to prove you've done some illustration. A sad fact of life is that you will always be judged by the weakest piece in the port. If, on the other hand, you have a well-defined art style, you may wish to showcase that talent. Being selective in this manner, however, also has a risk: you may be excluded from certain jobs because you will not be perceived as a generalist.

Young designers tend to include too many pieces in the port. Doing so may make you appear disorganized or unsure of yourself. Remember the old saying: "Too much of a good thing." Most interviewers will know whether you are qualified for their position after viewing just a few pieces, so don't waste their time. I learned this lesson the hard way once, when I was asked during an interview to stop my presentation, which had gone on for too long. It was very embarrassing!

Organizing Your Portfolio

How you organize your portfolio is almost as important as the work you choose to include in it. As with the résumé, you can arrange your art chronologically or categorically. Using the chronological system, you arrange your projects with the most recent work at the front of the port and continue in reverse order by date. This is a logical way to order your work, but use it only if you're confident the first piece in your port is a strong one. Also note that this style of arrangement works best if all the pieces are in the same category. If you have a wide variety of work, then the categorical system may be a

Ask yourself these four questions about every piece you are considering for inclusion in your portfolio:
1. Technical ability: Does this piece demonstrate the use of techniques appropriate to the particular art form?
2. Aesthetic content: Does the piece adequately and accurately express feelings, emotions, and/or a state of being through the content and form of the work?
3. Composition and design: Does the piece show that you understand the principles and elements of good design?
4. Conceptual basis: Does the piece effectively communicate ideas and theories in your area of expertise?

better choice. This system allows you to divide your portfolio into well-defined sections. A graphic designer, for example, might arrange his or her work into sections such as logo design, collateral pieces, or editorial spreads. An illustrator might instead divide the port into book jacket designs, political cartoons, and fine art pieces. The categorical system also allows you to prioritize the pieces that are the most relevant to the job for which you are applying.

Professional Portfolio Presentation

I want to begin by saying it doesn't really matter which style of portfolio you choose as long as it thematically supports your work and creates a professional appearance. The following are some factors to consider regarding which port case is right for you:

Most cases are about 1 to $1\frac{1}{2}$ inches in depth, but if you have a lot of work or some bulkier pieces, you might need a deeper case.

This portfolio, made by Pina Zangaro, is named Rossano. It is a fashionable way to display your work and comes in both black and brown. These portfolios are compatible with all major brands of sheet protectors, mounting sheets, and adhesive hinge strips.

• STYLE	SIZE
Vinyl or leather handle and zipper cases (Uses sleeves)	8 $\frac{1}{2}$ x 11 11 x 14 14 x 17 17 x 22 18 x 24
Aluminum attaché cases (Holds boards)	(small) 12$\frac{1}{4}$ x 15$\frac{1}{4}$ (large) 12 x 18
Bookcase portfolio cases (Gray or black; holds boards)	8 $\frac{1}{2}$ x 11 11 x 14
Book-style portfolios (No handles)	8 $\frac{1}{2}$ x 11 11 x 14
Screwpost aluminum portfolio	8 $\frac{1}{2}$ x 11 11 x 14 11 x 17 14 x 17
Three-ring binders	10 x 12
Flip charts	11 x 17 17 x 22

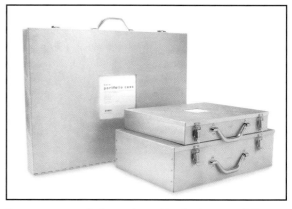

Contemporary and ultramodern, this aluminum portfolio case protects your work and looks good as well! Photographs of Pina Zangaro Portfolio Products.

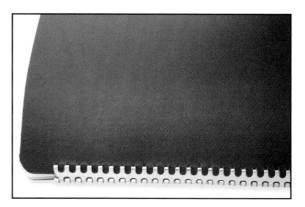

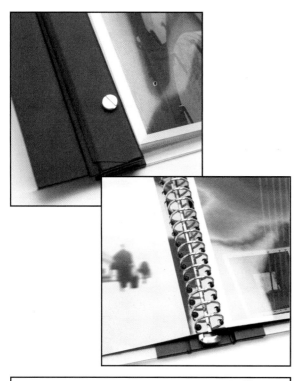

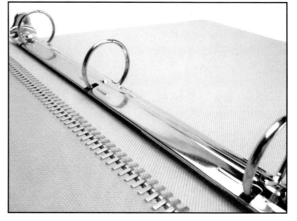

This case uses industrial-grade black PVC with a woven nylon backing. The stainless steel lacing gives your design work an extra bit of sophistication.

This lightweight acrylic portfolio case offers a clean, contemporary look. You can expand the portfolio's capacity to hold art with standard screwpost or ring binders; these offer you the ability to expand the portfolio to include additional work.

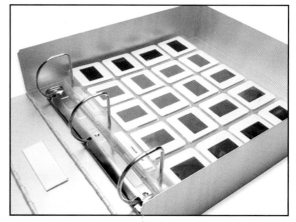

Here is a terrific case to hold traditional photography slides. You can see that this case has a lot of room to hold your work.

Buy the best binder or case you can afford. To check out different portfolio options, visit an art (or craft) supply store in your area. You may also find several options at a business supply store, where you will see a full spectrum of sizes and formats. Or visit a few of the many art stores on the Internet.

You certainly do not have to use a traditional presentation case. If your work is unusual, perhaps consider a more avant-garde style, such as one made with steel exteriors; or a fashioned wooden case, designed to look as if it came from the Wild West. If you're very handy, you might even consider constructing your own case. Just make sure that your nontraditional look doesn't overshadow the work inside.

Should you show your portfolio work on mat boards or set inside of sleeves in a book? The answer is simple: use whichever method is easier and more convenient for you. Both styles of display allow you to replace the art, to keep your selections up-to-date. Boards, though they tend to be heavy, allow the viewer to pick up the work and examine it closely. Furthermore, boards make it very easy to rearrange your pieces based on the job at hand. In contrast, the portfolio book is much lighter and easier to carry, but it is difficult to find one whose pages don't "catch" when they are repeatedly turned. The better-made port cases that don't rip your pages tend to be quite a bit more expensive. So before you choose one of these, insert your artwork in the book and turn the pages. Do they move easily without crimping

the binder? Also consider whether the book or the case is awkward to handle; if so, you will feel clumsy during an interview. One final word of caution: whether you select a book or a case, make sure that it holds the art securely in place.

There is nothing more exciting (or nerve-racking) than the moment when the prospective employer opens your portfolio case for the first time. Help both to calm yourself and to make it easy on the interviewer by choosing the design portfolio that best meets all of the above criteria.

To give you a jump start on shopping for a portfolio, pages 54–55 detail a number of different sizes and styles of portfolio cases.

Here are some Web sites that can help you find the best portfolio to suit your needs:

Star Filing: www.star-filing.com
Filexec Products: www.filexec.com
Prat Paris: www.prat.com

Pay Attention to Detail

A major factor in developing a professional presentation is choosing a unifying theme or style to link what's in your portfolio to the style of the case. You can do this graphically by using a consistent page color, border design, or logo. But whatever you do, don't draw attention away from your work. Avoid wild patterns or loud color schemes that take the viewer's eye away from the

The CD case is another opportunity for you to showcase your design talents. This sleek cover is a progressive way to hold your digital portfolio.

A flip-book makes it easy to display pieces to a larger group because the work can be propped up. All you have to do is flip the sleeves to reveal each piece. (Sabrina Serrano, Fashion Design, Spring 2003.)

• **Ink-jet Tips**

If you have an ink-jet printer, don't set up the paper in a stack to feed through the printer. Why not? Because when the paper emerges from the printer, the ink is still wet. If you run the paper through automatically, one page after another, the ink is going to smear and you'll be wasting time, money, and supplies. Print each page individually and give it time to dry; and, by all means, keep wet pages separated—ideally, in a room with very low humidity. Give the prints a day or so to dry thoroughly before you mount them in your portfolio.

Two more tips: Be aware that ink-jet papers will fade in time. To maintain the quality of your prints, store your work in a dark area, out of direct sunlight. And keep your unused paper as dry as possible.

focal point of the port—your art. Most portfolio cases come supplied with black or gray paper inserts. You can usually change these, but always opt for neutral colors. Believe it or not, there's been a major debate among artists as to the color of these sheets. Most artists still believe that black is best. It showcases the art. Of late, however, I have heard a great deal of talk about other colors such as gray (as the new black!). Don't be surprised when you hear your friends discussing this particular issue quite heatedly. Ultimately, choose the color system you think shows off your work to best advantage.

Prepare Your Work for Viewing

You have your portfolio case, so now let's talk about how you're going to prepare the actual artwork. If you are a graphic, interior, or fashion designer, many of the pieces you have created are probably on disk. (We'll talk more about fine art in a moment.) The images must be printed, but which method is best? Should you use a home printer or a commercial printer?

Using a Home Printer

There are many fine color printers available for the home market today. Epson, Hewlett-Packard, Brother, Minolta, Lexmark, Canon, and Olympus all make high-quality ink-jet printers. Though these printers can be a bit slow, the price can't be beat, and the results are spectacular. All sorts of papers are available for these machines, from photo glossy to holiday card stock, from

T-shirt transfer paper to large-format papers. There is definitely a printer and a paper for you.

Take some time to research which printer will best suit your designs. If you will be doing a lot of large-scale printing (for example, 11 × 17 inches), you will probably want a printer that is capable of handling oversize sheets. Then you will be able to print full size and trim down to the correct size. That way your pieces will look as if they have a "full bleed" to the edges. This makes a very professional presentation. And speaking of professional, that is the name of the game. It doesn't really matter which printer you use, as long as your final outputs look great.

Once you have selected a printer, you will have to decide what kind of paper you want to use. You can achieve striking results with both glossy and matte paper stocks, but which one should you choose? A good printer alone can't guarantee fabulous color prints, but a little knowledge about paper, along with some printing hints, will net you great results.

Ink-jet paper comes in a range of different weights, textures, and colors, so before you buy, again take the time to research what each one has to offer. Go to your local computer or office supply store and take a look at the samples provided by the manufacturer. Many computer and business stores have Saturday demonstrations

Typically, an artist may expect to spend anywhere from $150 to $500 for printing the art, making the slides, buying the portfolio case, compiling a stationery package, burning CD-ROM disks, and producing other materials (such as self-promotional pieces). But that cost may be much lower, depending on how much you can accomplish at home versus how much you have to outsource to print shops such as Kinko's or other local business supply stores. Print shops charge an hourly rate based on how much time you spend sitting at their computers. And should you require additional services, such as scanning your art, expect to pay from about $5 to $12 per scan. This price range depends a lot on the quality and resolution of the scan (although you can generally negotiate an hourly rate if you are doing the scans yourself using the shop's equipment).

If you do need to use a print shop's computer, arrive prepared and organized. As I just said, you are going to be charged by the hour, so you don't want to waste any time. Each scan takes about one to two minutes, so costs can add up pretty quickly. Another word of advice: don't waste time color-correcting or resizing your images at the shop if you have a computer at home. Save your work and leave as soon as you are finished scanning. Those extra minutes will really add up!

If you are creating a digital portfolio, expect to pay for materials such as the CDs themselves, the jewel cases to put them in, and duplication and printing costs (should you decide to label the CDs with your

Here is a great example in which the art on the cover is in harmony with the CD and the business card.

name and logo). These costs can vary but generally run about $0.35 for the do-it-yourselfers to about $3.50 each with a minimum order of 500 through a CD specialty company. Color-printing a multicolor logo, for example, will increase the cost by about $0.20 per color.

The good news is that once you have completed the portfolio, you have incurred the bulk of your costs. Maintaining a portfolio is never as expensive as initially creating it. As you develop new pieces, you simply have them printed and add them to your port.

conducted by the manufacturers' representatives. If possible, view a printer demonstration and make your choice based on the outputs you are given. If you can't see samples of the printing results, don't buy the printer. If no demonstrations are available, ask the store personnel to print something for you, preferably one of your designs.

Paper, as I just noted, is available in both glossy and matte stocks. Glossy paper was invented to produce prints that mimic the typical photograph. It generally produces a deeper, more intense color. Semigloss paper can also be purchased should you wish to produce work with a more understated shine. Matte papers feature a low degree of gloss. They are good when your intent is to produce softer, subtler shades of color in your design. Matte papers typically are available in lighter weights, good for printing, say, a brochure that will be folded. Glossy papers, because of their heavier weights, are difficult to fold cleanly.

Most ink-jet printers allow for only one-sided printing. If you have a document that requires two-sided printing, such as a folder or book, you need a printer that can ink both sides of the page. Printing on both sides involves a difficult and frankly irritating process of trying to align the paper perfectly in the print tray in hopes of getting it right on the first pass. Then you have to flip the page over and feed it back into the printer facing in the right direction. This primitive trial-and-error process all too often results in misprints and paper jams. There are many laser printers that will print on both sides automatically, but you sacrifice quality of ink for the two-sided print. Laser printers often cost quite a bit more than ink-jet printers, too. The higher the print resolution (that is, the quality of the output), the more costly the unit. In the long run, your double-sided artwork (and your wallet) will benefit from a cost-effective printing by a professional business store.

Using a Commercial Printer

What if you can't afford to buy a printer? No problem! There are many small print shops, such as the aforementioned Kinko's, Staples, or Office Max. They have color printers and bindery equipment available for your use. You bring in the file on disk or CD, sit down at one of their computers, and output your work. You are charged for only the time you're logged on. And you can work whenever it suits you, as most of these shops are open 24 hours a day.

You may find that purchasing a specialty printer for developing your digital art may be more costly than simply selecting a dependable digital printing service. These services cost a bit more than a home printer, but they have several advantages. They save you a lot of time and trouble. Instead of sitting and waiting while your home printer cranks away at your piece, you drop off a CD and the print house does the work, freeing your time to address more pressing issues (such as picking out that portfolio). The quality is excellent. The commercial inks now available from a professional print house are made to last decades without fading or discoloring. Prints created by a home printer do not have that long life span, mostly because professional print houses use commercial-grade archival paper and ink in the printing process.

There are also many online services that will print your digital photos that you may wish to include in your portfolio. You prepare your photos—making the necessary corrections to get good image quality with your favorite photo-editing software. Then you simply save your images (usually in JPEG format) and upload them over the Internet to the photo printer's Web site. The completed pictures are mailed directly to you and usually arrive in two to five days.

If you need results faster, almost every modern drugstore or photo store offers digital printing. You take your digital memory card to the store, insert it in a freestanding photo kiosk, and select from the menu of available options. This allows you to pick and choose just which images you wish to print and gives on-the-spot results. You also have the option of leaving your memory card with the employees, and they will complete the process for you. No more blurry throwaway images for you! Digital photography technology has given you the power to keep what you want and discard the rest. Whichever method you choose, you will find the quality of your professional images well worth the extra effort.

Mounting Your Work

Now that you have printed your design work, how do you mount it? There are two different ways to display your art: flush mounting and matting. In the past, artists always used the matting system. An opening just slightly larger than the artwork would be carefully cut in the mat material. The art would then be slipped into place in between the mat and a board placed just under the piece. It was a little like making a sandwich. Though the presentation was highly professional-looking, the two boards made each piece of art heavy and bulky to handle. Therefore, these days, mats are used primarily for displaying fine art in homes and offices.

Flush mounting is a much more practical solution for those who wish to display their work on boards (as opposed to on paper sleeves in a port case). The work is carefully centered on the board. A fine mist of spray mount (a type of glue) is spritzed lightly on the back of the art. The art is then pressed to the board.

What if you have a lot of awkward pieces that need to be pulled out and examined, such as cards, packages,

Kwesi Williams created this illustration and portfolio pocket. As you can see, this is a great way to show off your work.

• How Should You Display Artwork for Interviews?

The answer to this question requires a bit of thought. Let's begin with the size and weight of your case. Remember, you'll have to carry it from interview to interview, so, as cautioned earlier, keep size in mind when you shop for a case. Color is also an important consideration. You want the case to show off the work, not overwhelm it. Select a neutral color. (Most artists prefer black.) Some portfolio cases come with stands or easels, enabling you to prop the work up. These are quite effective, but they can be a little awkward to work with until you get accustomed to the setup. Most people prefer the old-fashioned way: standing and looking over the work as it is presented page by page.

product samples, or booklets? In this case, you must strive to create a portfolio that is professional yet manageable and practical. Portfolio sleeves require that you reach inside to pull out each piece. To make things more manageable, create a clear pocket holder for the piece to nest in until you are ready to remove it. If you feel that a 3-D piece, such as a package, will not be seen in its best light, build the piece, then shoot a picture. That shows the 3-D piece in full relief.

Displaying Three-Dimensional or Folded Pieces

Three-dimensional art pieces, such as clay worked to create backgrounds, and constructed pieces, such as packages or pop-up cards, can cause unique display problems. Art pieces such as sculpture, folders and brochures, and package designs must be exhibited as effectively as possible to accommodate their dimensionality.

Let's examine package design first. Most pieces of packaging are fully articulated—that is to say, "in the round." This presents a unique challenge. How do you convey the full sense of the art in a two-dimensional environment? There are two answers:

1. You could photograph the piece from all sides, then generate a series of slides or prints. In this way, the viewer would be able to see the piece from all angles. A series of mounted prints would allow you to represent the art from many different angles.

2. You could videotape the piece. This method, too, gives you a way to show the piece from all sides, but in choosing it, you run the risk of not being able to play the tape during the interview (the employer might lack the proper equipment). Therefore, a videotape should be used only to supplement the printed work (or converted to a digital QuickTime movie to be placed inside a digital portfolio).

What about folded pieces such as catalogs? The best way to hold these pieces is to use folder pockets and corners. They provide a practical way to keep your pieces firmly in place until you are ready to bring them out for further examination. These pockets are useful for most of your bulkier pieces. Small corners are also sensible for

This superb package, designed by Fernando Velasquez, requires special display treatment for a portfolio. As you can see, Fernando photographed the piece and added extra support pieces. The entire project was mounted in a book to really highlight the design work.

pieces that may require a lot of handling. They serve to keep your work from sliding around in the portfolio.

Once you have decided which of the display methods to use, carefully measure the board or paper insert so that once the system is in place, it will present properly.

Protecting Your Work

A portfolio that features a lot of photography generally consists of prints, color slides, and tear sheets. Most photographers go to great lengths to protect their work.

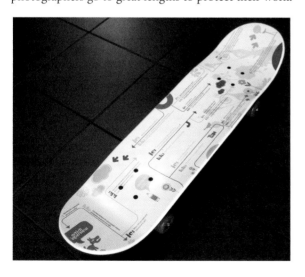

Frequently, prints are window-mounted between white or black boards, then slipped into acid-free sleeves, to ensure that the art is not harmed. Some artists prefer to laminate their photos between two sheets of clear plastic. This fully protects the art, and any smudges can be easily wiped off. Black card masks are excellent for color transparencies. They come in an assortment of sizes and allow the viewer to see many different pieces (both horizontal and vertical) on one page.

If you are a professional photographer, you may have a selection of tear sheets. Tear sheets are provided to the photographer by the publication once a piece has been

Jenna Ebanks designed the graphics on this skateboard and had them applied directly, creating a truly unique portfolio piece. This piece had to be photographed from a variety of angles in order to best show off the design.

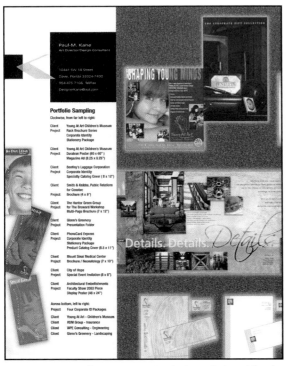

Here is a section from a promotional piece designed by the award-winning graphic designer Paul Kane. His design skills are clearly apparent; hence, this piece would make an excellent way to showcase his portfolio.

selected to appear in print. They can include anything that has been published, from a magazine editorial to a print ad. Tear sheets are usually placed in plastic sleeves inside a good-quality display book. Because most tear sheets are produced in a standard size, the 14- × 17-inch display book is a good option. It is just large enough to hold the work and forms a nice black border around the art.

As discussed earlier, for most designers, the design case with a zipper on three sides and a ring-binder mechanism on the spine is the most popular format for carrying work. But for the photographer, this may not be a practical solution. Because photos need to be seen up close, they must be removed. For this reason, professional photographers prefer briefcase-style portfolio cases with a hinged lid and an open interior. These are more flexible for displaying different-size pieces. You may also wish to place your photos in a miniportfolio. These small ports are designed to sit inside a larger case. They use the same spiral rings as the large case but feature smaller pages just the right size to best show off the work.

One additional option is to consider a custom-created book of your photos. Low-cost technologies allow you to develop and print a softcover or hardcover book. The quality is so high that they are virtually indistinguishable from commercially printed books. How do the companies accomplish this? With extremely high-resolution printers from Hewlett-Packard or Xerox. These printers can reproduce the colors of your photos faithfully, and because they can print across several pages, they are quite cost-effective.

There are a number of different companies for you to investigate, all of which offer the ability to create your photography book directly from their Web site. You create the design of your book from provided templates, upload the file, and a bound book complete with a rich, colorful printed cover sleeve arrives in about two weeks. One of the best is Blurb (www.blurb.com), which creates books directly from your PDF files. The results are beyond belief!

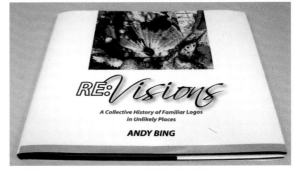

Andy Bing has created a beautiful book of his designs using the services provided by Picaboo. Not only is the color reproduction work excellent, but the book can also be made with a wrap-around cover to create a most professional presentation.

The Apple Web site also offers a terrific service—iPhoto Print Products. iPhoto uses preset templates and works with both Macs and PCs. You drag your photos or art onto template pages, add text and captions, hit a button, and voilà—your newly created book arrives in a few weeks. The software also lets you create calendars and greeting cards of your photography or your art, for that matter—great for giveaways.

The process of getting a book printed at Picaboo (www.picaboo.com) is easy as well. Not only can you work with templates, but Picaboo allows you to completely customize your book by creating your own page layouts. Picaboo is designed to work with PCs.

There are other ways to create photo books as well. Snapfish (a division of Hewlett-Packard; go to www.snapfish.com) and MyPublisher© (www.mypublisher.com) both offer some great features. MyPublisher© gives you the ability to create a coffee-table-size photo book that is quite remarkable. MyPublisher© also offers eight unique book styles and more than 200 page layouts from which to choose. There are choices of color for your book's pages, and you can even order leather covers. Plus, MyPublisher© has a plug-in for iPhoto. Snapfish creates photo books as well as mugs, mouse pads, notebooks, keepsake photo plates, barbecue aprons, and calendars. Any of these items might make terrific self-promotional pieces to help people remember you and your designs.

Lulu (www.lulu.com) is yet another publishing option. Its Web site has a very thorough step-by-step process that will enable you to create a professional book design featuring your photography. You pick a design and add captions to explain your ideas. Lulu offers templates you can follow, or you can send a PDF file of your designed book and simply have Lulu print it, at the same prices.

MyPublisher© offers a variety of options for your book designs and can be used with both Macintosh and PC computers.

• Portfolio Tips: Summary

- Include only your best work.
- Include only recent work—from the past two or three years.
- Create a diverse and broad range of work—that is, demonstrate your experience.
- Consider writing short explanations about your work.
- Resist the urge to use fancy or strange typefaces! Make sure your text is readable.
- Check and recheck for spelling errors.
- Don't crowd large images—for example, a three-ad series on one page.
- Don't shrink large posters of oversize layouts down.
- Use neutral-color pages in your presentation case.
- Always include your rough book or concept journal (described later in this chapter).
- Never let the pages you select to hold your designs detract from the art. Use smooth or matte papers.
- Do not use distracting borders around your designs.
- Put your best work first in the portfolio; likewise, put some of your best work last.
- Keep everything in proportion—nothing too large or too small.
- Make sure that all images are aligned with the edge of the page; do not make your interviewers tilt their heads.
- Make sure your portfolio is always neat and clean.
- Purchase a portfolio case large enough to house your art comfortably.
- Keep your portfolio and your art in a dry place.
- Strive to be different—explore beyond the obvious.
- Let your personality, perspective, and passion show. These are the things that make for distinctive portfolios!

One thing is for sure: your newly created book will really catch people's attention. A book implies a certain level of importance. A book looks significant. It will not only make your work look its best but get more attention as well.

Additional Display Guidelines

You might use the guidelines here as a checklist as you begin to compile your portfolio. Not all of the guidelines will apply to you or to every piece of your art, but they are good reminders of the professional viewpoint.

- Insofar as possible, include only original work in your portfolio. Stay away from photocopies, as they are inferior to ink-jet outputs. Once a printed piece has been copied, it tends to lose its sharpness—the color washes out. It is far better to take a photograph of the piece. Then your work will always be crisp, and you can alter the photo size to match the portfolio.

- Consider using cover sheets. The cover sheet is usually a small piece of paper that offers the viewer an explanation of the nearby art or comments on the scope of the project. An artist involved in a group campaign frequently provides explanations of a design project using this method. Perhaps you were involved in a graphic design project—for example, a

This innovative little package display, designed by Tiffany Braguta, is difficult to capture in pictures. Nevertheless, it is important to try to feature the piece in its best possible light, by taking a series of photos from different angles so that the viewer can see it from all sides.

promotional package; you helped create a piece but had only limited involvement. A cover sheet accompanying the work would enable you to give a short explanation of the role you played in the production of the piece. Cover sheets aren't always necessary, but they can be an effective tool in portfolio design.

- Display pieces that demonstrate knowledge of your industry. Even if your portfolio comprises mostly student work, that does not mean it should look amateurish. As an example, a graphic designer must always be concerned with how art is produced. Don't, then, design a full-color brochure with two spot colors and a varnish that only the top 5 percent of American corporations could afford to print. It might look interesting or exciting, but it might also cause potential employers to wonder whether you could make practical decisions on behalf of their clients and their bottom line.

- Keep it clean! This may seem like stating the obvious, but when I tell you some of the things I have found in the portfolio cases I have evaluated, you'll understand why I include this guideline: dog hair, coins, the smell of cigarettes . . . and worse—so much worse! Double-check your portfolio. Erase smudge marks from projects. If the pages are scratched and torn, the port will look old and unprofessional. I once had a student tell me that he was going for the "messy art look" as his port style. He ripped, tore, and burned his boards. They looked horrible. It might have struck him as a good idea, but the final product looked dreadful, which brings me to my next point . . .

- Always purchase additional sleeves for your portfolio. As you use the port, some of the plastic sleeves will get scratched or tear. Periodically, replace worn sleeves with new ones. You always want the port to look great.

- *Look at your portfolio with fresh eyes.* Turn a critical eye on your port. I know it's your baby and you love everything in it, but consider the viewpoint of the potential employer. Remove any material that could be offensive under certain circumstances. Bright, shiny sports cars with beautiful models might be great if you want to design for a car magazine, but you won't score any points with an in-house graphic design firm whose major clients are banks or hospitals. And stay away from controversial topics unless you can show both sides objectively. I'm not saying you can't display editorial work, but you must be sensitive to the opinions of others. Don't lose a great job over something that could easily have been avoided. Always have others evaluate your portfolio. If several people question the same piece, you really should pull it.

Portfolios for Different Design Disciplines

Each of the design disciplines uses the traditional portfolio in a slightly different way. This is due in part to the types of projects that each discipline generates. For example, a fine artist might generate large multipanel paintings or site-specific installations. A graphic designer might design large billboards. Sometimes the project centers around a kiosk at a mall or government center. Web sites are rich in multimedia and contain multiple pages. These are very difficult projects to capture in pictures. And the fashion designer will be creating clothing in both two-dimensional (on paper) and three-dimensional (on a model) forms. As the artist's needs change, the display method utilized must change as well.

Consider for a moment the portfolio of the fine artist. The painter, the printmaker, the photographer, and the sculptor each produces art of various sizes. Many of these pieces will be too large to fit into a portfolio. (Imagine carrying a 3- × 5-foot painting around.) Large-scale work requires special attention. The artist has several options. As you already know, he or she can take a series of slides that show both the size and detail of the piece. These slides can be mounted in special photo sleeves that serve to showcase the work, which are then inserted in the portfolio case. Other options are available as well. Some fine artists feel it is important to show the art on a computer at the interview and so will bring a laptop along to display their work. An artist may also print a piece as large as he or she feels is necessary to properly show the scope of the work. As long as the

prints fit easily into the portfolio case, the work will be properly displayed.

Graphic designers will also need to give some consideration to challenging display problems. A beautifully designed three-dimensional package has to be displayed to show all sides of the project. This would require the artist to display the piece in flat two-dimensional form and in finished form. The artist could take a picture of the final package as it would appear on a shelf to show the application.

Architects and interior designers frequently prepare boards for clients that are 24 × 36 or even 30 × 40. Although it is possible that the work may be kept in a large format, such work is frequently reduced to accommodate the interview process. Design models will be photographed from a variety of vantage points and the photos mounted on boards to show the design from various angles. Drawings of the design in process are included to show the project from concept to completion.

The Sketchbook

You know you are a remarkably talented, creative, and incredibly insightful artist and designer, but now you have to prove it in the professional arena. To help you do that, in addition to your portfolio, it's a good idea to provide a sketchbook. Your sketchbook (sometimes known as the rough book or concept journal) is a compilation of doodles, quick ideas, drawings, sketches on the backs of napkins, musings, visual references, and anything else that shows how you conceptualize design. Think of it as a record of your brainstorming process in action. Employers know that great ideas typically evolve slowly, from careful thought coupled with research into the customers' needs. They like to see this thought process.

You don't have a sketchbook? Start developing one now! Employers will not hire you based on a pretty portfolio alone. They also want to know how you arrive at your designs. And, unlike the portfolio, you don't have to worry about the appearance of your sketchbook. It may very well be messy, and that's perfectly acceptable. The purpose is to show the development of your ideas in your sketchbook. In fact, it's advisable to show alternate solutions to each problem. Your first idea was

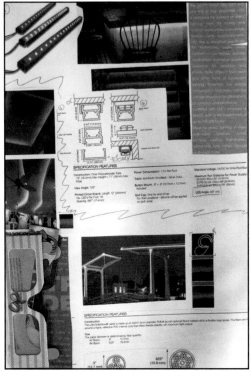

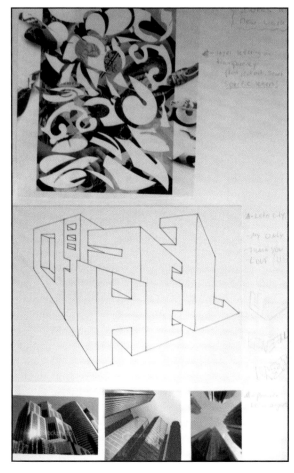

above Here are a couple of pages from Kelly Bennett's sketchbook. It's full of doodles and researched images. This type of sketchbook shows your development process for a project.

below Iliena Popow lets us see the process she uses to solve the problem of creating an ad for a product called Juice Time. It is important to show the steps taken to design a complicated piece.

unlikely to have been the final one, so be prepared to show how you went from point A to point D or F or even Z. And try to keep the sketchbook somewhat organized, to more clearly demonstrate your process.

The Artist's Statement

As part of the portfolio process, most art students are asked to develop an artist's statement before they are permitted to graduate. The artist's statement is an essay that describes the artist's philosophy. Usually, the statement discusses the meaning of processes or techniques involved in art making.

In preparation for writing this statement, take a moment to think about what you want to achieve with your art as well as what kind of message you are trying to communicate as your portfolio is viewed. Your objective is to promote yourself in a way that sets you apart from other artists. Thus, your artist's statement should give the reader compelling insights about you.

The statement usually includes the artist's college history, from freshman year until just before graduation, and frequently discusses the influences of other artists. If you've been out of school for a while, you can also refer to your most recent influences. The point is, you want anyone who reads it to gain valuable insights into you and your work. The following subsections will help guide you in creating your artist's statement.

Artist's Statement: Catherine Ramey

I work with imagery, which utilizes the intensity of nature as a motif for spiritual and psychological being. The organic inferences evolve from my experiences cultivating a lush garden in upstate New York. I start with a form, but the form is no more or less important than the feeling that surrounds it and the deeper and more enduring intangible that cradles that feeling.

The source of a piece is a convergence of linked relationships. It is the still and demanding afternoon light on the lower garden and the deep and awkward letting go of my aging mother. The beginnings of a painting are an amalgam of memories, a shaft of light, a shadow, a tender remembrance of the day. I gather and return to these moments of emotional impact.

Once something is laid down, a stratum of building begins through adjusting a color tone or an edge, again and again. Sometimes the traces remain as a pentimento. I work the surface with various implements and mediums to create a physical density and luminosity.

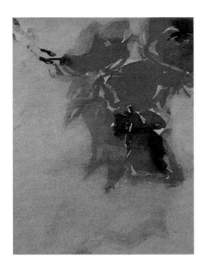

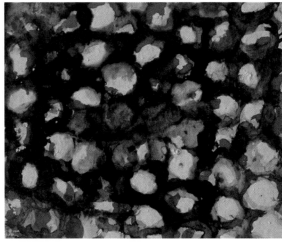

Catherine Ramey has created these exquisite images, entitled Meadow Son #9 and Laying Seed #6.

These paintings are mainly concerned with sculptural forms painted with light. My concerns were with finding relationships with forms that would hold their own with the forms around them and also relate to the space that the viewer occupied.

This work is for me an extension of ideas first brought to painting by Paul Cézanne, added to by Braque and Picasso, and examined by the abstract expressionists and the formal painters of the 60s, 70s, and 80s, the ideas of how to bring pure form back to painting.

Mark LaRiviere finds that his influences come from the Impressionist era. Here is a piece entitled *Blue and White*. Visit his Web site at www.marklariviere.com.

Introduction

The first paragraph of the artist's statement sets the stage for all the information to come. It should be informative but brief, giving some insight into your art and your philosophy of art making. Invite the reader to learn more about your goals and ambitions. You want to pique his or her interest. The first paragraph should be only three to five sentences long.

Body

The purpose of the body is to discuss several of your pieces and provide the reader with some insight into your art-making process. The pieces you choose to talk about will be the focal points of your statement. Therefore, for each piece, provide critical information, such as the title and dimensions of the work, the medium utilized, and why you included the piece. Explain each piece. Discuss your ideas, and describe your artistic vision. Communicate your inspirations and influences and how they intertwined to produce the final piece.

As you describe the art, provide some analysis for the reader. Use artists' terminology that helps to characterize the piece, such as color, negative space, texture, movement, and emphasis. Interpret the piece for the viewer. Clarify the message that is being communicated. Mention well-known artists who have influenced you and your work. Be passionate about what you have to say. Help the reader to understand why you believe the piece to be a successful work of art. This may be an uncomfortable thing for most of you to do, but you must learn to promote yourself.

The accompanying sidebars present two examples for you to examine.

Final Thoughts

As you close your artist's statement, draw some conclusions. Be honest and direct in expressing your final thoughts. The statement should not be so erudite or difficult to comprehend that you lose the reader's interest. And never make excuses for your art.

Before you distribute your statement, ask some professionals in the field to read it. Invite and consider their thoughts and criticisms. Fine-tune your statement as necessary. Your artist's statement may just be one of your most effective promotional tools.

An Interview with Andrea Lubell

Andrea Lubell is the marketing and advertising consultant for the Lubell Group. Ms. Lubell holds a bachelor of science degree in business from Ithaca College, Ithaca, New York. Ms. Lubell started in marketing but decided to move into project development and marketing. She moved to Florida and started an advertising and marketing firm, which was primarily involved in launching new products. Ms. Lubell is also actively involved with Women in Distress and assists in the organization's fund-raising efforts. She currently sits on the board of directors for the nonprofit group Meals on Wheels. You can visit her Web site at www.lubellgroup.com.

1 **What qualities do you look for in an applicant?**

Professionalism and good computer skills/knowledge and familiarity with current software.

2 **In your opinion, what makes a successful interview?**

Coming to agreement to work on a project together.

3 **Has the Internet had an effect on your interview process?**

Yes . . . [It provides] the ability to review portfolio items online, and it eliminates the need to have face-to-face meetings.

4 **What are the five best things job candidates say that impress you during an interview?**

1 They are deadline-oriented.
2 The client gets what they want, not what the artist wants.
3 Flexibility—review what type of work they do best and what they have experience with.
4 Understanding how to price for a broker relationship.
5 They are Mac-based, not PC, with a strong familiarity with programs.

What are the five worst?

Don't tell me you know how to do something and let me figure out you are lying. For example, if I ask if you know how to design display graphics and you answer yes, you'd better know what resolution is expected, formats are normally used, et cetera.

5 **What are skills that really help all artists succeed regardless of their specialty?**

- Ability to understand what the client wants.
- Juggling, working multiple jobs in tight time periods.
- Understanding the printing process and working within the parameters/specs provided.
- Being organized.

6 What advice would you offer to designers looking to impress you with the presentation of their work?

Have a variety, be able to explain what the job or assignment was that the art was created for, and the work needs to be commercially acceptable, not necessarily pretty (although it might be).

Designer's Challenge 1

Create an artist's statement that describes your graphic design philosophy or art-making skills. The statement should comment on your inspiration. It should also mention which artists, either contemporary or historical, have influenced your work. The accompanying sidebar presents an example to jump-start your writing.

Designer's Challenge 2

Create a newsletter for an organization. The colors and type chosen should be appropriate for the client. Design a new masthead for the client. Use a multicolumn format with pictures that support the copy.

Here is an excellent newsletter designed by Amanda Grieve. She shows you the "before" and the "after," and you can really see the difference! (Amanda Grieve, graduate, Sinclair Community College.)

Code of Honor

The knight traditionally stood for honor and a code on how to act. For deeds that should be done—for doing what's right, not what's right for you. That seems to be lost in today's world. By placing iconic images of armor in a contemporary setting, the viewer is forced to contemplate the place of these images and what they stand for. Do they still mean what they once did, and how does that relate to our self and our world today?

These drawings and paintings bring us face-to-face with this question by bringing the romanticized ideals of chivalry, and right, into our world. We idealize the world of the knight, and indeed the knight himself, through stories of "might for right," not "might makes right." Was it ever truly that way, or is the very idea of chivalry just an idea? Even if these were just ideas, are not the concepts of responsibility, respect, and compassion worth our time? Are the qualities expressed by each of these pieces noble parts of man to be strived for or just unrealistic dreams of a past that never was?

These two pieces are by Howard T. Katz. On the left is a sketch for a painting entitled *Code of Honor: Valor*. The drawing shows the value of keeping a sketchbook to work through ideas. The piece on the right is the finished painting that was produced as a result of the sketch. The final painting is part of a series designed to explore the traditional code of chivalry and asks the question, "Does chivalry still have a place in today's society?"

5

The Digital Portfolio
CD-ROMs, DVDs, and Web Sites

We live in a digital world. Cell phones, the Internet, cable television, personal digital assistants (PDAs) such as the BlackBerry and PalmPilot, all plug us in and keep us connected. It won't surprise you, then, to hear that having a digital portfolio will give you a leg up on the competition. What employer could possibly resist a state-of-the-art presentation with sound and animation? A print portfolio is a great marketing tool, but a digital portfolio is an experience.

Armed with just a small CD-ROM or DVD containing your designs, you can easily apply for jobs anywhere. Want to relocate to another state? Simply send your CD or DVD to remote locations for evaluation. Or post your material on the Web or attach it to an e-mail.

Although this may sound great, the question is how to begin. I won't deceive you: an electronic portfolio can be challenging to create from scratch. There are many details you must consider—which computer program to use, which graphic format, file sizes, presentation styles, and copyright issues, to name just a few. Fortunately, once armed with some basic information, you will be able to create a terrific tool with which you can promote yourself. And that's the purpose of this chapter—to examine the process of creating both CD- or DVD-based and Web-based portfolios. In it, I evaluate the strengths as well as the weaknesses of each format so that you'll be able to choose the best program for the job. I'll also introduce you to some of the support software available for multimedia authoring.

CD-ROM/DVD- or Web-based Portfolio?

Any discussion of electronic design begins with the question, Which format should I use to create my portfolio? Should I create a Web site? Or produce a CD-ROM or DVD? The answer is, it depends. In fact, there is not much difference between the two formats. Both follow a very similar set of rules. The difference is one of speed. On the Web, files take longer to download, so they must be smaller in size. CD-ROMs and DVDs don't have the same speed restrictions; hence, files can be much larger. That said, with a little planning, you can create a project that works effectively in both formats.

The most important point to remember is that all interactive media-based projects are fundamentally the same. You create a user interface that allows the viewer to navigate through your résumé and art projects. The final products may differ, but the interface principles remain the same. We'll take a closer look at some of the problems associated with the various forms of multimedia a bit later. For now, let's consider some of the software necessary to create an interactive portfolio.

The best way to create a successful electronic presentation is to produce a portfolio that is not reliant on any other program. With a stand-alone presentation, the original software need not be present in order to view the work—for example, a Web site or a CD or DVD that automatically launches your presentation without the need for additional software. Several programs are available to help you build an interactive portfolio. Some are easy to master, while others require a bit more effort. All will help you achieve your goal: to create an interactive portfolio. Before we explore some of the more popular programs, let's evaluate the strengths and weaknesses of the two formats.

The CD-ROM- or DVD-based Portfolio

For all intents and purposes, a CD-ROM (compact disc read-only memory) or a DVD (digital video disc) can be considered simply a storage device for your designs and résumé. Whatever your specialty—fine art, photography, graphic design, or interactive design—a CD or DVD can be used to display your work. As a simple art

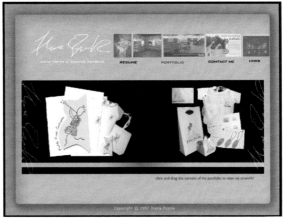

The Internet makes it possible for your work to be viewed at any time from virtually anywhere in the world. Here is the digital portfolio of Iliena Popow.

storage device, a CD or DVD lists all the files that contain the various elements of your portfolio. The user double-clicks on any of those files, which opens the creation program to display the file's contents.

The primary disadvantage of this method is that the viewer must have the software you used to create the art, or he or she will be unable to open the file—unless you have created a file that will run as a stand-alone program. Fortunately, there are now several different ways to make your files "play" without dependent software. We will talk more about these solutions later.

One major advantage of creating a CD-ROM- or DVD-based portfolio is that you can reproduce it as often as necessary. As soon as a hot job prospect comes your way, you "burn" a CD or DVD containing your work and send it quickly on its way to the potential employer. Most new computers today come with CD or DVD burners that enable you to reproduce your work in a matter of minutes. If you have an older computer, you can buy an external CD or DVD burner for under $100. Or you can have your digital portfolio reproduced at most local print shops.

The CDs themselves are inexpensive—about $0.49 per disc. And if you buy in bulk, you can reduce the cost to about $0.25 per disc. Furthermore, CDs are lightweight, so it doesn't cost much to send one through the mail, a real savings if you plan to do a bulk mailing. And for a professional touch, you might want to consider buying a software package that will enable you to create special CD labels with your contact information. Some of these programs will also allow you to add graphic images. Then you can include the logo you use on your business card. Very professional!

A CD-ROM can hold about 700 megabytes of data. That is a lot, but it is not unlimited. A Photoshop file sized to 11 × 17 (a typical two-page spread) and created at 300 dots per inch (dpi) is typically about 24 megabytes (for definitions of these computer terms, see the accompanying sidebar as well as the glossary at the end of the book). This means that you will be able to store about 26 images on your disk. If you plan to display larger images or want to run an authoring program, you will have to dedicate more space.

A DVD holds 4.7 gigabytes, in contrast to the 700 megabytes that a CD can hold; however, the associated costs are higher. The average price can run $2 to $3 per disk. This is because the discs can be written to on both sides. In addition, some discs are rewritable. The good news is that thanks to the latest technologies, you can customize these DVDs by burning logos onto the media with a compatible drive's laser technology. This laser precision and detail means no more unprofessional-looking marker scribble or messy adhesive labels to center.

The single biggest problem associated with a CD or DVD is the time required to load large images. Fortunately, this problem is not insurmountable. It just requires a little knowledge and creativity.

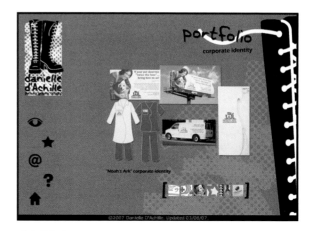

Danielle D'Achille has created this whimsical Web site that really reflects her design sensibilities. She even has some hidden areas for you to discover.

The Web-based Portfolio

Using a Web-based portfolio is probably the fastest possible way to promote your abilities as a designer to potential employers. Anyone interested in your work can log on and visit your Web site in a matter of seconds, from anywhere in the world.

A well-designed Web-based portfolio generally consists of a main (or home) page, which contains links to other areas of the site. In many ways similar to the CD or DVD, a Web site offers the viewer a variety of ways to navigate and interact. Like the CD- or DVD-based portfolio, a Web site is created in a nonlinear fashion. What does nonlinear mean? It means you can move about a Web site in any manner you choose. You do not have to follow a preestablished interface that goes only forward but not backward.

Designing for the Web does, however, have its own set of unique problems—first and foremost, speed. Art created for the Web must take dial-up user limitations into account. Any file that takes too long to download risks losing the visitor's patience. Clearly, you don't want the viewer to click away from your site out of frustration.

Other Web portfolio issues you'll have to address include the following:
- *Color:* Dramatic color shifts occur between print and Web-based output. There are color differences between displays on PCs and Macs as well.
- *Typography:* There are fundamental differences between fonts available on the PC and the Mac.
- *Copyright:* You have to protect your material as much as possible from theft. A few tricks will help keep your files safe.
- *Ease of navigation:* If the viewer can't figure out how to navigate your site quickly and easily, he or she will soon leave. (We will deal with such technical problems in detail in Chapter 6.)

Size and Speed: Primary Criteria

As I've already stated, working with media files can be challenging for the simple reason that they are big. Really big! This is especially true of large-scale images, sound, and video files. For example, a 24-megabyte Photoshop file prepared for print would never be acceptable as a digital file. Why not? Let's say you have a project that you plan to publish both on the Web and on a CD or DVD. (Remember, file size makes a big difference in this situation because the Web is much slower than a CD or DVD player.) Now assume that your final project size is 2 megabytes. Depending on the method of transfer, here's a chart that shows how long it would take to download that file from the Internet.

Now add to those numbers the amount of people on the Web at any given moment. At certain times of the day, only a few million may be online, but at other times, there may be many, many more. Think about rush hour on the expressway. It takes a long time to get home when everyone else is trying to do the same thing. The Web is like that. A file that streams nicely across the country late at night may take twice as long in the middle of the day. And most folks are pretty impatient these days. They will wait only so long before jumping to another site. So if someone would have to wait 50 seconds to download your project, that's probably expecting too much.

Now let's consider that same 1-megabyte file on a CD. The ability to access information on a CD depends on several factors, including drive speed of the player, buffer size (memory), and how fast that disc can get up to full spin speed. To clarify, let's say that drive speed is represented by an X factor, where each X indicates an access speed of 150 kilobytes per second. As an example, a 40X CD-ROM drive can access information at a rate of up to 6 megabytes per second. (The fastest transfer rate commonly available is about 52X, or 10,350 rpm and 7.62 megabytes per second, though this is only when reading information from the outer parts of a disc.) That same 1-megabyte file can be accessed in a fraction of a second. At least, that's the way it's supposed to work. The problem is that the CD has to get "up to

ACCOUNT TYPE	SPEED	BITS PER SECOND	TIME REQUIRED TO DOWNLOAD 1 MB (SECONDS)
Dial-up	56 Kbps	56,000	143
ISDN	128 Kbps	128,000	63
Broadband	1 Mbps	1,000,000	8
T1	1.5 Mbps	1,500,000	5

speed" (known as spin speed) in order to access the file. This works well for single files, but if you want to take multiple files (such as your entire Web site, with its multiple file links) and burn that group of files on a CD, the CD will have to "ramp up" every time your portfolio accesses a different area.

DVD players have become more prevalent in recent years and provide faster transfer speeds than CDs. A typical 16x DVD transfers data at a rate of up to 21.6 megabytes per second. If you are going to be accessing multiple files, you are better off with the newer technology. If you have only one large file on the disc, the faster speed will not be a big help.

As you can see, you have to give a lot of thought to how you approach your initial files. You must always keep in mind the viewer, and how long he or she will be willing to wait to see your project.

Deciding Which Multimedia Authoring Program to Use

There are a number of terrific multimedia programs on the market today, offering an impressive range of features. The newest multimedia software features floating palettes with "drag-and-drop" capacity. You decide on the look of the project, and the software helps you to create the interface. Let's peek inside a couple of these packages and find the one to suit your needs.

Linear versus Nonlinear: Choosing a Presentation Program
PowerPoint: Viewing from Point A to Point B

One of the most popular presentation programs on the market today is Microsoft PowerPoint. PowerPoint is a relatively uncomplicated program used to create portfolio slide shows as well as simple Web sites. Both images and type can be imported to preexisting templates (or to those you create from scratch). The newly created "slides" can then be controlled via buttons or by creating a timed presentation. You can also demonstrate the process of creating a portfolio piece from sketch to completed project with a transition build. This allows you to sequentially add art images one picture at a time on a single slide. This is a nice effect if you want to show the evolution from concept to finished piece. Neat transitions such as "wipes" and "dissolves" can take you from image to image; and you can add music to enhance the experience. Simple animations are also possible if you want to add a little something extra.

PowerPoint is easy to learn. Most important, for many designers, PowerPoint will be all they need to quickly create an electronic portfolio. One of the program's most useful features is the ability to save your material as a PowerPoint Show. This feature allows you to take your finished electronic portfolio and export it as a stand-alone environment. Once you select PowerPoint Show from the Save As options, the PowerPoint Viewer is embedded as part of your presentation. Potential

Abbreviation	Stands For	Pronounced	Use When Describing Bytes	Approximate Number	Actual Number
K	kilo	*kay* or *killa*	kilobyte (KB)	A thousand bytes	1,024
M	mega	*meg*	megabyte (MB)	A million bytes	1,048,576
G	giga	*gig* or *giga*	gigabyte (GB)	A billion bytes	1,073,741,824

Note: K (kilo) = 1,000; M (mega) = 1,000,000; G (giga) = 1,000,000,000.

When you look at the storage capacity of a drive or a CD or DVD, these numbers all start to mean something: a CD holds 700 megabytes, a DVD holds 4.7 gigabytes, and a hard drive holds anywhere from 20 gigabytes to 120 gigabytes.

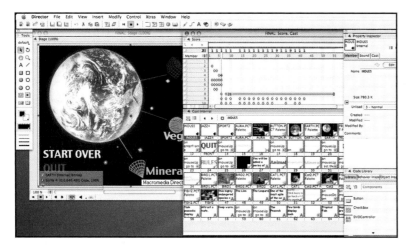

Adobe Director offers a powerful scripting capability that makes it possible to create a nonlinear presentation. This interface is for an interactive children's quiz game.

employers viewing your portfolio will not need PowerPoint in order to look at your work. They need only double-click the starting icon, and the slide show begins.

The main drawback to PowerPoint is that it is mainly designed as a linear program. That means a slide show can be run only forward and backward, one slide at a time. If the viewer wishes to revisit an earlier image, he or she will have to sequence through each of the in-between slides to get there. The program has grown up in recent years and can now be used to create simple nonlinear programs, but it takes a bit of work, and the self-running show doesn't always operate quite the way you expect. This can frustrate the viewer, who may be unwilling to backtrack in this fashion. PowerPoint can also use your basic show to create a Web site, but any of the program's cooler features, such as sound or animation, must be sacrificed to make the file Internet-ready. Typically, effects such as superscripting, subscripting, formulas, and footnotes will not make a successful transition to the Internet either. Still, PowerPoint is a great little program if you need a quick and easy presentation for your work.

The Flexibility of a Nonlinear Presentation

If you want to make it easier for your viewers to navigate your portfolio, you'll need to prepare a nonlinear presentation, one that allows them to "bounce around" your portfolio. A viewer might first look at your résumé, then visit your "gallery." Once in your gallery, he or she may veer off into minigalleries, where more of your designs are on display. At any time, the viewer can, simply by clicking, move directly to another area of your port without having to back out of the section he or she is currently viewing.

Nonlinear authoring programs offer additional flexibility. They give you the ability to import many different file types, so no matter what your area of design, chances are that you will be able to transfer your projects into a format that these programs will understand. With these and many more features, such multimedia programs can really showcase your work. You can design almost unlimited interface styles. You can make the project as friendly and approachable as you wish. In sum, nonlinear programs are very attractive to potential employers. They offer a sophisticated way for you to display your work, and they demonstrate your level of design expertise in the process.

Several programs are currently available to create nonlinear portfolios. Two of the more popular programs are Director (formerly Macromedia Director) and Flash (formerly Macromedia Flash), both now owned by Adobe.

For many years, Adobe Director has been the program of choice for multimedia authoring. Director serves many different purposes and professions; it not only enables you to build your digital portfolio, but it can also help you to create simulations, tests, and even games. What gives Director the edge over other authoring programs is its capability to handle a wide range of media. Director can import all sorts of graphic formats, music, even long-format video and 3-D.

Consider, for example, how effective it would be to take one of your sculptures or architectural drawings and model it in a 3-D space. (Programs such as 3ds Max [from Autodesk], form•Z [from AutoDesSys], and Maya [from Autodesk] can be used to create the model.) You could then import the project to Director, where the viewer could look at your model from all sides.

A word of caution is in order here, however. Director has a higher learning curve than many other authoring programs. But once you master it, you'll find it to be very flexible and capable of producing quite sophisticated interface designs. Director uses a computer language called Lingo to create what are called "markers." These markers represent the various sections of your interface. (Note: Although you can create a digital portfolio without using Lingo, you'll need it in order to employ all the program's best features.) Check out the example of Director in the accompanying illustration.

For those who prefer to create multimedia with as little programming as possible, Adobe Flash is the program of choice. Flash utilizes a highly graphic interface that allows you to create an interface in a relatively short amount of time. Floating palettes abound, to make your design work easier. And the programming code, ActionScript, used in Flash helps you control major sections of your project. Although ActionScript can be difficult to learn, Flash makes it easy on those of us who are nonprogrammer types. All sorts of scripts come pre-built to help you on your way. These snippets of code, called behaviors, allow you to control parts of your project without actually having to write in the ActionScript language—meaning you don't need a lot of programming knowledge to build your portfolio. Templates are also included, to help you with the creation of slide shows and video presentations.

One of the most important reasons for using Flash is speed. Flash employs vector-based technology to create interfaces. (A vector image is made up of many individual points arranged by the underlying math of the graphics program. Because they are math-based objects, vector graphics can be output at any size without sacrificing quality.) This enables you to produce dazzling animations, yet keep file sizes down to just a few kilobytes. What does that mean? Little or no wait time at your Web site or on your CD or DVD.

But what really sets Flash apart from other multimedia authoring programs is its flexibility. Are you an architect? Flash can import files from AutoCAD. Do you have files created in graphic programs such as Photoshop or Illustrator? No problem. Flash can import files from those programs as well. Moreover, a wide range of features makes it easy for you to use the program to suit your individual needs. Animators enable you to create cartoons for the Web. In fact, Flash can help you create projects that go way beyond portfolio

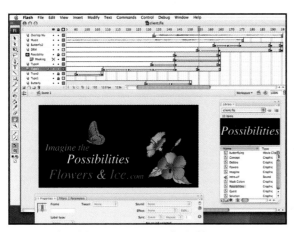

Flash has the ability to maintain multiple libraries so you can share assets among different files. This can really streamline your development process.

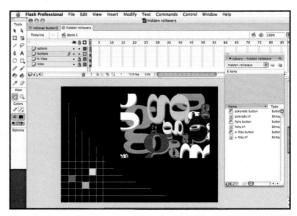

This Flash interface features a "rollover" effect. The viewer rolls the mouse pointer over one of the buttons located at the lower left and artwork pops up on the screen.

design. Corporations can extol their fine consumer products with Flash-based demonstrations; weather and stock information can be sent graphically to cell phones or PDAs; and kids are encouraged to learn facts about the world with clever Flash-based games. Flash has become so popular of late that you'll hear people refer to their projects as "Flashed."

Which Program Is Right for You?

So which type of program should you choose—linear or nonlinear? The answer is, it depends. Each program has strengths and weaknesses, advantages and disadvantages. If you find the thought of doing even minimal programming daunting, then PowerPoint may be the clear choice for you. If, however, you can double-click to generate a few lines of code, you might be surprised at how easy Flash is to learn. And, of course, the more time you spend working with a program, the more sophisticated your interface will become as a result. It is easy to create a quick little interface, but the really great ones take time (lots of time). So if time is of the essence, choose the quickest route possible to your final project.

Master of the Web: Choosing a Hypertext Markup Language (HTML) Program Editor

Just as there are a number of multimedia authoring programs that can help you to design an interactive CD or DVD, there are numerous programs to help you design Web pages for your projects. Though it is possible to design Web pages using nothing more than a simple text editor, most experts agree that using what's called a drag-and-drop program will simplify the process considerably. The code generated by these text editors isn't always perfectly clean; nevertheless, they do offer powerful design and programming tools.

Adobe Dreamweaver

Let's take a quick look at the most popular HTML editor on the market today—Adobe Dreamweaver (for-

In some ways, creating a Web site is similar to producing a CD-ROM or DVD. Images, text, and sound are combined to create a series of "clickable" pages. Many designers use both multimedia authoring programs and HTML editors to create a total viewing experience.

merly Macromedia Dreamweaver). What makes Dreamweaver unique is that it enables you to create layouts that don't look like ordinary Web designs. This gives you free rein to be an artist without worrying so much about how the layout will look once it is uploaded.

Once upon a time, the HTML Web design market was filled with competition, but not anymore. In recent years, Adobe Dreamweaver has become the program of choice. Dreamweaver features a drag-and-drop-style HTML editor, with extensive layout tools, and its features and results are spectacular. Adobe products are well integrated, meaning that Dreamweaver works well with Flash and Photoshop (not surprisingly, since Adobe produces all three products).

Dreamweaver is notable for the clean HTML code it creates. Using the program, you can work directly in code view, in a page-layout mode, or in a split view where you can see both your code and the preview, as shown. With Dreamweaver, you can manage your Web site with ease and efficiency. In addition, should you ever decide to become a more advanced HTML designer, Dreamweaver provides excellent support for scripting languages such as Active Server Pages (ASP, special embedded scripts that can be written for Web page development), JavaServer Pages (JSP, a scripting language for creating interactive Web pages), PHP (Hypertext Preprocessor, used to create shopping carts), and ColdFusion Markup Language (CFML, one of the main languages used to design Web databases).

Dreamweaver has just about every authoring tool you can imagine. Dreamweaver provides the ability to create designs using the latest HTML and XHTML/CSS extensions. It comes with preinstalled behaviors that enable you to create rollover effects that can add some punch to your designs. It allows you to link live to the host site, which in turn allows you to use FTP (file transfer protocol) to send your files directly online. Dreamweaver also comes with a powerful "Find and Replace" feature, which permits you to find and replace words throughout the site with just a click or two. Dreamweaver adheres to all United States government Section 508 rules regarding accessibility for people with disabilities

And then there are the extensions—an extensive collection of prewritten codes that add functionality to your Web design. There are menu-builder extensions that help you create any kind of pop-up or drop-down Web menu with no coding experience. Additional applications create pure CSS (Cascading Style Sheets) galleries and slide shows with fluent navigation and image transitions. They are generally customizable and fit most site layouts. Small animations can be created for the top and bottom of your windows with the help of still more free plug-ins. All it takes is some time and a bit of effort.

Adobe Acrobat

Adobe Acrobat is especially useful for graphic designers who are comfortable with page-layout software. Using Acrobat, you can create files that rework layout-style pages (such as QuarkXPress and InDesign) into Web links. The program converts those files into a special format called Portable Document Format (PDF, a cross-platform file format that accurately displays font and graphical elements contained in a publication). The program can also embed multimedia content such as sound and movies. And because fonts cause one of the biggest problems facing multimedia designers (standard TrueType fonts on PCs do not always work on Macs),

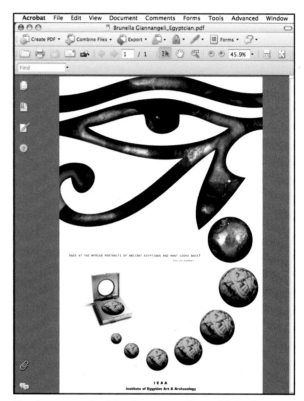

Here is an example of Acrobat output. Once a file has been created in Acrobat, you can open it and examine it in Acrobat Reader. (Poster created by Brunella Giannangeli.)

Acrobat embeds font information directly in the document. This lets you create documents that will look just as you intended, no matter who reads them and regardless of the platform. Acrobat works well with Microsoft Office, and the program allows you to convert most Word, PowerPoint, and Excel files. Acrobat can also make PDFs of copied-and-pasted Web pages (but only in the Windows version). Both the Mac and PC versions of the program can import 3-D objects created with AutoCAD.

Moreover, using Acrobat, pages can be created that contain index links, enabling visitors to click on any link and immediately be taken to its corresponding page. Acrobat also has the capability to reduce file sizes (which means they download more quickly) and is great at creating electronic magazines. Once a document has been designed in Adobe InDesign or QuarkXPress, it

Just a bit of searching on the Internet will uncover a virtual plethora of HTML editing programs that are designated as "freeware" or "shareware." You'll see names for software programs such as Nvu, Amaya, SeaMonkey, Taco, HTML Kit, CoffeeCup Free HTML Editor, and Arachnophilia, but what does that all mean to you?

Let's start by defining what these programs are. Freeware and shareware are software programs available for download from the Internet. Freeware is, as the name suggests, free for your use. Shareware, on the other hand, is software that you can try out for a specified period of time, after which it is available for purchase. Freeware can include games, small widgets for your desktop, small snippets of programming code, or minor program upgrades. Generally speaking, these types of programs do not come with software manuals, but they are usually pretty easy to use. Sometimes the author will maintain a Web site that offers some technical support by way of a discussion forum, or, in some cases, the author may answer your questions directly.

Freeware has become a popular way to develop a program. The creator begins by writing a basic version of the program. As the developer continues to refine the code, new versions are released. You can download each of these interim releases and check for potential problems (called "bugs"). The version will be designated something like .8a, 1.2b, or 1.3.1. As the program is refined, more features are added. Eventually, the program may be offered for a small fee. At that point, the freeware has now become shareware. You may see a license agreement when you decide to download your program or code. This end user license agreement, or EULA, tells you if there are any restrictions on usage and usually asks you to give credit to the programmer if you place the program on your Web site. The agreement may also specify that you must not alter the written code. Each license is specific to the author.

If you decide to download something, be it freeware or shareware, it is very important to be familiar with the site. All sorts of computer viruses can come along for the ride if you're not careful. Be sure to run a virus-check program on your new software as soon as you complete the download.

One other category of software is "open source software." This type of software is similar to freeware. The big difference is that the code that powers the program is open and available for modification. One of the most popular examples is osCommerce (www.oscommerce.com). This software package was developed to enable you to create your own shopping cart without having to learn a complicated programming language such as PHP (Hypertext Preprocessor) from scratch. It is not always the easiest route, but using open source software can save you time in the long run.

One final category of software is public domain software. Public domain, as the name implies, is software that is not copyrighted. As with open source software, you can modify it as you wish. Additionally, you can distribute it to anyone and everyone. Games often fall into this category. You will occasionally be asked to give credit to the original programmer or source, but the software itself is yours to use and distribute.

can be easily converted into an Acrobat document. The new page can move seamlessly to the Web, where it becomes available for viewing.

Making a Choice

Which program should you buy? The choice, of course, depends on what you want to do and how much you are willing or able to pay. Graphic designers would do well to learn PowerPoint or Acrobat, as both programs do a good job of creating very basic Web pages that follow layout rules they are familiar with. These two programs are also efficient at designing a small site that features a fair amount of static content. If, however, you are a budding techie who intends to move into programming environments, then Dreamweaver is your best bet. It has the capability to work with the most modern computer languages, offers a full suite of programming code, and allows you to create sites that feature electronic shopping carts.

Putting It All Together: Additional Software Options

You have created a design portfolio. It may consist of printed pieces, along with 3-D pieces such as sculpture or package design, drawings, slides, and/or photographs. Now you must convert that print portfolio into a digital format. Where do you begin? How long will it take? How do the different programs work together? To answer those questions and more, in this section, we'll examine some of the programs that can help you to convert your work to a digital format.

As you have learned, the building blocks for any multimedia project center around the final environment you are targeting (Web or CD/DVD) and the authoring software you have selected. To finish the final project, you will need additional support software, and choosing the correct program and file format is important to produce a successful project.

The software necessary to complete the transformation from print to digital generally falls into three categories: raster-based programs, vector-based programs, and page-layout programs. The following subsections provide a quick rundown of the features of these types of programs.

Raster-based Programs

Raster-based images (sometimes called bitmapped graphics) are created pixel by pixel within a grid of pixels, or points of light. These images have a fixed resolution, which is defined as the dpi (dots per inch), determined when an image is first created. A typical screen resolution is 72 dpi. Any image you create or modify at a set dpi should never be resized, because each of the individual pixels is fixed, or absolute, in size. Any attempts at resizing will make the image appear "soft." Raster-based images are great for continuous-tone

images such as photographs, as they allow for smooth gradients and subtle detail.

Adobe Photoshop

In the raster-based category, Adobe Photoshop is without doubt the leading image-editing program on the market today. Photoshop comes with powerful tools to create and manipulate images. Its list of features is impressive. There are tools for color correction and auto removal of dust and scratches. One particularly interesting tool is the Healing Brush. It erases wrinkles, minor skin defects, and other small flaws from images of the human face. And Photoshop's selection of special effects provides endless possibilities for image manipulation. There are filters to create special effects such as clouds. You can create natural-looking watercolors, charcoal, and chalk drawings. Other features such as layer masking and a spell-checker really smooth your work flow. There are dozens of books on the market covering literally every aspect of this feature-rich program. You will always find more to learn, and it will always be fun.

Photoshop works in conjunction with many of the popular scanners and cameras, allowing you to import your images directly into the program—a real time-saver. Moreover, the program offers several formats for saving, and there are numerous options for exporting your images to other authoring programs. The program has a steep learning curve, but it is so worth the effort!

Adobe Photoshop is the industry standard when it comes to image manipulation, and it's easy to see why. Its full set of sophisticated features makes it easy to create complex images.

Photoshop also comes bundled with a set of Web preparation tools, which help you to prepare your files for display on the Internet. You can customize each picture by specifying the levels of compression for saving. There is also a function that allows you to create "image slices." These mini pictures can be saved as sequentially numbered files that can then be brought into Dreamweaver and dropped into layout tables. Very useful! The program also gives you constant feedback on the time that would be required to download an image. This "real-time" feedback is very handy for Web designers.

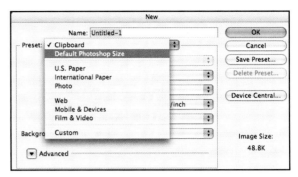

Here is a typical setup page in Photoshop. Notice that you are offered a wide range of options for the initial page setup.

Corel Painter

But perhaps you're looking for a program that is geared more toward fine art than graphic art. In this case, Corel Painter might be a good choice for you. Corel Painter is what's known as a *natural media painting program.* As such, it offers a large assortment of media to work with—including oils, acrylics, colored pencils, felt pens, chalk, charcoals, crayons, and airbrushes—to create realistic artwork. Each of the program's tools mimics the features of the real medium, right down to the particular thickness and type of brush. You can also select the "paper" type (such as watercolor or charcoal) for your project. You then apply the medium to the paper, where it acts as it would in the natural world. Did I mention there are 400 different brushes? Painter includes a function that keeps watercolors "wet" even when you save a painting and come back to it later. And the paintbrushes are pressure-sensitive; that is to say, they work with drawing tablets to control the amount of paint or the thickness of the lines you apply to the drawing. Corel Painter has the ability to detect pressure-sensitive pens and tablets, such as those created by the Wacom Company. Just as you would press down on a pencil to produce a darker line, a pressure-sensitive pen creates that same darker line in Painter. Very realistic effects are just a touch away.

There are even tools to enable you to create traditional compositions using the same methods learned in school. These features—the Divine Proportion tool and the Rule of Thirds—are additions to the program that help you to create paintings just as the masters did hundreds of years ago. These compositional aids really help you to visualize your design as you begin the creation process.

The program also comes with lots of filters so that you can include additional effects in your designs. Painter also has features that will help you move your designs to the Internet. You can produce rollover color button effects and create files that can move seamlessly to other Web programs such as Flash. There is also a preview command, which offers you a "live" preview before you upload your project to the Internet.

Vector-based Programs

Vector-based drawing programs are very different from raster-based programs. They use math to describe the points or shapes that make up an image. (Fortunately, you won't have to know these mathematical equations.) The advantage of using math to describe a shape is that it doesn't have a set resolution. Furthermore, file sizes are very small, and the images may be resized as much or as little as necessary. All that said, vector-based programs have one major disadvantage: they are terrible for converting continuous-tone images such as photographs.

Vector-based programs include Adobe Illustrator and CorelDRAW.

Adobe Illustrator

For many years, Adobe Illustrator has set the standard for vector-based drawing programs in print production. This professional graphics program enables image creation with clean PostScript output (very important in the print industry) and tight integration with Adobe Photoshop. The program lets you create new pages with either print, the Web, or a CD or DVD in mind.

Illustrator also offers a superior set of drawing tools to design amazing effects. The Warp effect tool allows you to customize text in unique ways. A 3-D tool allows you to create complex drawings from even the simplest shapes in one or two clicks. The Magic Wand allows you to select objects (especially useful for type) in your document with a set of attributes that you like and reproduce those attributes directly onto another shape. The Magic Wand also makes it possible to specify which attributes to look for, including fill color, stroke color, stroke weight, opacity, and blending mode. You can put 3-D effects on most objects to make them look more dimensional. The Mesh tool helps you to create the smoothest blends you've ever seen.

Illustrator supports the use of symbols to create and update complex drawings. You create an object (such as a wheel) and define it as a symbol. Once that symbol is created, it can be placed over and over throughout a document. There are cool creative effects that can be produced using symbols as brushes. Let's say you design a snowflake. With that one initial shape, you can specify such variations as size, rotation, tint, and transparency. You can make amazing effects with very little effort. If you are a professional designer or artist looking for a stable, powerful drawing program, look no further than Adobe Illustrator.

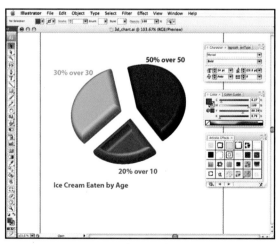

When it comes to vector-based illustration, there is no doubt that Adobe Illustrator leads the way. The interface is straightforward, and the options are boundless.

Once upon a time, Illustrator was very testy about working with Web-authoring programs such as Flash and Dreamweaver, but that is changing now that Adobe owns them all! The program can slice your images for direct use in any Web design program. Layers you create while drawing can be brought directly into Flash and kept as layers—a very useful feature indeed!

CorelDRAW

CorelDRAW continues to be a cost-effective way to "set up shop" with everything you need for drawing and Web animation. CorelDRAW is easy to master, and it ships with a superior interface and features set. Working with vector-based images can be difficult, so one of the most useful features of the program is its capability to quickly join multiple paths into a single object. It also features pressure-sensitive Smudge and Roughen Brushes and excellent filters, which can add bulge and ripple effects to an object. Text is easy to control, and using CorelDRAW, you can also embed graphics within a paragraph of text. PowerTRACE and Smart Fill are two tools to help you create a vector-based illustration from a raster-based photo. These tools are intuitive and easy to use. With the Smart Drawing tool, CorelDRAW also attempts to draw refined shapes for you when you freehand-doodle on the screen. Draw a loop, and CorelDRAW turns it into a perfect ellipse. It can be a lot quicker to develop a drawing than using the traditional shape-drawing tools. CorelDRAW also does a good job of creating and optimizing Web images and can generate rollovers for Web design. In sum, the product offers a number of great features, including enhanced drawing tools, text tools, fills, textures, patterns, and interactive tools.

Adobe Fireworks

Adobe Fireworks is a bit of a hybrid program. It utilizes both raster-based and vector-based capabilities to create pictures. It is also a full-scale image creation and manipulation program, similar to Adobe Photoshop. Live Effects is the Fireworks answer to manipulating text to create some pretty cool effects—all in real time. In Fireworks, every aspect of a graphic—including text, objects, and image maps—is fully editable and can have

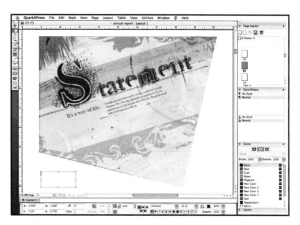

Adobe Fireworks is a great choice if you intend to move your designs from either Illustrator or Photoshop. The three programs integrate tightly to give you more drawing options than you would have with any one of the programs alone.

When it comes to page layout, QuarkXPress has long been considered at the head of the pack. The latest version allows you to create Web pages directly from your page layouts. Here is an annual report created by Frances Gonzalez.

effects applied at any time. For Web-based design, Fireworks offers a good assortment of tools, including image slicing (which cuts an image into separate segments to prepare it for HTML) and JavaScript rollovers. The ability to optimize graphic interchange format (GIF) images with browser-safe colors, as well as the capability to import files from Photoshop, Illustrator, Dreamweaver, and CorelDRAW, make Fireworks a good program choice. There is some speculation that Fireworks may be discontinued, since it was acquired by Adobe in 2005. In many ways, Fireworks duplicates the features of Photoshop, so the design community is waiting to learn what Adobe has in store for this venerable design program.

Page-Layout Programs

Page-layout programs are unique, in that they act as holders of many different kinds of file types. Pages are created using images, vector illustrations, and charts from spreadsheet programs. Once upon a time, QuarkXPress ruled the publishing universe. Lately, however, an up-and-coming challenger has given Quark a run for its money. Let's take a look at the contenders.

QuarkXPress

QuarkXPress is the cream of the crop when it comes to layout programs. Most newspapers, magazines, pam-

phlets, and posters today are created with this program, and with good reason. QuarkXPress features a clear, easy-to-understand interface, and it comes with a complete set of type tools and the capability to work with complex pages. Of late, Quark, the maker of QuarkXPress, has turned its attention to the Web design market. The program now includes features that allow you to produce Web pages that contain hyperlinks, image maps, and rollovers. You can also choose compression settings for your images on an individual basis, to gain more control over your pictures. Exporting HTML in QuarkXPress is straightforward, but you will have more control over the look of your final Web pages with an HTML editor. Still, for designers comfortable with the program, this is a good starting point.

InDesign

Adobe InDesign is another excellent page-layout program. InDesign is a relative newcomer to the page-layout market, but it has already won legions of followers thanks to its clean interface, which is so much like its companion program, Illustrator.

Much like QuarkXPress, InDesign offers a full set of page-layout features. It makes excellent use of the familiar Illustrator/Photoshop-style interface and offers several of Illustrator's vector-based tools. Images can be dragged directly in from either program, bypassing the

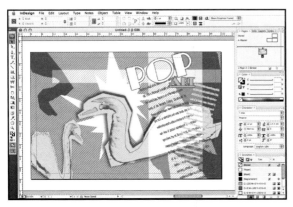

Michael Solis demonstrates how Adobe InDesign simplifies the work of preparing images and type for page layout. The program allows you to create multiple layers for special effects.

import step that is usually required in other programs. InDesign is especially strong at previewing images in a layout. You can view images in high-resolution mode or in the quicker Typical Display mode. InDesign also enables you to perform multiple undos—a very useful capability! InDesign writes relatively clean code, although, as with QuarkXPress, you are still better off using an HTML editor. InDesign can also convert your tagged image file format (TIFF) images to graphic interchange format (GIF) or Joint Photographic Experts Group (JPEG) files on the fly when you export them. InDesign, like all Adobe software, is well integrated into the work flow for designers. It works extremely well with all of Adobe's other software packages, making this program a solid choice.

Program Review

At this point, you've been introduced to a number of programs, all designed to, in one way or another, enable you to produce your digital portfolio. To help you sort through all the information, you can use the "Software Evaluation Form," found later in this chapter, to make notes about each of the products we've discussed.

Once you have completed this form, which will give you a basic understanding of the software available for multimedia authoring, you will be ready to make a buying decision. I suggest that you include at least one vector-based and one raster-based program, along with an authoring package, based on your final output. At one

point or another, I have used all of the programs discussed above, and they all feature outstanding options for the digital designer. That said, here are my personal recommendations:

> For raster-based image creation: Adobe Photoshop
> For vector-based image creation: Adobe Illustrator
> For page layout: QuarkXPress or InDesign
> For CD-ROM authoring: Flash
> For Web design: Dreamweaver

Here are some additional points to ponder when you are evaluating software:

- How user-friendly is it? If you have only a couple of weeks to design the interface, you probably won't have time to learn a complex program. Look for programs that offer tutorials and help screens. Ask yourself, "Can I figure out enough of this program to design an effective interface in the time I have?" And consider purchasing a book that offers lots of visual instructions.
- Does the program feature good text and graphic options and an easy way to manipulate text? Does it let you choose from numerous fonts, colors, sizes, and styles? Can type be "broken apart" into vector-based shapes that no longer require the font?
- What graphics features does the program have? Can you produce special effects, such as "warped" or 3-D?
- Does the program come with any prebuilt options, such as animations?
- Can images be readily imported from other programs and manipulated?
- Does the program accept sound?
- Which sound formats are available within the program?
- Can you import sounds and music from other sources?
- Can you modify the sound once it is inside the program?
- What level of interactivity does the program offer?
- Is the authoring program linear or nonlinear? Will linear design be enough to satisfy you, or will you require a more advanced authoring environment?
- How much does the software cost?
- Can you purchase the software with a student discount?
- Are free trial versions available?

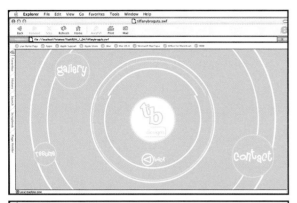

This enjoyable interface, designed by Tiffany Braguta, is reminiscent of design from the 1950s, with its colors of aqua, yellow, and blue. It is clear to the user which options are available.

- Will a "light" version of the program be enough to get the job completed? How much do upgrades cost?
- Can you edit images within the program?
- Does the software come with a spell-checker and thesaurus?
- Will the program self-check for programming errors?

Now that you know a bit more about authoring programs, you are almost ready to design your digital interface, and in the next chapter, you will begin the process of building your digital portfolio, but, first, let's turn our attention to a more complete discussion of Web design.

Planning Your Web Design Project

Though, as I've said, designing an interface for the Web and for a CD or DVD are similar, there are a few

Engaging, charming, and downright fun! This interface, designed by Douglas Waltman II, offers lots of visual interplay and a great deal to explore.

• Web Site Evaluation Form

| 1 | Name of Web site | URL: www._____.com | Does the URL make sense? |

| 2 | Is there an opening page? Did you like it? | ● Yes | |
| | Is it appropriate for the site? | ● No | (If not, why not?) |

| 3 | Does the site open quickly? | ● Yes | |
| | | ● No | |

| 4 | Do a thumbnail sketch of the site. Compare it to the other sites you visit. | | |

| 5 | Does the home page reflect the overall message of the site? | ● Yes | |
| | | ● No | (If not, why not?) |

| 6 | Does the home page require a lot of scrolling? | ● Yes | |
| | | ● No | (If not, why not?) |

| | List the design elements. Do they work to support the theme of the site? | 1. 2. 3. 4. 5. | |

| | Do the links make effective use of color? | ● Yes | |
| | | ● No | (If not, why not?) |

| 7 | Do the links make sense? | ● Yes | |
| | | ● No | (If not, why not?) |

| 8 | Do the links work? | ● Yes | |
| | | ● No | (If not, why not?) |

| 9 | Is the text easy to read? | ● Yes | |
| | | ● No | (If not, why not?) |

| 10 | Are there frames? Do they work? | ● Yes | |
| | | ● No | (If not, why not?) |

| 11 | Is there good content? | ● Yes | |
| | | ● No | (If not, why not?) |

| 12 | Is there a background color or graphic? Does it work? | ● Yes | |
| | | ● No | (If not, why not?) |

| 13 | Is there animation? Is it effective? | ● Yes | |
| | | ● No | (If not, why not?) |

| 14 | Is there sound? Does it support the theme of the site? | ● Yes | |
| | | ● No | (If not, why not?) |

| 15 | Were links included to other sites such as colleges? | ● Yes | |
| | | ● No | (If not, why not?) |

| 16 | Was there a contact page? Does the e-mail work? | ● Yes | |
| | | ● No | (If not, why not?) |

| 17 | Did you have any technical difficulties? List them. | 1. 2. 3. 4. 5. | |

| 18 | What is your overall rating of this site? | 1 = Needs a major overhaul. 10 = It rocks! | |

• Software Evaluation Form

Program Name	Main Purpose of the Program	Technical Features	Learning Curve
Microsoft PowerPoint		1. 2. 3. 4. 5.	
Adobe Director		1. 2. 3. 4. 5.	
Adobe Flash		1. 2. 3. 4. 5.	
Adobe Dreamweaver		1. 2. 3. 4. 5.	
QuarkXPress		1. 2. 3. 4. 5.	
Adobe Acrobat		1. 2. 3. 4. 5.	
Adobe Photoshop		1. 2. 3. 4. 5.	
Adobe InDesign		1. 2. 3. 4. 5.	*continues*

Program Name	Main Purpose of the Program	Technical Features	Learning Curve
Corel Painter		1.	
		2.	
		3.	
		4.	
		5.	
Adobe Illustrator		1.	
		2.	
		3.	
		4.	
		5.	
Adobe Freehand		1.	
		2.	
		3.	
		4.	
		5.	
CorelDRAW		1.	
		2.	
		3.	
		4.	
		5.	
Adobe Fireworks		1.	
		2.	
		3.	
		4.	
		5.	

special considerations. When it comes to proper planning, the key is to ensure that your Web site design goes as smoothly as possible.

And to help you to focus your thoughts and design ideas, I want you to do the following exercise: visit at least five portfolio Web sites, and complete the "Web Site Evaluation Form" (presented in this chapter) for each site. The purpose here is simple: how can you design a site if you don't know what you want or like? You need to take time to check out sites by other artists such as yourself and identify what works and what does not at each site. Pay particular attention to the overall design, graphics, speed, and ease of navigation. (Note: Don't worry if you can't answer all the questions here. You will be able to after you read the next couple of chapters.)

Now, don't just sit there. Start brainstorming! Grab a sketchbook, start drawing, and don't stop until you like what you have created. Ask yourself, "What is the mood I am trying to create?" Simple, outrageous, or elegant— it doesn't really matter. But one thing's for sure: you can't begin to create the interface until you know what the site will look like. Good design equals good navigation. Put yourself in the employer's shoes. What will really grab the visitor's attention? An effective opening?

Examples of your work? A clean navigational system? The success of your site depends primarily on the logic you apply to the introduction and first page. The next chapter is devoted to design techniques, so stay tuned for more on this shortly. But, for now, consider these questions:

- Do you have a site map, and does it make sense?
- Do you have the skills necessary to create the interface you have designed?
- Are you getting your message across?
  - Does your choice of colors, graphics, and fonts support your design theme?
  - Do you include a logo on the site?
  - Can your designs be grouped into logical categories?
  - Should you include image descriptions and photos?
  - Do you need music or video?
- Do you have the following items?
  - An updated résumé that uses effective action verbs and good typography?
- A gallery of your designs? At least 10 to 15 outstanding pieces should be available for viewing.
- A description of each piece?
- Do you have a contact page?
  - How do you want prospective employers to contact you? Via e-mail? Telephone?
  - Did you indicate this information somewhere on the site?
- Is it fast?
  - If it takes more than ten seconds for the first page to load, you'll lose your viewer. Do not design Web designs that require images larger than 50 to 80 kilobytes. In the case of Web interface design, smaller equals faster.

If you are serious about designing a portfolio Web site, and you follow all the steps outlined in this book, you will create a winning site.

An Interview with Blaise Nauyokas

After graduating from California State University, Long Beach, in the early 1980s with a BFA in graphic design, Blaise started his career at the legendary Cross + Associates in Los Angeles. Eventually he entered LA's advertising scene as an art director, winning accolades for work on automotive, television, and movie studio accounts.

By the late 1980s, Blaise moved south and joined San Diego's most creative advertising agency, Franklin & Associates. There he produced award-winning work for the San Diego Padres, the San Diego Union-Tribune,

McDonald's, and the San Diego Convention Center, to name a few. In time, he accepted a position as associate creative director at the Arnold.Buck agency, creating concepts for numerous home builders, communications companies, and the fashion industry. In the early 1990s, Blaise left to start his own advertising and design business and, in 2000, incorporated his business under the name BrainShine. His focus on advertising, design, and new media has led to increased success as the business continues to grow. Today Blaise is the president and creative director of BrainShine advertising + design + new media, with a diverse list of international clients. You can visit his Web site at www.brainshine.com.

Blaise Nauyokas has freelanced as a senior art director for all of San Diego's top agencies. He's also been a guest instructor at the Advertising Arts College, teaching classes in art direction, copywriting, and design. (Blaise Nauyokas, President and Creative Director, BrainShine advertising + design + new media.)

1 What qualities do you look for in an applicant?

Since we tend to prejudge a person by their looks, I would start with that. Present an air of professionalism—dress nicely; speak well; and present a clean, organized portfolio. Before I even see the work, I can tell a lot about the candidate's qualities: if they are not attentive to detail in their appearance, I have little hope they will do so in their work. Secondly, I need to see an understanding of what my agency does. Don't bring a portfolio that's not appropriate to the kind of work we do. A little research online will tell a candidate if a firm will be a proper fit for their style. And lastly, I want to know that my new hire has the computer skills necessary to work here. That's harder to demonstrate, but the portfolio pieces should give me a sense, and the candidate's presentation of skills should tell me what I need to know.

2 In your opinion, what makes a successful interview?

Candidates must know what they are trying to achieve—what their goals are, their strengths (and weaknesses), what kind of position and salary they are seeking. Ultimately, the portfolio is key as to whether the person will be hired, but a clear understanding of themselves is a strong indicator as to what kind of employee they will be.

3 Has the Internet had an effect on your interview process?

Yes. I generally prescreen applicants by asking to see their work either on a Web site they may have created or via an e-mailed PDF portfolio. If I'm impressed by the level of work, I will meet with them in person.

4 What are the five best things job candidates say that impress you during an interview? What are the five worst?

Best
1 "The objective was . . . I solved it by . . ." (Thoughtful design!)
2 "I saw the work you did for your current clients. . . ." (Demonstrate a knowledge of my business.)
3 "I'm here to learn." (Maybe not those exact words, but demonstrate you're open-minded to the way we do things.)
4 "Thank you for your time." (Recognize that the interviewer is a busy person.)
5 "I'll work for minimum wage." (Just kidding, but know what your salary needs are.)

Worst
1 "I don't really like this piece, but . . ." (Then don't show it!)
2 "My instructor said . . ." (Don't tell me how to feel/think.)
3 "This piece is kinda old, so it's not really my style now." (Then don't show it!!!)
4 When asked: "What kind of projects do you like working on?" Answered: "I dunno. I'll do anything." (Know what your talents are, what your passion is.)
5 "I really hate my current job. . . ." (I'm not your port in the storm. Show me you want to work here.)

5 What are skills that really help all artists succeed regardless of their specialty?

First of all, I'd rather that they not be called "artists," nor would I want them to think such. In this business, they are visual communicators. That means a full understanding of how brand building works—knowing how to match objectives with quality design in order to further a client's brand. I see far too many portfolios in which the design seems created more for the designer's pleasure. In great work, a creative solution is not only interesting to look at; it solves a client's problem.

6 What advice would you offer to designers looking to impress you with the presentation of their work?

Treat your presentation like a creative assignment. Be organized. Design your portfolio for maximum impact. Less is more—show only your best work. Know my business, and show me how you can contribute. Most of all, be professional.

challenge

Designer's Challenge 1

Create a photo collage using at least five different images. Use the advanced drawing capacities of your raster-based software program (Photoshop or Painter) to create a new, never-before-seen space scene. Construct it so that it looks as whimsical as possible. Invent planets, stars, and other space anomalies.

Here is a fantastic solution to this designer's challenge, brought to you by Kristalyn Burns.

Designer's Challenge 2

Design a label for a bottle. Select a country or an area and a product from that country or area. Create a label that will support the product. Include all relevant information, including ingredients (if necessary) and nutritional information (if needed).

A charming bottle of shells, designed by Amanda Grieve, brings back the sights, smells, and memories of a day at the beach. (Amanda Grieve, graduate, Sinclair Community College.)

6

The Digital Portfolio
Technical Elements

Now that we have spent some time looking at the various multimedia-authoring and support programs available to help you design your electronic portfolio, you may be wondering how these programs work together. It is at this point that the graphics file format comes into play, and in this chapter, you will learn how to analyze some of the multimedia industry's graphic formats. Fortunately, no matter what type of images you plan to add to your portfolio, the format selection process is pretty much the same.

But before we get started, recall from Chapter 5 that computer graphics programs fall into three main groups: raster-based programs, vector-based programs, and page-layout programs. But it is also possible to have what are called metafiles, a type of hybrid file containing both vector and raster images. (Flash and Fireworks, the multimedia authoring program, fall into this category.)

Preparing Work for Digital Presentation
Working with Raster-based Images
We'll begin with the use of raster-based images. Raster images, as you will recall, are produced by such programs as Adobe Photoshop and Corel Painter, as well as scanners and digital cameras. There are many different file formats to choose from, but the most common raster-based formats are:

Tagged Image File Format (TIFF)
Joint Photographic Experts Group (JPEG)
Graphic Interchange Format (GIF)

As you can see with these two images, bitmapped images (such as those created with Photoshop) always look pixelated. However, images created with vector-based programs can be resized as much or as little as needed. The images will always look crisp.

The format you select will depend on a couple of factors: the image itself (such as a photo requiring a lot of detail or a logo) and how the image is to be used (e.g., CD-ROM/DVD or on the Web). Remember, images created for print can be large, whereas images for the Web must be well compressed to enable efficient downloading. You also need to be aware that not every program is capable of importing every file format. In general, you are better off using the three formats listed here. It is important to use standard formats; otherwise, though your files may import correctly to an authoring program, they may not work well once the files are available for viewing.

Working with Vector-based Images

A vector-based image, remember, uses math to describe the points or shapes that make up the image. Common vector images include 2- and 3-D architectural drawings, illustrations, flowcharts, logos, and fonts. The advantage of using math to describe a shape is that the image doesn't have a set resolution, so the file size tends to be much smaller; hence, vector-based images can be transformed or resized more easily than raster images. Vector images are typically created and displayed within

drawing and animation programs. The images generally consist of lines, curves, and other shapes, which can be assigned colors and given outlines or other special effects such as drop shadows.

Common vector-based formats include:

Scalable Vector Graphics (SVG)
Shockwave Flash (SWF)
Encapsulated PostScript (EPS)

Working with Page-layout Files

A word of warning: page-layout file types present a problem. Neither the InDesign (.indd) nor the QuarkXPress (.qxd) file extension is fully compatible with most multimedia programs. As a general rule, you will have to export the page-layout file into another program as an intermediate step. The file can then be saved in a more universal format that the authoring programs will understand. For example, a file created in QuarkXPress can be exported as an EPS or a PDF file to Photoshop. Once in Photoshop, the file can be saved as a JPEG. Now the file is ready for digital usage. InDesign can also export your file as a PDF, but although that format is quickly making inroads, it is still not completely accepted in the multimedia world. Most likely you will be using the PDF to move the file to Photoshop so that it can be converted to a JPEG.

In very basic portfolio design, without all of the features programs can provide, PDF files can be downloaded and burned to CD (PDF is not the best choice for Web design). Page layout formats include:

Encapsulated PostScript (EPS)
Portable Document Format (PDF)

Working with Metafiles

A graphics metafile is a computer file that contains a set of data records describing a graphical image. These files may contain either bitmapped or vector graphics data. They are also used to describe information about layout, fonts, and graphics to a printer or display device. Metafiles transport graphical information between different types of computers and computer applications. There are different types of metafiles, including page description language (PDL), Computer Graphics Metafile (CGM), Encapsulated PostScript (EPS), and PDF. Vector formats such as Flash or SVG can also function as metafiles, because they are capable of including raster information. The most common metafile format is:

Shockwave Flash (SWF)

Coordinating Graphic Formats

By now you're probably feeling as though you're swimming in alphabet soup—EPS, TIFF, PDF, CGM, and so on—but, fortunately, all this comes together fairly easily.

It all begins with the final output. Once you have determined how your portfolio will be viewed, you can select the authoring program that will best serve your needs. Whatever authoring program you choose will have import requirements and restrictions. Knowing these in advance allows you to work backward as you prepare your images electronically for the digital portfolio. In a moment, we will take a file from the beginning to its final destination in an authoring program, but first, let's examine some of the import requirements for each of the multimedia packages. (Note: This is not a complete list, but it will serve to highlight some of the formats you may encounter in your travels through multimedia design. An asterisk indicates a popular format choice.)

Microsoft PowerPoint
Joint Photographic Experts Group (JPEG)*
Tagged Image File Format (TIFF)
Macintosh (PICT)
Windows Bitmap (BMP)
Encapsulated PostScript (EPS)*
Graphic Interchange Format (GIF)*
Windows Metafile (WMF)

Adobe Flash
Joint Photographic Experts Group (JPEG)*
Tagged Image File Format (TIFF)*
Photoshop proprietary format (PSD)
Graphic Interchange Format (GIF)*
Macintosh (PICT)
Windows Metafile (WMF)
Encapsulated PostScript (EPS)*
Windows Bitmap (BMP)
Waveform audio (WAV; cross-compatible between Mac and Windows)*
QuickTime movie (MOV)*
Flash Player (SWF [Shockwave Flash])*
AutoCAD 10 (DXF [Drawing Interchange Format])*
Silicon Graphics Image (SGI)*

Adobe Director
Joint Photographic Experts Group (JPEG)*
Tagged Image File Format (TIFF)*
Photoshop proprietary format (PSD)
Graphic Interchange Format (GIF)*
Macintosh (PICT)
Windows Bitmap (BMP)
QuickTime movie (MOV)*
Rich Text Format (RTF)
PowerPoint (PPT)
Waveform audio (WAV; cross-compatible between Mac and Windows)*

Dreamweaver
Graphic Interchange Format (GIF)*
Joint Photographic Experts Group (JPEG)*
Flash proprietary format (SWF)*
Portable Document Format (PDF)*

Cascading Style Sheets (CSS)
QuickTime movie (MOV)*
Waveform audio (WAV; cross-compatible between Mac and Windows)*
Extensible Markup Language (XML)
Director Shockwave proprietary format (DCR)*
Hypertext Markup Language (HTML)
Microsoft Excel proprietary format (XLS)

Inserting, Resizing, and Moving Graphics

Creating and working with images designed for multimedia is quite different from working with images for other media. You already know that file size plays a big part, but there are other technical considerations. One of the most important decisions you must now make is screen size, because this will determine all later choices you make when you resize each of your projects. My first word of advice here is to resist the temptation to use the default size of the multimedia-authoring program. The reason is that you must make a selection based on the final application—that is, whether your material will be displayed on the Web or on a CD or DVD. Why? Because each of these environments uses a different page-layout configuration. Let's examine the differences.

The page layout you initially select for Web and CD-ROM/DVD design will be based on two factors: (1) the size of the monitor and (2) the screen resolution. Your electronic portfolio will be displayed under a variety of different conditions. For example, it may be viewed by potential employers whose monitors are set to 800 horizontal × 600 vertical pixels. Other companies may have their monitors set much higher, to, say, 1024 × 768 and beyond. Some companies will have screens as large as 21 inches, whereas other potential employers may look at your work on screens that are only 15 inches. As a multimedia designer, you need to be sure your project will display properly regardless of the circumstances.

And never assume that the people viewing your portfolio will have updated equipment or use the same programs you have on your computer. Take my friends Bob and Robert. Bob is into technology big-time. He owns three desktop computers plus one laptop. He also has the latest digital camera and printer, and everything is networked. When you design for someone like Bob, you need not be concerned about whether your project will display to its best advantage. But my other friend, Robert, is just the opposite. He hasn't bought a new computer in almost five years, and his monitor is only 15 inches and displays at 640 × 480, which is seriously out-of-date. Plus, his eyes are weaker, so he needs larger type. But as long as Robert can surf the Net, he's happy. My point is, you may well encounter both Bob and Robert types when you submit your electronic résumé, so it's a good idea to keep this diversity in mind. According to *Browser News* (a weekly newsletter for Web site designers: www.upsdell.com/BrowserNews/stat.htm) and W3Schools (a Web site for people with an interest in Web technologies: www.w3schools.com/browsers/browsers_display.asp), the percentages of people using the most popular screen resolutions break down as follows:

800 × 600	8 percent
1024 × 768	48 percent
Higher	38 percent

You might be wondering why this is so important. When you create pages that are larger than the size of the monitor on which they will be viewed—that is, pages that exceed the viewable area—artwork may be cut off or in some cases disappear. So keep these recommendations in mind to ensure that all of your artwork displays properly, even under less-than-ideal conditions.

Which size should you select? For CD-ROM or DVD design, the answer is pretty clear. A project created at 1024 × 768 has the best chance of being seen in all its glory. For Web design, you must factor in the browser window title bar at the top, the scrollbar on the side, and the possible size of the monitor being used. These additional elements take away some of your design "real estate." Thus, to design a Web page for a monitor set to 1024 × 768, choose a size approximately 984 × 728. When the project is loaded into a Web browser, it will fit well for most viewers.

Compressing Files to Reduce Size

Most completed design projects do not conform to either Web or CD/DVD size requirements. Sculpture, paintings, clothing designs, and interior renderings are created for a client, not for multimedia. They have to be converted to digital information. And although many graphic design projects are already in digital form, they are usually not in a size that conforms to a specific multimedia format. And, as I've mentioned numerous times, typically, the files are huge. Here's why.

As I explained previously, raster-based images are created pixel by pixel within a grid of pixels, or points of light. Each pixel contains information that helps define the color. As such, they tend to be quite large. For example, a typical file created to be printed would utilize a 24-bit red, green, and blue (RGB) image. Each image uses 8 bits of data for each channel of color, for a total of 256 possible values for each color and 16.7 million colors. To print, graphic files must be converted from RGB to CMYK (cyan, magenta, yellow, and black). The CMYK file now has four channels of color information, so these files are still larger. Even a 24-bit image created with the digital portfolio in mind would be 1024×768 pixels as a page size and would result in a file of around 2.3 megabytes. That's way too large for your purposes. For example, a poster created for, say, an upcoming festival might be designed to be 24 inches $\times$ 30 inches at 300 dpi (again, that's dots per inch), in CMYK format, for a file size of 247.2 megabytes!

Screen resolution also plays a role in a raster image's file size. Most graphic design image files are created at 300 dpi. Files created for the Web are always 72 dpi. Obviously, a 300-dpi file will be substantially larger than a 72-dpi file. Always keeping in mind that time is a factor in your multimedia presentation, there are several different techniques you can use to reduce the download time for your viewers. The first is to apply a compression system to the image. With a little work, the image size can be dramatically reduced.

Image-compression systems can be either lossless or lossy. Lossless compression has been around for some time. The system is generally applied to file types such as TIFF, LZW, and PKZip. It compresses files through algorithms that reduce file size. A lossless compression can reduce an image to approximately 50 to 75 percent of its original file size. When extracted from the compressed condition, the file is completely restored to its original state, with all of its original information intact. Although the lossless system is great for archiving files, it is not useful for multimedia work, because the files will still be too big and the format is not generally accepted by Web browsers.

In contrast, lossy compression can dramatically reduce the size of your files. Depending on how much compression you apply, the image can be reduced to as little as 1 percent of its original size. This is achieved by removing small to large amounts of pixel information contained within the file. However, the end result is the loss of both information and quality. The higher the

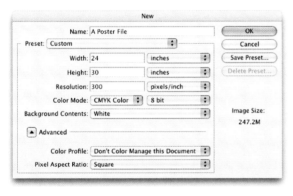

As you can see, the difference in file size between the poster design and the Web design is significant. Any files created at such a large size will have to be reduced to fit the limitations of the Web.

compression, the more visible the degradation of the image. If you open a JPEG, alter it, and resave it, there will be about a 10 percent loss of information. Open and close that resaved file a couple of times and you will end up with graphics garbage! To maintain file quality, always save your multimedia files in their original format (TIFF, EPS, etc.) and compress them under a different name at the last minute. File formats that utilize lossy compression (JPEG) should be used primarily for display on the Web and on a CD or DVD.

In general, JPEG compression is very useful, but there are certain conditions under which you do not want to apply it. Some programs will attempt to apply compression for you when you first output the file, and you never want to apply compression on top of compression. Your image quality will really begin to degrade. We will talk about this potential problem, along with some solutions, in more detail a bit later.

Using Color Spaces for Multimedia Design

A color space is simply the range of colors that a viewer has available. The color space for a graphic designer is CMYK. CMYK projects are typically used for work that is intended for printing, as ink on paper. For a multimedia designer, the color space is usually RGB. The RGB

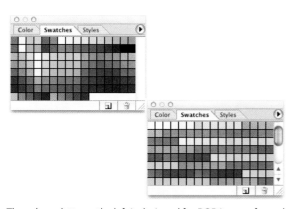

The color palette on the left is designed for RGB images for multimedia presentations, and the palette on the right represents the color space for Web design.

color space is applied in files that are created for use on-screen. Here is the reason why. When the Internet was first being developed, most monitors were limited to a palette of 256 colors (known as "Web-safe" colors). Any additional colors were automatically eliminated. Despite the fact that today's monitors can display millions of colors, many Web designers still use the original Web-safe palette (although with the newer Internet speeds, higher color palettes are increasingly used for design). In fact, many Web designers use index colors, derivatives of RGB color but with an even more limited palette. Using index colors enables the multimedia designer to produce a project that will be seen in its proper colors under the most diverse conditions possible. It also assures the fastest possible download.

Which color space should you select? Use RGB for all multimedia projects, including CD-ROM/DVD and Web design. Use "Web-safe" colors for Web design once you gain some technical proficiency.

Transferring Artwork into the Computer

The key to successfully transferring art into the computer is to know which programs work together in the most efficient way. Sometimes this is quite easy, requiring just a couple of mouse clicks. Other times the process requires a bit more knowledge about the programs and how they work together. To clarify this concept, we'll step through a couple of projects.

Two-Page Editorial Spread for a CD or DVD

Most graphic designers have completed a couple of magazine design projects. Typically, the programs utilized to complete such projects are Adobe Photoshop, Adobe Illustrator, QuarkXPress, or InDesign. A project such as this may exist on boards, but for the purpose of this discussion, we'll assume it is archived on a CD/DVD or flash drive (a type of small, lightweight storage device). We'll also assume that the project is in digital QXD format (QuarkXPress's native file format), which is not compatible with any of the multimedia gram). Before this PDF file can be used in a multimedia-authoring program, however, it will need to have the following five changes applied to it:

1. *It must be resized to fit a 1024 × 768 screen.* And if the final resolution is 1024 × 768, the file will actually have to be sized slightly smaller to allow for the placement of other items on the page, such as navigational buttons.
2. *It will need to be converted to RGB format.* Although Photoshop gives you the option of opening the file as either CMYK or RGB, it is better to first open the file as a CMYK and then convert it, because the colors will remain truer to your original layout.

programs, so the file will need to be converted. There are two different ways to accomplish this.

The important first step is to move the archived file to your hard drive. To begin the process of converting your editorial spread, you must export the file to a program using either the "Save Page as EPS" or "Print to PDF" method. Using the first method, the file will be exported as an EPS. The file can then be opened in Photoshop or other raster-based programs.

The second method converts the editorial spread file to a PDF. This file will also open in Photoshop. In this method, you must select the Print command from the File menu. Once your dialog box is open, select the Printer option at the bottom of the dialog box. A second dialog box will appear. This box will allow you to select PDF as your choice from the list of printer options. Once you click Print, you will be prompted to select the location where your new file will be saved. After the file has been converted, it can be opened in Photoshop (this works pretty much the same in all versions of the pro-

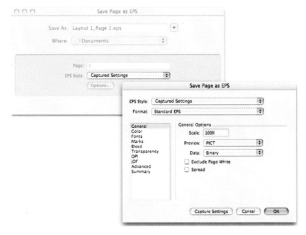

QuarkXPress's Export as EPS option allows you to select from a variety of color space and display options. These will be available once the page has arrived at its final destination.

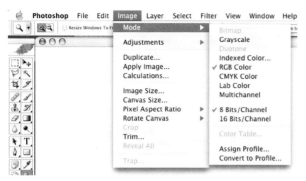

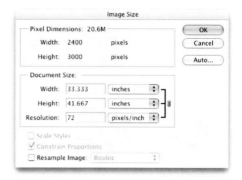

As you can see, there are a lot of different choices when it comes to color and design. T-shirt designers prefer the Indexed option, whereas graphic designers usually choose the CMYK option, and multimedia artists use the RGB option. The one you select will depend on your final output.

3. *The file must be resized to 72 dpi.* You have the option of selecting 72 dpi when you first convert the file, but I recommend completing each step separately. This gives you the opportunity to try out different settings.
4. *Save the file as a TIFF or a JPEG.* I usually select TIFF for Adobe Flash. Why? Flash can apply a JPEG conversion for me when I publish the final interface design, and I can instruct Flash as to how much compression I want the file to have.
5. *Import the TIFF file into Flash.* The final destination for the editorial spread is the Library, Flash's holding area, where it will be when you are ready to insert it in the final project.

A 3-D Package Design for a Web Page with a Digital Camera

For our second example, we'll assume you want to display a series of images that show one of your recent package designs from all viewpoints. For this type of art, we have to start at a different point than we did for the editorial spread.

First, the project has to be photographed, and for this step, we're going to assume it will be done using a digital camera. This will simplify things considerably, because it eliminates the hassle of running to a store to have the film developed, then scanning the image. All you have to do is transfer the photo from your camera to your computer. Let's get started.

The Image Size dialog box is where you "resample" (reset) the dpi of your layouts. All images created for either CD/DVD or the Web must be saved as 72-dpi files.

1. *Take the photographs.* I recommend you take several photos from different points of view. Your package design is three-dimensional, so you will want to showcase it from several vantage points. If possible, use a scrim. (A scrim is fabric that serves as a background. It looks opaque when lit from the front but is actually semitransparent when lit from behind.) You can always use a large white sheet that has been pressed. (No wrinkles are acceptable here!) Don't rush. Take time to consider the best way to show your work. You will need to determine the dpi your camera uses to "capture" (see step 2). It has different quality settings

Boxes and other three-dimensional designs have special needs. When building a portfolio, it's best to display the fully articulated box, but having an extra copy that lies flat in your case is a good backup plan. These clever boxes were designed by Priscilla Giler.

for different types of photographs. Consult your manual for dpi equivalents. Remember, you are ultimately trying to achieve 72 dpi. Some cameras also allow you to control how the image is saved. If possible, save it in an uncompressed format. This might be TIFF or as an unprocessed image (RAW, a native format of many digital cameras).

2. *Capture the photographs.* A digital photograph is downloaded to your computer via a flash memory card. The card is usually loaded into a small reader, where the file can be transferred to your computer. Once on your computer, the file can be opened by a raster-based image program, such as Adobe Photoshop. Photoshop has a nice feature that allows you to "browse thumbnail images" of all your photographs.

3. *Rotate the photographs if necessary.* If you had to turn the camera sideways to photograph the entire image, you may need to rotate the photo to its upright position.

4. *Use the RGB format, and make sure the file is 72 dpi.* Most digital cameras use RGB as their default when capturing pictures, but it's best to check and make sure. If you captured the image at a higher setting than 72 dpi, be sure to change the file.

5. *Resize the photos to fit a page for a monitor set to 1024 × 768.* A good starting point is 984 × 728.

And, as I mentioned a bit earlier in this chapter, if the final destination is 1024 × 768, the file will have to be sized slightly smaller to allow for the browser window and the placement of other items on the page. Some artists like to display the image as a thumbnail first. Then, when the visitor clicks on the thumbnail, a larger version of the picture opens on the screen. This feature is quite easy to implement. Create the image in the large size you want, then size it down to a thumbnail and save it a second time under a similar, but different, name.

6. *Save the file as a JPEG.* JPEG compression is always best for the Web when photographs are involved. But you'll have to decide how much compression to apply to the image. Use the lowest possible setting that won't detract from the quality of the image, always keeping in mind that the smaller the file, the faster the download. Most Web designers try to keep their image size under 50 kilobytes. You can, however, create a file as large as 80 kilobytes, but only if you have no other choice.

7. *Import the JPEG file into a Web design program.* This is the final destination for your photographs. Import the small and large JPEG images and bring them onto your newly designed Web page.

Linda Weeks created this marvelous display showcasing her design talents. Not only did she create the package designs, but she produced the visual display for the packaging as well. As you might imagine, a display such as this requires a lot of extra work to be properly shown in a portfolio.

This display piece, designed by Linda Weeks, would be best shown in her port with a series of photographs that capture all the angles.

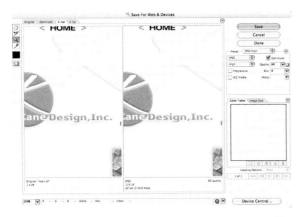

Using Photoshop's Save for Web feature, you can view your files under many different conditions. Here you see the before and after of a compression system imposed on the picture.

The Lowdown on Downloads

You've been there; we all have. You've gone to a Web site that sounds interesting to you, and now you sit staring at your monitor waiting . . . waiting . . . waiting. Finally, an image appears. But it's blurry. You click one of the icons to head to the next page. When you get there, not only is the text small but it's white reversed on a black background, so you can barely read it. On the next page is an animated image. But it never stops spinning, and the colors are blinding. On the last page is a large button, which is obviously meant to be a link. You click it, but nothing happens. Finally, you leave the site in frustration, vowing never to return.

Don't let this happen to visitors to your Web site. Although images are an important part of interface design, you must be careful not to let them frustrate your visitors. You want their experience to be aestheti-

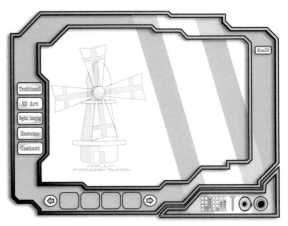

A well-designed Web site looks great on the screen yet still has a quick download time. This one was created by M. Milton.

cally pleasing, but don't make them wait forever for the experience to begin.

Rules for Using Images for Your CD/DVD or Web Site

Of course you'll want to include buttons, pictures, image maps, thumbnails, logos, and other images in your design interface, but you must use caution in this regard. Simply put, don't get carried away. A picture may be worth a thousand words, but not if the viewer has to wait a thousand seconds to see it. I've said it before, and I'll say it again because it's so important: smaller images equal faster downloads.

• The Importance of a Master File

As you begin to develop all of the support material for your project, remember to always keep the original, or master, files. I cannot tell you how many times I completed a freelance job for clients only to have them change their mind at the last moment. CD or DVD burners and low-cost zip disks make backing up your files a no-brainer.

• A Bit about Bit Depth

Bit depth is the number of bits used to store information about each pixel. The higher the depth, the more colors are stored in an image and the larger the file. Most images are scanned at 24 bits to retain the maximum color definition for the image.

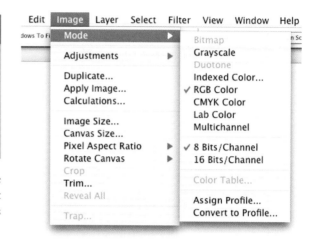

Not only does the image look good, but the file size is conveniently small. The following subsections present some tips to help you keep your interface downloads lean and mean.

Resize Your Images and Icons

When you are creating graphics for an interface, do not use images that are any larger than the actual size of the final design interface. For example, if the final page size of your interface is 800 × 600, any graphic you use should size well under that amount. If you have a photograph that's 4 inches × 5 inches, at 300 dpi, you will need to resize it to under 800 × 600; and make sure to change the pixels to 72 dpi. Most raster-based programs will help you complete this step. These programs offer you a "live" preview as you work with the image.

Test the image in the interface. Make sure it looks as clear as possible. The object is to make the file small while retaining clarity. Yes, it involves a lot of extra steps, but it must be done.

Lowering bit depth is a great way to reduce file size while still maintaining quality.

Optimize Your Images

As you have already learned, the two most commonly used image formats are GIF (graphic interchange format) and JPEG (Joint Photographic Experts Group). GIF is best for graphics that have only a few colors; JPEG is best for photographs. These formats can be optimized in other ways to decrease download times. For example, if you have a picture with a white border, remove (or crop) the border to eliminate that space. By doing so, you will reduce the file size.

Test the JPEG files at different compression levels. Sometimes a file will actually look better at reduced sizes if you blur the image slightly before the compres-

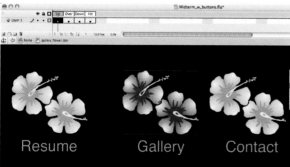

This rollover effect on the Gallery button was created in Flash. When the user's mouse pointer rolls over the flower, it changes color to indicate that there is a clickable icon that can be used to navigate to another area of the interface.

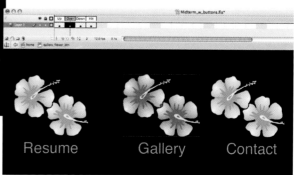

sion is applied. Find the lowest acceptable level that still maintains the original quality of the image. If you have a scanned image, chances are it has a high bit depth applied to it. Reducing the bit depth will decrease the file size. (See the sidebar on bit depth.)

Use the Same Icons Again and Again

Using the same graphic or icon repeatedly on different pages within your interface decreases download time, especially when you use authoring programs such as Flash. The reason is that there's less new information for the system to load, so naturally it will load faster. And if you are clever about the repeated use of graphics, no one will notice.

Use Thumbnails

As I mentioned briefly earlier, thumbnails are miniature versions of the larger images inside your interface. When the user clicks on one, a full-sized version of the image appears. Either the larger image is reduced in a graphics program and saved under a different file name, or the image is reduced directly in the authoring program. Once the thumbnail is inserted into the digital page, it can be linked to the larger image. Creating a thumbnail saves the user download time and keeps the overall file size small. The small thumbnails also allow the visitor to select which images are of particular interest while navigating the interface.

Slice Up Your Images

Slicing up your images is another little trick that also serves to speed download time. And it's easy, too. Take your image into a raster program such as Photoshop or Fireworks and break it up into small chunks, then save each minifile. Each image will display as it loads. This gives the user the (correct) impression that things are happening a bit faster.

Don't Overanimate

Flash and Director files, JavaScripts, GIF animations, and scrolling marquees can be a lot of fun, but they are doomed to failure if no one ever sees them. These files, as you know by now, can become gigantic, and the more

• Stay on the Right Path

Take a moment right now to look at your computer desktop. Are files scattered all over the screen? If so, you need to clean things up. When it comes to interface design, it is imperative that all your files reside in the same folder. HTML creates "paths" (or trails) for your files to follow. If you create a link for a file that works on your home computer but doesn't work once it is uploaded, you have probably changed the path without realizing it.

Here is an example: MyHardDrive>Myfolder>MyNewWebsite>MainStuff>picture.jpg. The picture.jpg file is buried deep inside the computer in the area called MainStuff. Nothing wrong with that, but as you start to upload the file to the Web, you realize that you need to rename one of the folders, so the path now reads: MyHardDrive>Myfolder>MyNewWebsite>Images>picture.jpg.

This is now an entirely different path as far as your Web page is concerned. The Web link that was established is looking for the folder "MainStuff," but that folder no longer exists because you renamed it.

If you have created any links on your page that look for the original path to load that picture, nothing will load. Why? Because the HTML code will still be looking for the old path.

What's the solution? Create subfolders within the main site folder for your project and make sure those names are exactly the same as they will be once the project is uploaded. If you move images and pages around after the folders have been created, your links will break.

animations you insert on your page, the longer it will take to load. And aside from the lengthy download time, overuse of animations will make the page look unprofessional, which is the last thing you want. I recently visited a Web page that had five animations. I didn't know where to look! You want your interface to be the star, not the animations.

Scaling the Learning Curve

At this point, you may be asking yourself, "How long is it going to take me to learn how to do all this?" Of course, that depends on your patience and your tenacity. Some authoring programs have a pretty steep learning curve, and you will need to spend however long it takes to become proficient using them. You have a lot of pictures to coordinate in the computer. You must design an interface. Yes, it is a lot of work, but the reward will be your beautiful electronic portfolio.

What kind of time commitment are we talking about? Although I have produced complete projects in as little as about 20 hours, I have also spent as much as 45 hours. But I consider this work a labor of love. If you are enjoying the challenge, you will hardly notice the time you spend.

If you find yourself overwhelmed by all this information and feel you need training from an expert, don't hesitate to sign up for tutoring or for a class at your local community college. You will find a variety of classes offered, including on many of the software programs mentioned in this book. Or cruise your area bookstores. Dozens of books are available on every conceivable software program on the market. The Internet is another great resource. There you'll find user forums and tutorials for virtually every need. In short, do what you have to in order to get yourself up to speed in as short a time as possible.

An Interview with Steph Doyle

Steph Doyle is the principal/creative director of DelineateDesign. Doyle is both a graphic designer and an illustrator. His specialties are brand identity, print and Web design, and commissioned illustration work. In his own words: "I am also currently experimenting with different mediums such as linoleum cut block printing, letterpress work, silk-screening, and various types of photo manipulation projects. I can also shoot a decent photo every now and then as well." You can visit Doyle's Web site at www.delineatedesign.com and his blog at stephdelineated.blogspot.com.

1 What qualities do you look for in an applicant?

I look for someone that has strong communication skills and a professional work ethic, is confident, willing to share information and learn from others, and [has] a proven track record as a team player.

2 In your opinion, what makes a successful interview?

I would say a strong book and the way the candidate presents their work. I want to see the process a designer goes through to solve a problem to come up with a final conclusion. I also look for designers that have a strong sense of concept. I really enjoy a designer's portfolio that makes me think to myself, "I wish I had thought of that."

The next thing is a potential candidate asking a lot of questions and comfortably interacting during the interview.

To me, there is no such thing as a stupid question. I see an interview as a learning process and want to know that the candidate is interested beyond the average job search. I am also very impressed when a candidate presents specific knowledge about my background and my work. That tells me they do their homework and are willing to go that extra step to get specific information to accomplish projects above and beyond what I would expect.

3 Has the Internet had an effect on your interview process?

Yes. I frequently visit Web sites to seek out and learn as much about a potential candidate as possible before I actually talk to that person. A Web site, in my opinion, is the initial first impression that can either make or break the candidate. If I don't see anything strong in the first few samples, that candidate goes to the bottom of the pile. I also enjoy reading case studies on a site. They offer a nice snapshot of the design process and allow me to understand the designer's way of thinking.

4 What are the five best things job candidates say that impress you during an interview? What are the five worst?

The Five Best Things

1 Would you mind if I contact you in the future for further information?
2 It is imperative that I arrive ten minutes early to everything.
3 I would like to take on other responsibilities outside of my assigned position to gain experience.
4 I thrive on short suspense deadlines; they bring out the best in me.
5 I enjoy working in a team environment.

The Five Worst Things

1 I am not a morning person.
2 I hope you offer a lot of sick leave.
3 I work better alone. People irritate me.
4 I get stressed out easily.
5 I don't work overtime.

5 What are skills that really help all artists succeed regardless of their specialty?

Good time management skills, excellent written and oral communication skills, and finally, excellent people skills. I have worked with a lot of designers and illustrators in the past. In my opinion, those that have succeeded have the ability to multitask, communicate effectively, and at the same time get along with everyone no matter what the situation is. Bringing in doughnuts on Friday mornings doesn't hurt either.

6 What advice would you offer to designers looking to impress you with the presentation of their work?

Candidates should have a well-thought-out book or Web site. I want to know what role they played in the production of the piece and to see what they have done when a client needed something that wasn't flashy or cool. Providing case studies and a sample design brief that define the thought process would definitely impress me. I am also very impressed with pieces that are designed strictly with type. I want candidates to show me how flexible they can be and show variety in their presented work.

Next, design around a concept. I have seen many nicely designed pieces that lacked a concept or didn't communicate the message with strength. Candidates should ask others to look at their work and seek out advice from mentors and peers alike. They should ask questions when seeking critique to see if the piece is sending the intended message. And they shouldn't be afraid to ask what they could do to improve their work.

Designer's Challenge 1

Invent a new animal. Using images and either Photoshop or Painter, create a mythical animal or creature. Make sure that no one can detect that any photo manipulation has occurred.

Kristalyn Burns creates this whimsical owl-dog. Or would that be a dog-owl? Notice that it is impossible to see where the images begin and end, making the design look as authentic as possible.

Designer's Challenge 2

Devise a product that might come in different varieties, such as juice or pasta. Design a series of color-coordinated boxes that hold the entire product line together but still maintain the individual nature of each product.

Valentin Miloje demonstrates a first-rate solution to this design problem. Not only do the colors work to support the product, but the look and feel make it instantly obvious that it's all from the same company.

7

The Design Phase

What do potential employers regard as the most important element of your digital portfolio? If you answered creativity, you're right. But they're looking for much more. They will examine your portfolio as a reflection of your logic, vision, versatility, artistry, and computer skills.

A well-designed electronic portfolio gives the viewer a better understanding of your particular design strengths and knowledge. The way you choose to arrange the portfolio gives the viewer insight into your intellectual and organizational skills. In the end, the employer is not going to want a designer who does only what is asked for but someone who is willing to go the extra mile. An innovative electronic portfolio reveals that you are willing to push your own creativity in an effort to keep producing higher-quality, more innovative work. An accomplished digital portfolio says, "If you ask for two comp designs, I'll come back to you with three."

To help you produce that kind of digital portfolio, this chapter explains the process of planning, with a focus on the theory and use of color.

Organize, Organize, Organize

I've stressed the importance of being organized in earlier chapters. When it comes to developing an effective electronic portfolio, planning your overall interface is the most important effort you'll make, and it begins well before the design process. Simply put, the more time you spend conceptualizing and gathering the parts of your electronic portfolio, the easier it will be to assemble the components.

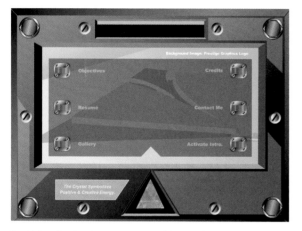 

Don't be afraid to let your sense of humor shine through, as Kwesi Williams does here.

There are a number of organizational strategies you can employ to make the multimedia part of your life easier. Begin by gathering all your project materials together. Sift through all that work and select the best for inclusion in your portfolio. Let's call this your artist inventory checklist. (Chapter 4 discussed this process in much more detail.) Always keep in mind that this work must represent the best of what you can do, so be very selective, with a focus on articulating your vision. Remember, your work should not only highlight your skills and abilities but also reflect your artistic philosophy. If you have other projects you were involved in, such as copywriting or marketing, you may include them as well, even if no actual artwork was involved. There are clever techniques available to showcase those accomplishments in your digital port.

You should have already completed your résumé, ready for conversion to a digital format. Don't forget to include other materials such as logos or artwork created on a more personal level in your inventory checklist. The many images throughout this book will offer examples of these components. Finally, select 15 to 20 pieces for your digital portfolio.

Know Where You're Going

After you have chosen which projects to include, you need to determine the best way to arrange them for the multimedia presentation. You are going to have a lot of information to include in your final portfolio—your projects, résumé, list of awards and accomplishments, along with your contact info. All of these materials have to be organized into a coherent system. Here is a list of some sections that you might consider including in your port (and have a look at some of the examples in this chapter that show these elements as they appear in an actual interface):

Summary of qualifications
Objectives
Employment history
Artist's statement or design philosophy
"Gallery": a body of work
Sketches, drafts, and works in progress
Education
Honors and awards
Community service
Memberships, certifications, and achievements
Letters of reference
Letters of recognition
Contact links

And all this material has to be in some logical sequence. The best way to begin is to map out the major sections of the portfolio, then create subcategories. Let's call it the "divide and conquer" strategy.

There are many ways to approach the task of organizing the material for your digital port, but I think it's best to start by listing all the possible categories. Don't

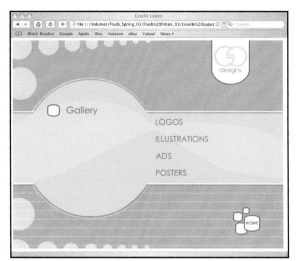

Clean, crisp, and uncomplicated, this portfolio by Giselle Lopez accomplishes everything necessary for a good design.

worry at this stage how long the list is or if certain categories overlap. Your goal is to arrive at a complete inventory of everything you might want to include in the digital interface. Then start sorting by subject matter. You might want to sketch out this information, or you might prefer to cut and paste the categories into groups.

Don't stop after one attempt. Try out several different systems. When you think you have one that will work, refine it a little further. Some of the items you list may fit into more than one category, so take some time to determine the best way to combine the material. For a graphic designer, the list above might be arranged to look like this:

Main or Home Page
Résumé
    Summary of qualifications
    Objectives
    Education
    Employment history
Honors and awards
    Community service
    Memberships, certifications, and achievements
    Letters of reference
    Letters of recognition

The gallery
    Sketches, drafts, and works in progress
    Graphic design
        Editorial spreads
        Poster designs
        Annual reports
        Package designs
        Logos
        Photography
    Personal art
        Paintings
        Drawings
Contact links

The next step is to develop a visual schematic to assist in the arrangement of the major sections—a flowchart. A flowchart maps how that list you just created will be represented in your portfolio. It helps you to visualize a clear arrangement of material that will make it easy for anyone to navigate your portfolio while still offering something unusual and unique. In short, think of a flowchart as a way to visually index the contents of your portfolio.

Take a look at the flowchart designed for the Web in the accompanying illustration. The interface shown here was developed by Giselle Lopez. Notice that the interface offers a clear way to navigate to the home page.

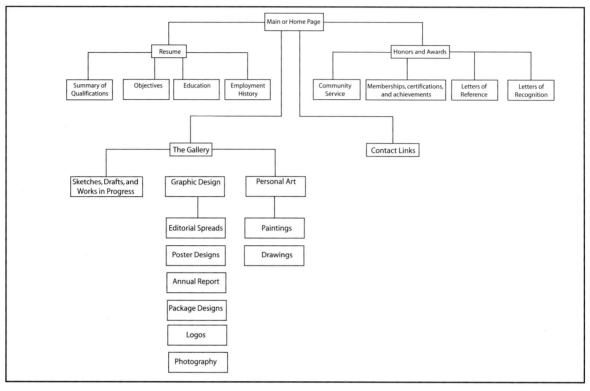

The flowchart for a portfolio might look like this.

Next time you're online, visit a couple of Web sites with the express purpose of concentrating only on how they are arranged. Ask yourself the following questions about each site: Is the organization of the information clear? Do you find it easy to navigate the site? If so, consider sketching a flowchart to describe that site. It will help you to visualize how different sites are compiled. And keep in mind, there is no one right way to develop a flowchart. It's simply a tool to help you once the actual work begins.

Gather Your Art

It's time to get your project off the ground. By now, you have your art projects, rough book, sketches, photos, boards, sculpture, and anything else you need to begin the process of multimedia design. You have taken the time to inventory your projects, and you have selected the pieces you want to include in the port. You must now convert the art to a digital format.

If the art is two-dimensional, a scanner is ideal. Most scanners can control the size and dpi of the image as it is converted. This will save you some time. The more functions the scanner can perform, the easier it will be for you to finish the prep work on the file once it is in the raster editing program. Whenever I scan artwork, I take some time to figure out the size of the final file. Then, with the art on the scanner, I input appropriate dpi numbers and reduce the file enough so that it fits comfortably within the layout. This shortens the time I have to spend in Photoshop (or any other program), and that small effort makes me more productive.

Art that is too big to fit on a scanner presents a special challenge. Package designs, billboards, large-scale renderings, and point-of-purchase displays (those terrific 3-D displays you see in supermarkets featuring promotional products) all require a different approach. Larger pieces will need to be photographed with either a digital or traditional camera. Digital photos can be downloaded directly into the computer. Traditional photos will have to be developed, then scanned. Large flat pieces can be scanned in segments, then merged back together in Photoshop. There's quite a bit of prep work to get all your art ready for the authoring program, but it's important to take your time and get everything just the way you want it.

Remember to keep backups of all digital art. Once the images have been captured and saved, create extra copies! Burn CDs or DVDs, copy to a zip disc, save to an external hard drive—use whatever method you prefer to archive your work, but do it. Here's why it's so important. Suppose you want to save your work for the Web. The art will be saved as a JPEG. As you will recall, the JPEG format compresses art by eliminating extraneous pixel information. If you keep an original version of the art before you create the JPEG, you will always be able to alter the original. You will have to do this more often than you might imagine. As your portfolio needs updating, for example, you may find it necessary to change dates, colors, or the size of the art. It may also take a couple of tries before you have the piece in just the right size.

Designing a Visual Theme: Making Your Portfolio Unique

All the art is properly scanned, sized, and saved. You have created a flowchart for your interface and selected a multimedia-authoring program. The next step is to design a visual theme for the interface, to tie the project together. Through the use of color, buttons, sound, images, and type, you will give a viewer a complete art and multimedia experience. This presentation is every bit as important as the art itself. In the same way that showing a beautiful painting in an inappropriate frame will detract from its beauty, a poorly designed presentation will detract from the designs you worked so hard to produce.

There are countless ways to present information. Which way you go depends on how you want to present yourself. Are you playful or serious? Do you fancy yourself traditional or avant-garde? Do you like lots of color or neutral shades of gray? Your personal style sense is a good place to begin the design process, but there are other factors. The art you will be showcasing also influences the look of the interface. Pieces that feature a lot of bright colors need to be shown against neutral background colors. Keep in mind that it is always about the art, not the interface.

Take care in making your style and theme choices. Never forget that your portfolio will be viewed not only directly but indirectly as well. This means that your port will also give viewers insight into the underlying meaning of who you are and how you perceive yourself as an artist. What you may see as a really innovative idea for an interface may patently offend others. Consider your audience at all times, and steer clear of themes that might be viewed unfavorably. An interface can be fun and innovative yet carry a serious message. Remember the retro fifties look you saw in Chapter 2? Music, colors, and type characteristic of the decade created an amusing presentation. You, too, can create an interface based on novel motifs or unconventional ideas. Think about your hobbies, cultural heritage, and places you might like to visit. Do whatever you have to do to get your creative juices flowing.

You might consider an opening theme, similar to how so many television shows use a theme song. It's their signature. Even a simple animation will dazzle the spectator. We have been talking a lot about the overall look and feel of the main (or home) page of the digital port, but you can also design an opening that will set the tone for everything to come. While it is not mandatory to create an introduction for your port, a clever one hints at your skills as a multilevel designer. A well-designed opening gives your viewer an engaging and interactive experience—a "wow" experience. It creates the environment. So take some time to sketch, storyboard, conceptualize, and sketch some more. Figure out the best approach for your introduction and start creating it.

Once the opening is complete, you will need to design your home page, the pivotal area, or hub, of your site. From the home page, the user navigates through the rest of the site, discovering the many sections you have produced. Therefore, it is the most important of all your pages. Remember, first impressions are the most important. The information you present on this first page should demonstrate a clear understanding of the user's navigational needs. Home pages generally contain the design elements listed below.

Dan McCauley shows you his navigational strategy in a way that integrates extremely well with the overall design of the interface.

(Observe some of the interface examples in this chapter as a starting point.)

Your name
Clear links to other pages
Effective use of color that creates a unified design
Images that serve only to support the design
Common interface design elements

What is the most important part of your home page? Your name! Place your name in a prominent location. Remember, the portfolio is about you; your name may be in logo form or created with type, but it must be there. Place any other elements you wish on the home page, but make sure your name is right up there where the viewer can see who created the awesome portfolio.

Navigation: How to Get There from Here

Navigation is all about the users. Buttons, navigation bars, and text provide visitors with the tools to go everywhere on your site from wherever they are at the moment. A well-designed set of graphic links within your portfolio pages will direct users beyond your home page.

Make sure navigation buttons and bars are easy to understand. Do not assume that users will "hunt around" for a hidden link. And make all navigation buttons consistent throughout the site. Never design anything without considering how it will function for users. You can create several different types of links, such as buttons, bars, images, text rollovers, and image maps. Each of these represents a design metaphor. Use any of the methods you wish as long as each method supports the overall design. Buttons should always be small and quick to download. We'll discuss them further in Chapter 9.

Of course, you can always make your own buttons! Take a look at a few I designed with Photoshop and Illustrator. It's not that difficult. Armed with a little knowledge, you can design some great buttons just by combining different colors and shapes.

In Camilo Montilla's interface, the building blocks always appear in the same location throughout. It is important to create a theme that works at all times to support your message.

Anabella Feaugas uses a stylish color set that allows the images to stand up on their own. Notice the clear navigational strategy of images at the bottom. If you roll over any of the small images, a larger version pops up.

Photoshop is a great resource for button design. These buttons were created with the Styles palette and the Webdings alphabet. The Styles palette offers you a vast variety of premade color systems designed specifically with Web-safe colors.

Dreamweaver comes with an option that allows you to create Flash-animated buttons. Each button can be customized with the type of your choice. There are many different buttons styles available.

You can buy buttons that are ready to use. As I mentioned previously, there are lots of Web design clip art packages on the market. But as I also mentioned, the problem with such packages is that everybody else has access to them. That said, let me tell you about two great Web sites: ButtonGenerator.com (www.buttongenerator.com) and ButtonBoost.com (www.buttonboost.com/startweb.html). At these nifty sites, you can customize buttons and Web-ready menus based on their designs. You can also choose to create a multiple-state button, which offers an up, down, and over effect. This makes it much easier for the user to see when the button is active and will link to somewhere else. Everything you need to create a button is just a few clicks away. A variety of fonts, colors, and button styles are available for you to choose from, and the final results are worth the effort. The accompanying illustrations show just a few of the many buttons ready for you to modify.

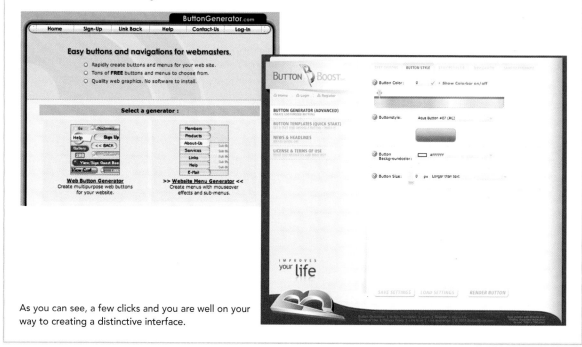

As you can see, a few clicks and you are well on your way to creating a distinctive interface.

A basic button is generally a circle, square, or rectangle that represents a link to another area of the portfolio. Buttons may include informational text and may be three-dimensional or stylized graphic symbols called icons. For example, as shown in one of the accompanying illustrations, you might use an icon of a small house to indicate the link back to your home page.

A navigation bar is used to display a collection of buttons. As such, the navigation bar usually resides at the top or bottom of the page. So-called text buttons are not buttons at all but rather text that acts as a link. Text buttons are frequently designed to change colors (known as rollovers) when selected, to indicate their function as a link. Small images can also serve as links. They can be created to change colors or morph into another image when selected. An image map is a picture with several links or "hot spots" embedded in the file. When the user's mouse passes over the hot spot, it changes in some way to suggest a link to another area.

Here are several other sites that give you the opportunity to generate custom designs for free:

Cool Text Graphics Generator:
    http://cooltext.com
Free AlphaButton:
    www.free.alphabutton.com/index.php
FlashButtons.com: www.FlashButtons.com

There are also a number of Web sites that offer relatively inexpensive programs to generate your buttons. Here are a few to check out:

Just Buttons:
    www.lincolnbeach.com/justbuttons.asp
Crystal Button: www.crystalbutton.com
1 Cool Button Tool: www.buttontool.com
Xara Webstyle 4:
    http://site.xara.com/products/webstyle/
Likno Software: www.likno.com

Using Color Effectively

Much of what we know about color today began in 1666, when English scientist Sir Isaac Newton discovered the nature of light and color. At that time, the general consensus was that color was a mixture of light and darkness and that a prism (a transparent optical component with flat, polished surfaces) simply acted to color the light. Newton was able to set up a prism near his window and project a stunning color spectrum of light 22 feet onto the far wall. Thus, Newton was able to prove that a prism can act to separate colors into individual wavelengths or colors.

Although every element on your home page contributes to the cohesiveness of the design, color plays the most important part. Color is a major form of communication. Color can symbolize and trigger emotions and associations, both positive and negative. Color adds impact. Color points to what is important for the viewer to see and understand. Color (both in type and as a background) can act as a unifying theme. In short, effective color use can really distinguish your interface; ineffective use can jeopardize your message.

• I Can't Write Code. Now What?

You know the feeling. You see a really cool Web site and wish you had the knowledge to produce something just as wonderful. Most artists are not programmers. That's where Flash components and Dreamweaver extensions come in. These bits of prewritten code can really streamline your development time. And the best part is that they require little or no coding.

There are Flash components that can help you create art galleries, scroll bars, and professional menus. Flashloaded (www.flashloaded.com) and FlashComponents.net (www.flashcomponents.net) are just two of many sites that offer components.

Extensions allow you to add new features and capabilities to Dreamweaver above and beyond the program's normal functions. There are extensions to create feedback forms and lots of different navigation menus. Project Seven (www.projectseven.com/extensions/listing.htm), Dreamweaver Fever (http://dreamweaverfever.com/extensions), and Adobe Exchange (www.adobe.com) are several sites to visit in your quest for extensions.

These various miniprograms range in price from free (always a good thing) to $50 or more.

As an example, think about Valentine's Day. What colors come to mind? Now think about fall in Vermont. Can you see the color of the leaves? Color is important in all aspects of life. So-called green rooms are used in Hollywood to relax actors. Red is used in restaurants to stimulate appetite. Department store designers have found that reds, blacks, and blues have a positive impact on impulse shoppers (positive for the store, at least). However, the interpretation of a color depends on many different factors, such as age, gender, cultural background, training, and personal experience. Men react to color differently than women; they tend to prefer blue and orange. Women like red and yellow. In general, red, orange, and yellow are considered to be "exciting" colors; purple, blue, and green are thought to be "calming" colors.

The Psychology of Color

All this is by way of saying that selecting color for your portfolio should be based on how you want to market yourself. Don't use a color simply because you like it. Recognize that the colors you choose will have an effect on each person viewing your portfolio, regardless of his or her background or culture. To help you in this regard, let's examine briefly what's called the psychology of color.

Red and Pink

Red suggests excitement, strength, passion, or courage. But it also has implications of violence and aggression, as it may trigger images of blood or war. Studies have demonstrated that red can even raise blood pressure. In China, red symbolizes luck. In India, red is the color of purity (used in wedding garments).

In most Western cultures, pink symbolizes innocence, romance, and femininity. Pink often conjures images of softness and sweetness, such as of a baby. It is also thought to be calming and tranquilizing.

Orange

Orange is a warm and vibrant color; hence, it evokes warm and cozy feelings or images of an autumn afternoon. But orange has also been shown to stimulate the appetite, and it symbolizes health. Because orange has radiant qualities, it is often used for attention-getting purposes, such as on caution signs.

Yellow

Yellow, as you might imagine, signifies sunshine, warmth, and happiness. Yellow is considered a positive, bright, cheerful, and optimistic color. But it has its "evil twin," as it can also symbolize cowardice, dishonesty, betrayal, jealousy, covetousness, fearfulness, or deceit. Give a yellow rose to your friends; it is a symbol of friendship and is not as "passionate" as red ones. In Asia, the color yellow is considered to be sacred and imperial.

Green

Green is seen as a refreshing color that symbolizes growth and abundance. It also represents health, freshness, new growth, and tranquility. Green is powerful, too, in that it communicates wealth and so is frequently used by banking institutions. Green's "bad" image comes from its link to the negative emotions of jealousy or envy, as well as to lizards, toads, and other creepy-crawly things. In China, a green hat may mean that a man's wife is cheating on him. In China and France, it is not a good idea to use green for package design. In India, green is the color of Islam.

Blue

Not surprisingly, the color of the sky and the sea is considered calming. It communicates trust, wisdom, generosity, reliability, conservatism, security, cleanliness, order, loyalty, dignity, and intelligence. Blue is known to be an appetite suppressant and can also be used to con-

These two screens are from the digital portfolio of Jennifer Worley. She likes to use strong contrast as a way to showcase her art.

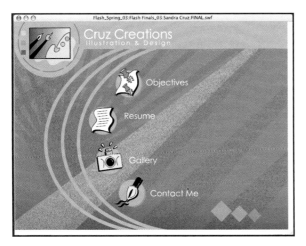

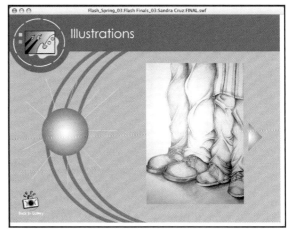

This beautiful interface, designed by Sandra Cruz, shows her love of illustration both in the main image and with her drawing on the "Illustrations" page.

note depression and melancholy. Blue is one of the few colors that is universally accepted by all cultures. In China, blue is associated with immortality. For Jews, blue symbolizes holiness. Blue is a protective color in the Middle East. In ancient Rome, public servants wore blue clothes.

Purple

Purple is a soothing yet powerful color, as it is associated with royalty, wealth, and creativity. It is also considered spiritual and mysterious. Lighter shades of purple are thought to represent romance and nostalgia. In ancient history, purple dye was created by gathering the mucus from the gland of a snail. It took literally thousands of snails to produce one small batch of the color, making purple the color of choice for wealthy nobles. Unfortunately, purple can also suggest cruelty and arrogance. (For a good example of the use of the color purple, take a look at the images by Sandra Cruz.)

Black, White, and Gray

Black is a very powerful color in that it connotes so many things: power, elegance, and sexuality; death, evil, and mystery; fear, unhappiness, and grief. Black is frequently used in packaging design to convey product sophistication; it is also used to invigorate other colors. It is stimulating in small quantities.

White is considered to be a cheerful color that reflects innocence and purity, hence its widespread use in weddings and christenings. It also connotes spirituality and cleanliness and is used to express youth and vigor. We think of white as the color of "the good guy" in westerns. And in contrast to most Western cultures, it symbolizes mourning in Eastern cultures. In Japan, white carnations signify death.

Gray is a conservative color that implies intellect and symbolizes a conservative point of view. It is considered a dignified color that speaks of maturity and dependability. It is also considered to be a futuristic color and so is used frequently for technology-related design concepts. It is currently a very "in" color in Web design. But

Bellatrix Martinez demonstrates that design can use neutral colors and still be very innovative!

gray can also be depressing and may symbolize sadness, old age, and decay.

Brown

Brown is a natural color that depicts earthiness or the outdoors. It brings to mind the rich image of coffee or chocolate. Brown also may be used to represent the future, as it makes people think of comfort, credibility, and stability. It is a restful color. And in India, brown is the color of mourning.

Color and Your Portfolio Interface

Ever since Sir Isaac Newton demonstrated that light was responsible for color, artists have been fascinated by its arrangement and use. However, Newton's most useful idea was his theoretical arrangement of colors around the circumference of a circle. Using his theories of light, Newton arranged primary colors (red, yellow, blue) opposite their complementary colors (e.g., red opposite green). In this way, he suggested that opposite, or complementary, colors could be used in effective ways to enhance each other through optical contrast.

After evaluating your approach to the colors you will use for your interface, the next step is to determine which colors can be used together and how to use them. Color choice will, of course, always come down to personal preference, but there are some guidelines you should follow to ensure the best response from the widest possible audience.

Limit the Number of Colors: The Three-color System

Too many colors will give the page a too-busy feel, and the viewer will find it difficult to locate the important information. Too many colors also can make the eyes tired. Conversely, using too few colors can make a page boring or uninteresting. Color should be used to draw viewers in and encourage them to see more, to see it all.

One good way to limit the use of colors yet still produce an interesting interface is to use the three-color system. That means you design your interface with a primary color, a secondary color, and a highlight color. The primary color is the main color of your design. It will occupy most of the design space. Therefore, it should be neutral and blend well with your art. Used correctly, the primary color sets the tone for the overall design portfolio.

The secondary color supports the primary color of the design and as such usually is similar to the primary color. Secondary colors are created by combining a primary color with a neighboring secondary color on the

Complementary Colors

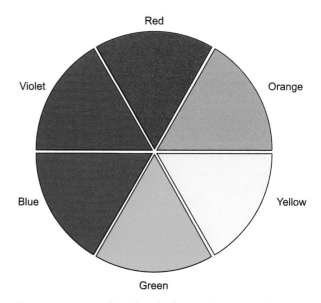

As you can see on this color wheel, complementary colors are any two colors opposite each other on the color wheel. Used together, they tend to vibrate, so employ them sparingly.

Keep in mind that about 8 percent of the population is color-blind. The most common form of color blindness is centered around an individual's inability to distinguish between red and blue. This mainly occurs in men. Between 1 and 2 percent of men have difficulty determining the difference between blues and yellows. Interestingly, fewer than 1 percent of women suffer from any form of color blindness. Choosing colors without regard to contrast virtually assures that this particular segment of the population will not be able to see your layout as you designed it. Make sure there is strong contrast between the text and the background (as shown in the accompanying examples). And be sure to visit a Web site such as Color Oracle (http://colororacle.cartography.ch) that specializes in checking Web pages for ease of use for the vision-impaired.

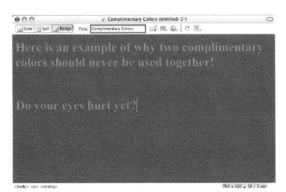

Stay away from complementary colors in CD/DVD or Web design, where they can cause type to vibrate, making it difficult for users to focus.

This is the layout shown on the left without color. A color-blind individual would have difficulty reading text under these conditions. Squint your eyes and look at your design. If the colors seem to blend into one mass of gray, you need to rethink your use of color.

color wheel. They usually are analogous or next to each other on the wheel; for example, blue and blue-green (a tertiary color) are two analogous colors. They are related but not the same. Whenever analogous colors are used, one color generally acts as the dominant color while the other colors are used as accents.

Tertiary colors are made of any primary and secondary color mixed together. They are usually expressed as blue-green or yellow-orange. When creating an analogous color system, one primary, one secondary, and one tertiary color are generally selected.

The highlight color is chosen to emphasize a particular section of the page. It is usually a color that contrasts with the primary and secondary colors yet complements the others used in the rest of your portfolio. The accompanying illustration shows why complementary colors can ruin a Web page. Complementary colors—two colors opposite each other on the color wheel—make the page very difficult to read.

Complementary colors never look good in CD/DVD or Web design. The type will "vibrate," and the user will have difficulty focusing on the colors for any length of time. Highlight colors are pleasing to the eye when used in small amounts. On the color wheel, the complement of blue would be orange. Be careful not to get carried away when using contrasting colors. Orange type on a blue background, for example, will be extremely difficult for your viewer to read. What you want to do is contrast the complements. For example, use peach and sky blue together to evoke an outdoorsy feeling. Look at the examples presented here for ideas on how to use complementary colors effectively.

Another approach is to use split-complementary colors—that is, the color on either side of the complement.

Jair Acevedo uses an architectural approach to this interface. The overall effect is that of a floor plan coupled with a galaxy.

The colors are broken into two colors that are adjacent to the main complementary color. The split complement of blue would be orange-yellow or orange-red. Split combinations tend to be less vibrant and add some variety to the page.

Think Soft and Monochromatic

Your color selections do not have to be bright. Selecting softer versions of colors will enhance the subtlety, finesse, and readability of your site. Warm colors (yellows, reds, and oranges) will come forward on your page. Cool colors (blues and greens) will recede. Mix both together to build additional interest. Colors created with a light value (white added) tend to be viewed as contemporary or less serious colors.

A current trend is to use monochromatic color schemes in multimedia design. That means using a single color plus tints and shades of that same color. This creates unity in a design and can be very powerful when mixed with one accent color. And colors with black added can impart drama to a Web site. But never place black on pure white, as this is very stressful on the eyes and will cause viewers to exit your project. Soften the contrast between the text, visuals, and background to solve this problem.

Use Web-safe Colors

When creating your electronic portfolio, always keep in mind that there are color limitations for projects destined for Web viewing. As you know, the human eye can perceive millions of colors. And, technically, you can produce millions of colors on your screen. But you'd be wise not to do so, because Macs and PCs use completely different color palettes.

To solve the problem of displaying color graphics on different monitors, Netscape invented the browser-safe color palette. This palette includes 216 "Web-safe" colors that are common to both Windows and Macintosh computers. By using these colors, you can ensure that your Web site will display fairly consistently on different operating systems (Windows or Mac) as well as in different browsers, such as Internet Explorer, Apple's Safari, and Firefox.

All that said, this is less of a problem than it used to be, because today's state-of-the-art monitors are set to thousands or millions of colors. What hasn't changed, however, is that the more colors you use, the slower the download speed of your Web pages.

Use Background Images, but Only to Enhance Your Interface

My rule of thumb is, be careful when using background images. Why? They are distracting, they take forever to load, and they make text nearly impossible to read over a "wallpaper-type" background image. And pictures used as backgrounds have to be created the full size of a Web page, which might be as large as 800 × 600 pixels unless you create a small and textured image. This makes the overall file size much larger. In addition, HTML documents that feature background images have formatting problems, as the image must be "sliced" into segments before insertion, which also means extra work, more time.

One partial workaround is to use an image as a section of the overall page design. This keeps the file size small and ensures a faster load time. A smaller image also leaves more negative space on the page. It "opens up" the layout and produces a very stylish solution.

You could, for example, create a small, seamless image file (which stays small) to be used as a wallpaper element. The image is created as a repeating pattern

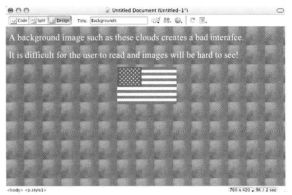

Backgrounds usually do more harm than good. This background must have seemed like a good idea at the time, but it interferes with the image and makes it hard to read the type.

once imported to the layout. Just make sure that the pattern will not compete with the other elements on the page. Contrast is the key.

If you are determined to have a background, create one that is subtle and that almost disappears, well, into the background! And stick with solid colors. In short, make sure the background doesn't overwhelm the main content of any pages.

Color Wrap-up

Let me close by reiterating the importance of considering the psychology and use of color before you construct your portfolio. A good way to do this is to find a Web page worth admiring . Analyze the color and see if you can determine what makes the page so attractive. The more sensitivity you develop to color and its impact on interface design, the more professional your pages will look. In the next chapter, we turn our attention to the importance of typography.

• Colors Giving You Trouble?

Are you having trouble finding colors just right for your design? No problem! Here are some Web sites that will help you to select colors that are sure to be compatible with one another:

Color Blender:
    http://meyerweb.com/eric/tools/color-blend
ColorMatch.dk: http://colormatch.dk
Colors on the Web:
    ww.colorsontheweb.com/spinwheel.asp
DeGraeve.com (Color Palette Generator):
    www.degraeve.com/color-palette

An Interview with Stephan Donche

Stephan Donche is a principal and creative director of viadesign, a design agency based in San Diego, California. The agency specializes in the creation of effective and targeted corporate communication materials, including corporate identities, publications, Web sites, and direct-mail and print campaigns. Over the last 20 years, the agency has won a variety of national and international awards for its outstanding work. Its clients range from small start-ups to large Fortune 500 companies. A graduate of UCLA, Stephan has served as a judge on a variety of national design award committees.

You can visit Stephan Donche's Web site at www.viadesign.com.

1 What qualities do you look for in an applicant?

At first glance, I expect the applicant to be on time, dress well, and have an outstanding portfolio. Also, any résumé left behind should have absolutely no spelling errors.

Then I look for the small things that make the applicant stand out. Does he or she speak a foreign language? Does he or she collect unusual objects? Does he or she show curiosity about the economy, world events, movies?

Does he or she sing in a punk band? Et cetera . . . What's important for any young designer is not to be afraid to share their unique background, their likes, and even their hobbies.

Finally, I look for an applicant that is not afraid to have a dialogue with me, ask questions, and be engaging.

2 In your opinion, what makes a successful interview?

One that is followed by a job offer.

3 Has the Internet had an effect on your interview process?

Yes, we pretty much expect applicants to have their portfolio online, which helps us screen them.

4 What are the five best things job candidates say that impress you during an interview? What are the five worst?

Best
1 Thank you for your time.
2 I've looked at your Web site. I am familiar with your work.
3 Hope you don't mind, but I also brought some thumbnails.
4 This was part of a team project.
5 Can I ask you some questions?

Worst
1 "Sorry for being late. I couldn't find a parking space." (Then come early next time.)
2 "This is not my best piece." (Then don't show it.)
3 "Would I be able to listen to my iPod?" (No.)
4 "I love the logo you did for Nike." (A great logo, indeed. Too bad my competitor did it.)
5 "I love garlic." (Me, too, but next time wait until after the interview before eating some.)

5 What are skills that really help all artists succeed regardless of their specialty?

More than [with] any other job, a successful designer needs to be organized, fast, money-savvy, and an excellent communicator.

6 What advice would you offer to designers looking to impress you with the presentation of their work?

Be yourself. And if yourself is smart, talented, and honest, then yourself, along with a little luck, will do well.

Designer's Challenge 1

Visit a well-known Web site. Critique the site for color, type, and appropriate message. Draw a flowchart that details how the site is laid out. Do you think the overall design is great, good, or needs help?

Designer's Challenge 2

Create a poster to advertise the Society of Typographic Designers exhibition. Using your best knowledge of type, design an appropriate layout to support the show. Include dates, times, location, Web site, and telephone number.

Frances Gonzalez has designed this dynamic solution to this challenge using a postmodern theme. The typography is bold and interactive.

8

Working with Type and Layout

The effectiveness of an innovative layout depends not just on your use of color but on your use of typography as well. As in graphic design, typography is one of the foundations of good visual design. Setting, or placing, type

involves the careful selection of a finely proportioned collection of lines and shapes, which are reproductions of the original letterforms. The correct use of type is just as important on an electronic page as it is in any other medium. Type must always be pleasing to look at and easy to read. As with other areas of visual design, there are rules to follow and limitations to be aware of when it comes to working with typography for an electronic purpose. Look at the two "Once upon a time" layouts. The one on the left is rather plain, while the one on the right is charming and appealing.

To work with typography successfully, you need to understand it. There is, of course, no "ideal type solution," but there are guidelines to follow to help you choose the right typography for any given situation. Legibility is the key to success with your designs.

A Brief Lesson on Type for Multimedia Design

Let's start with some terminology. In type design, there are typefaces and fonts. A typeface is a unified set of shapes or "glyphs" that form a complete alphabet system. Think of a typeface as all the letters: A to Z. In addition to letters, typefaces can include numerals, punctuation marks, and even fractions. Some typefaces, such as Zapf, include nothing but pictures or symbols. Now, a font comprises a complete assortment of the letters, numbers, and other characters of a design. This includes the type size and such features as bold and italic variations. (Font is often confused with the word typeface, which means literally "the face of printing

126

ABCDEFGHIJKLMNOPQRSTUVWXYZ
abcdefghijklmnopqrstuvwxyz

top Which of these paragraphs do you think would be more fun to read?

bottom The Gill Sans font looks like this. Notice that it's a clean, modern-looking type.

type," or all type of a single design.) As an example of a font, the accompanying illustration shows one called Gill Sans.

A font family contains all of the variations of one font, perhaps as many as 60 varieties. These variations might include italics, bold, extended, condensed, and small and regular caps. The accompanying illustrations also show Gill Sans in several different variations.

Fonts are generally grouped by category, based on common characteristics. Although there is some disagreement among designers as to what should be considered a category, for our purposes, type will be broken down into the following categories:

- Serif: Serifs are thin, short lines that stem from or at an angle to the upper and lower ends of the strokes of a letter. Serif fonts are used primarily for body text because of their legibility. They are easy on the eyes and hence do not cause eyestrain.
- Sans serif: Sans in French means "without," so a sans serif type is one that has none of the short lines that stem from or at an angle to the upper and lower ends of the strokes of a letter. According to most studies, sans serif fonts are more difficult to read. However, they are considered a good choice for headings and the Web.
- Modern: This category includes typefaces that feature strong contrast between thick and thin strokes

ABCDEFGHIJKLMNOPQRSTUVWXYZ
abcdefghijklmnopqrstuvwxyz

ABCDEFGHIJKLMNOPQRSTUVWXYZ
abcdefghijklmnopqrstuvwxyz

ABCDEFGHIJKLMNOPQRSTUVWXYZ
abcdefghijklmnopqrstuvwxyz

ABCDEFGHIJKLMNOPQRSTUVWXYZ
ABCDEFGHIJKLMNOPQRSTUVWXYZ

THIS IS GILLSANS IN BOTHE REGULAR AND SMALL CAPS.

top This is the Gill Sans font as a bold typeface.

middle Gill Sans Light Italic gives a totally different look to the letters.

bottom Here is Gill Sans in regular and small caps.

of each letter. Modern typefaces also feature strong vertical emphasis and fine hairlines on each letter.

- Display, novelty, or decorative: Typefaces in this category are designed to imitate brushstrokes or handwriting. Decorative or novelty types are most effective when used in larger point sizes for display. You often see them used as headlines and titles.

Using Type to Express Your Artistic Vision

If you have ever designed for print, you already know the power of type to express your ideas through the use of appropriate letterforms. In fact, type can be the focal point of your layout. Think of type as a kind of texture. This will help you to view type as a design element and allow you to focus on the visual representation of the words rather than the message. Just keep in mind that, like color, a typeface can either support or undermine your design, so you must choose wisely.

Display Type

Headlines, titles, subheads, and pull quotes are all examples of display, or novelty, type. Headlines are the most important. They show the viewer what to focus on in the display. Open your favorite magazine and find an article. No doubt you will take note of the headline or title of the article first. As you scan down the page, you notice the body copy, the bulk of any printed piece. The headline tells you what is important about that article and why you should be reading it. Subheads and pull quotes also give visual emphasis to a page and help direct the reader's attention, as well as divide the page into visually pleasing sections. The same rules apply to digital interface design as well.

Here are a few guidelines for designing headlines for a digital portfolio:

- The size of your headline suggests its importance. Choose wisely.
- Leave some white space around the headline. It gives your page additional impact.
- In general, use heavy, condensed sans serif typefaces in headlines.
- Don't underline headlines. (It will make them look like hyperlinks.)
- Use slab serif typefaces (fonts in which the serifs are solid straight lines) to suggest strength.
- Use rounded typefaces to create a more relaxed and friendly mood.
- Use large Modern typefaces to express sophistication.
- Use matching typefaces for headlines and subheads.
- Place pull quotes within paragraphs to break up long sections of type.
- And note that pull quotes work best when used in larger type sizes and that contrast makes them stand out.

Visual Organization

The accompanying figures show a Web page with the information blocked out and the same page with the information displayed. How does the first figure compare with the second one? What is the most important section of the page?

Squint while you are looking at the first image. Did you notice the shades of gray and the values in the

Times & Times New Roman
Garamond
Palatino
Caslon

Helvetica
Arial
GillSans
Myriad

Bodoni
Ellington
Didot

Brush Script
Edwardian Script
STENCIL
Sand

from top These are examples of serif typefaces.

These are examples of sans serif typefaces. Notice the absence of decorative line features.

Modern typefaces are designed to suggest a contemporary feeling.

Used in small quantities, display, novelty, or decorative typefaces offer interesting variations for your layouts.

design? Did you see those same patterns in the full-text version? I'm guessing that you did. It has been proved that, on a subconscious level, humans are always looking for patterns in the everyday world. In Las Vegas, players around the roulette tables guess which color is "due" to come up next. In psychology, Rorschach

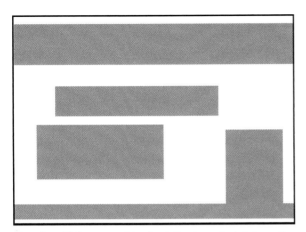

Here is a Web page with all of the important information blocked out by gray bars so that you can see the visual emphasis of the layout.

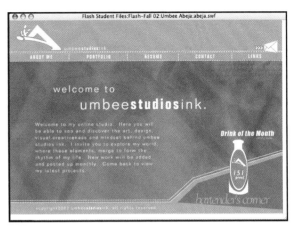

Here is the same page, designed by Umberto Abeja, with all of the information displayed. Notice how your eye travels around the page. This is known as "eye flow."

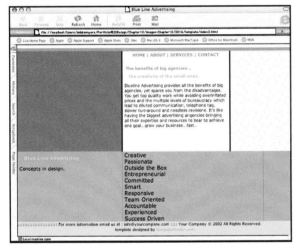

This is a dull Web page. The solid mass of unbroken gray makes it almost impossible to find the content.

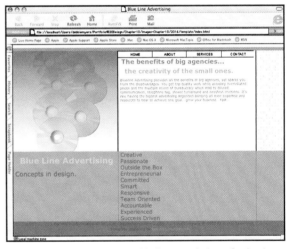

What is needed is contrast and balance. Splashes of color, large and small type, and images will prioritize the visual space.

inkblot tests are given to discover what a person "sees" in the "blot." Everywhere we look, we try to find patterns; and if we can't find a pattern, we will create one.

When it comes to your portfolio interface, you can think of yourself as an information architect. Type and images form the masses of shapes and color of your design. Everything you place on a page has a weight. Although the viewer probably will not perceive this fact at first, its patterns will become noticeable after a brief period. Those patterns will then become distinct

phrases and images. Once the page fully "emerges," the viewer will begin to pick out information that is relevant to him or her. Thus, the more difficult it is for the viewer to pick out what is important, the less successful your design will be.

This sequence is called the *visual hierarchy of design.* A visual hierarchy allows you to create a discernible system by arranging headings, subheadings, and images that give the page a structure. This then enables the viewer to understand the document's major structural characteristics at a glance. As a designer, you need to organize your menus, submenus, buttons, and text so that the appropriate elements receive the proper prominence you assign them in the hierarchy.

To clarify this concept, do this little exercise. Look at the accompanying pictures on the preceding page, the first of which shows an admittedly ineffective visual design for a Web page for Blue Line Advertising. Think about how you might improve it. Now sketch your thoughts. How might you rearrange the different elements to make a more effective design? A word of caution: don't allow the design to get in the way of the message. The second picture illustrates one possible way to improve the design.

Here are a few other tips to get you started:

- If it's essential, make it bigger. A headline created in a larger font says, "I'm important!"
- The more important the content, the higher up on the page it should be placed.
- Divide your information into clearly defined areas.
- Break up long sentences or paragraphs into bulleted lists.

The Importance of Consistency

Good navigation design is the first key to design success, as you learned in the previous chapter. Consistency is the second. Consistency lays a solid foundation for visitor interaction with your interface, making the experience comfortable and seamless. Approach interface design with the objective of making it elegant and easy to use. This is largely a matter of balancing the layout.

Consistency is achieved in a number of different ways. First and foremost, the person viewing your port should be able to understand the layout. You already know the value of a consistent navigational system. The same principles apply to backgrounds, page designs, and titles, as well as multimedia. The following subsections delve into some specifics of this important guideline.

Use Grids

Your interface must be functional as well as visually appealing. The idea is to draw the visitor into the material using a combination of words and pictures that all relate to your theme. A poorly designed page will make it difficult for the viewer to understand how to find items of interest. Therefore, positioning graphical and text elements consistently throughout your project (as Hilda Vazquez's interface illustrates) is vital to its success. A consistent layout quickly increases the user's confidence in navigating your digital port.

Time for another exercise: select three pages from three different Web sites. Try to determine whether a grid was used. How? Look for the placement of the different interface elements on each of the pages. What do you notice? Do you see a consistent design? Are the

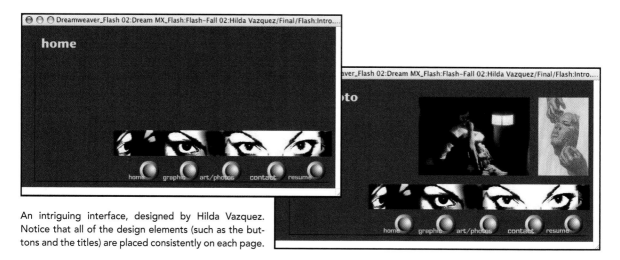

An intriguing interface, designed by Hilda Vazquez. Notice that all of the design elements (such as the buttons and the titles) are placed consistently on each page.

It's very tiring on the eyes to read text across the full width of the screen.

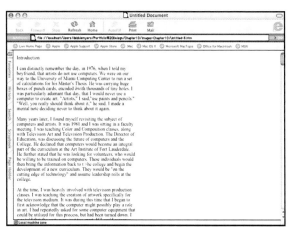

Notice the difference when the type is set in narrower columns. Less left-to-right eye movement means less strain on the eyes.

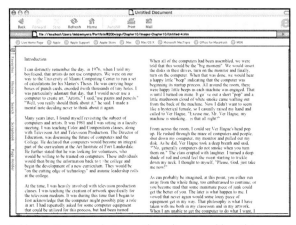

Add negative space between the columns and breathing room to the page. Things don't seem so crowded now, and nothing gets in the way of the message.

elements easily found and understood? The two pages from Hilda Vazquez's Web site illustrate the use of a consistent grid layout.

Put All Vital Elements "Above the Fold"

Most interfaces are designed for either a CD-ROM or DVD (800 × 600 pixels) or the Web (1024 × 768). The most important information should be fully visible on the screen and readable at a glance. Techies refer to this critical space as being "above the fold" (a carryover from newspaper lingo). This is where the most important information should always appear.

This amazing Web site, designed by M. Kathleen Colussy, is an excellent example of the use of white space and a grid. The site is easy to read and to navigate.

As a rule, that includes your name, the areas of the site you wish your viewers to visit, and major navigational icons. The idea is that the most important information should always be above the fold line or (in this case) fully on the screen, where it can be easily seen. Regardless of where the icons are placed (top, side, or bottom), as long as the critical information is available to the viewer, the navigational experience will be a good one.

Find three Web sites and compare them for visual cohesiveness, using the following worksheet to record your observations.

Name of Web Site	Common Interface Elements
1.	1.
	2.
	3.
	4.
	5.
2.	1.
	2.
	3.
	4.
	5.
3.	1.
	2.
	3.
	4.
	5.

Set Large Amounts of Type in Narrow Columns

As I've explained, large amounts of type that run across the entire screen can be really difficult to read. This restriction can present a design challenge if, say, your résumé comprises a great deal of text. One way to solve this problem is to create a "resting place" for the eyes. Break up the text space into narrow columns. You see this technique commonly used in newspapers. Just be careful not to place two long columns of text side by side. That will make it even more difficult on the viewer.

Use Subheads to Break Up Information

Your pages will be more visually appealing to your visitors if your design includes both headlines and subheadlines. Subheads break up large blocks of text and direct the reader to each section according to subject. This helps increase the overall legibility of the page. Without subheads, the user has more difficulty seeing major patterns quickly and therefore interpreting information. Subheads are considered essential when a design page contains more than 500 words.

Here are five more tips to help you design text and subheads more effectively:

1. Use color to make your subheads stand out.
2. Decide on a few important subheadings; don't use too many.
3. Use headings and subheadings consistently.
4. Don't boldface everything, because then nothing stands out.
5. Split up large amounts of text into more easily digestible chunks.

Design to Scroll or Not to Scroll

Users say they don't like to scroll. Studies say otherwise. What's a designer to do? You have two choices:

1. Create lots of short pages with smaller amounts of text on each page.
2. Create longer pages with lots of type on each page.

Each approach has advantages and disadvantages. Small amounts of text and a few links mean little or no scrolling is required. There are many who endorse this strategy. The only problem is that it may take viewers several clicks through a number of pages before they find what they are looking for. The same is true in backing out of the site. With fewer, but longer, pages, the user must scroll to advance through the material, but there are fewer links, hence fewer ways to get lost. The important thing to remember is that the visitor will scroll only if there is something worth scrolling for! Whichever system you choose, make sure it is straightforward; don't add anything that isn't absolutely necessary.

Make Good Use of White Space

White space (also called negative space) is the blank areas between the graphics and text in your design. White space is essential when large amounts of text are present, as it helps to guide the viewer's eye from one position to another. As you might imagine, uncluttered pages are easier to follow and therefore make for a more relaxing reading experience. Some of the most effective magazine ads feature beautifully designed pages with plenty of negative space. White space is also a great navigational tool, as it can tell readers where one feature ends and another begins.

Too often, inexperienced designers try to cram in as much information as they can. This is a mistake. Think of the most stylish house you ever visited. Chances are, it was that open space that really grabbed your attention. Now picture that same house with tons and tons of clutter—not a very attractive picture. White space is elegant and pure. Don't clutter up your design space with too many graphics. Keep the combined weight of the graphics down to about half of the available space. The Web page designed by M. Kathleen Colussy shown in this chapter illustrates how white space helps the visitor find key information.

Body Copy

Body copy is, of course, essential to page design because it comprises the bulk of your document. It's the magazine or novel you read. Lots of heavy use of type can make your design look dull and uninviting. Think about ways in which you can break up the page. Paragraphs, use of bold and italic type, and even color can help the reader to visually understand all that you have to say. As you might imagine, it is important to choose your body type with care. In general, stay away from heavy, decorative typefaces, since they are difficult to read in large amounts and cause eyestrain. As mentioned above, serif typefaces are generally best for body text that will be viewed in digital format.

Here are some other guidelines:

- Use sufficient leading (the space between lines of type) and paragraph breaks to improve the readability of the page.
- Use only one space at the end of a sentence. The two-space practice went out with typewriters.
- Justify text in wider columns—that is, set the spacing so that the lines come out even in the margin.
- Use hyphens and line breaks to fine-tune line endings.
- Guard against "rivers" (gaps of white space) in type. This problem is very common with justified text.
- Never allow two hyphenated lines in a row. It is considered bad design.
- Don't use double hyphens for em dashes (the long dashes).

The Psychology of Type

Our reactions to type are similar in many ways to our responses to color. We are influenced by past experiences and associations. Most people have an expectation about what type should reflect. Take a look at the examples of the type selected for the phrase "It was a dark and stormy night . . . ." Which one of these examples does not look right? Only one of these says "dark and scary." Even people who don't understand the intricacies of type sense the correct usage of letterform.

Imagine an upscale restaurant advertising itself with children's lettering. Doesn't seem like such a great idea to you? OK. How about a toy store with some grungy

It was a dark and scary night...

It was a dark and scary night...

It was a dark and scary night...

Certain fonts are ideal for evoking emotions and responses. Which of these do you think best expresses "dark and scary"?

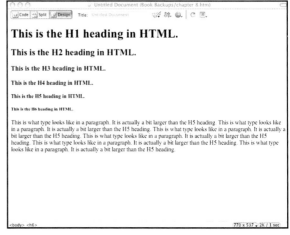

Here is an illustration of different type sizes displayed on a Web page using HTML.

type on the building? I think you see the point. Whenever you select type, you are not only using the type you think is correct but also relying on the perceptions of your viewers. A beautifully designed interface deserves an appropriate type choice as well. The next time you're about to use the default typeface on your computer, stop, think, and consciously choose the best type to support your message.

Successful Use of Type in Multimedia: Readability

Many different factors contribute to the successful use of type in multimedia. The first is size. Type must be larger on the screen than you might normally select for print, in order to improve the legibility of your carefully chosen words. The size you choose will then help to determine the amount and size of additional text elements you include. Color and contrast of the type will also have an impact on the readability of the page. Remember, type on the screen is much different from that used in print media.

Type size, line length, and alignment all contribute to the well-designed electronic page. Whereas print-based type is measured in "points," on-screen type is measured in pixels. Individual screen characters as pixels require a different measurement system. In Web design, for example, HTML uses H1, H2, H3, and so on, to designate type size. And a system called Cascading Style Sheets (CSS) is used to specify type by point size, percentage, or in relative units such as pixels, points, inches, centimeters, millimeters, and more. So designers have conceived a system of "browser-safe

fonts" for Web designers to follow. It is a very limited set, as you are about to see.

These are the fonts most likely to work in a CD- or DVD-based multimedia presentation on both a PC and a Mac:

> Arial / Helvetica
> Courier New / Courier
> Times New Roman / Times

Additional cross-platform options that generally work are:

> Arial Black
> Avant Garde
> Bookman
> Comic Sans MS
> Garamond
> Georgia
> Impact
> Palatino
> Trebuchet MS
> Verdana

And for Web design, here is a list of fonts (most of them shown in both lightface and bold) that are considered to be cross-platform and Web-safe:

Windows	Macintosh	Font Family
Arial	Arial, Helvetica	sans serif
Arial	**Arial, Helvetica**	sans serif
Arial Black	**Arial Black, Gadget**	sans serif
Arial Black	**Arial Black, Gadget**	sans serif
Comic Sans MS	Comic Sans MS	cursive
Comic Sans MS	**Comic Sans MS**	cursive
Courier New	Courier New, Courier	monospace
Courier New	**Courier New, Courier**	monospace
Georgia	Georgia	serif
Georgia	**Georgia**	serif
Impact	**Impact, Charcoal**	sans serif
Impact	**Impact, Charcoal**	sans serif
Lucida Console	Monaco	monospace
Lucida Console	**Monaco**	monospace
Lucida Sans Unicode	Lucida Grande	sans serif
Lucida Sans Unicode	**Lucida Grande**	sans serif
MS Sans Serif	Geneva	sans serif
MS Sans Serif	**Geneva**	sans serif
MS Serif	New York	serif
MS Serif	**New York**	serif
Palatino Linotype, Book Antiqua	Palatino	serif
Palatino Linotype, Book Antiqua	**Palatino**	serif
Tahoma	Geneva	sans serif
Tahoma	**Geneva**	sans serif
Times New Roman	Times	serif
Times New Roman	**Times**	serif
Trebuchet MS	Helvetica	sans serif
Trebuchet MS	Helvetica	sans serif
Verdana	Verdana, Geneva	sans serif
Verdana	**Verdana, Geneva**	sans serif
αβχδεφγηιφκλμν	αβχδεφγηιφκλμν	Symbol
✔︎ ✇ ☐ ♥ ♠ ♣ ☗ ■ ✿ ① ⚘ ✻ ✈ ! ●	✔︎ ✇ ☐ ♥ ♠ ♣ ☗ ■ ✿ ① ⚘ ✻ ✈ ! ●	Webdings
❀✸✳✶✷✳✶✷✶✷✶✶●○■	❀✸✳✶✷✳✶✷✶✷✶✶●○■	Zapf Dingbats

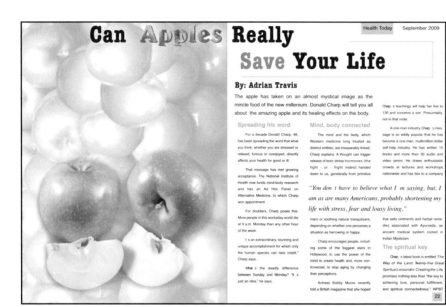

This editorial spread demonstrates how type can improve a layout. Although this page features three different typefaces, the page has interest and texture. Notice that some of the typefaces are used in their individual variations.

At this point, you may be thinking, "Why do I have to limit my designs to a small set of fonts? I have an awesome set of fonts on my computer!" The answer is simple: each browser can use only the fonts installed on that particular computer. This means that every visitor to your Web page needs to have all the *same* fonts installed as you've used in order to view the page properly. Of course, different people will have different fonts installed, so it is virtually impossible to ensure that your Web page will be seen properly unless you take the type issues into consideration.

I know you're probably confused at this point. Actually, it's quite easy, if you remember one simple rule:

Test often. Test widely.

By this I mean, test your project on your home computer. Then try loading the project on a machine at work or on a friend's computer—and ideally, on both a Mac and a PC. Look at the text on the screen. Is it readable on both operating systems? A mark of a successful digital portfolio is that it runs flawlessly on every computer and under every possible condition.

You must always strive to use type to effectively convey your message in a clear and concise fashion—yet you want your design to be original and attractive. This is a bit of a balancing act, I know. And you'll probably face limitations. Now you know that not all typefaces are available on every computer, and that a number of different companies produce type. Let's say you would like the text on your main page to be displayed in the Avant Garde typeface. In order for the text on your page to actually appear in this typeface, your viewers must have that font installed on their computers, or it will default to some other typeface such as Courier (which

Let's grow old together... that's the way life is supposed to be. You meet the love of your life, and live happily ever after, but what if your spouse leaves you alone? Worse yet, what if you survive your children, your friends and all of your relatives. How can you take care of yourself and protect your assets? The government is supposed to protect you with laws Checkpoints against any fraud that might be committed against you are supposed to be carefully regulated by law. But he law doesn't always work. Visit the case of Alice Martinez.

"The room was quiet, so quiet in fact, that I could hear the wine of the pipes of the apartment next door. I wanted to go there, to knock on that door, and ask for a little conversation- a little bit of life."

Martinez lives in Coral Ridge, Florida. She is now alone. Her two children, Robert and Mindy were killed in a freak car accident, in 1995. Her husband, Phil died several years earlier, in 1990. Martin always believed she would be looked after, "I thought that someone would always be there for me. Now, I go to bed at night and pray that I'll never wake up."

Here is an example of a typesetting error: two hyphens on top of each other at the ends of lines in body copy. Good typographers avoid too many hyphens in a row in a paragraph.

looks like typewriter text). The substitution may even result in words or paragraphs being cut off.

Another factor to consider is that Macintosh and Windows computers display at different resolutions. The resolution for a Windows computer is 96 ppi, which stands for pixels per inch. On a Mac, it's 72 ppi. In general, Windows computers can display smaller type with more clarity. In fact, type displays about 2 points larger on a PC. Really small type—say, 6 points—will be visible on a PC but disappear on a Mac. As you can appreciate, these factors can have a major impact on your carefully designed layout.

So how do you work around this type limitation? There are two techniques you can use to ensure that a typeface displays exactly as you intend it to on your page. The first is to turn the type into a graphic or bitmapped image. The second is to create a vector-based outline of the type. Graphic designers, for example, typically use the Create Outlines function in Adobe Illustrator to turn type into simple vector-based objects. Adobe Flash can perform this task as well using the Break Apart command. Once type has been modified to a raster-based or vector-based file, it no longer has to be installed on the viewer's computer to be seen. This solves most of the problems just described. But it does not address loading-time issues.

A classic typesetting exercise is to see how many ways you can express the word *no* in type. For example, you can scream "No." You can say "No" but mean "Yes." You can say "No" gently or whisper the word to intimidate someone. Combining color, type, and size are all ways to articulate the sense of the word you intend to convey.

Speed

You know by now how important speed is in multimedia design. Using type in its original form will always produce a smaller file size than using type that has been converted to either vector- or raster-based graphics. If you must convert type, a vector-based file is the better solution, as vector-based files are always smaller than raster-based files. If you must have a special look for your font, bitmapping your text may be your only choice, but recognize that you do so at the expense of speed. The best solution is to use the following typefaces that are common to both Macs and PCs: Times, Times New Roman, Arial, Courier, Helvetica, and Verdana.

You now know that when it comes to type, there are resolution and size issues. So, once again, the best solution is to test your pages on as many different computers, monitors, and Internet browsers as possible. Correct any discrepancies you find and all will be well.

The Importance of Line Length

Many studies have been conducted to determine the ideal conditions for type and readability. Some of these have centered on the issue of eyestrain, which I have mentioned several times now. It turns out that the length of a line of type is a major factor contributing to this discomfort. It is caused by the disruption to reading as your eyes move from the end of one line to the beginning of the next. As a designer, you want to minimize eyestrain for your viewers, so the best advice is to keep line length somewhere around 60 to 70 characters, although that is not a hard-and-fast number. A haiku on type by Professor Howard T. Katz, of the Art Institute of Fort Lauderdale, sums up the problem of eyestrain:

Eyes are red and swollen.
Watch out for the sharp serifs.
Typography hurts.

Type Alignment

I remember how hard it was as a child to color inside the lines in my coloring books. Placing type in a layout for your portfolio is a little like that. You want the layout to look clean and neat, but you don't want to be constrained by "lines." Although type alignment is not a particularly difficult undertaking when it comes to CD and DVD design, it is for Web design, due to the limitations imposed by HTML and CSS requirements.

Frequently, for example, you must design with tables, whose layouts use rows, columns, and cells to display tabular, text, or image data (think of spreadsheets). When type is placed within a table, it can be left-aligned, centered, or justified. As always, the readability factor comes into play. It is best to always set type left-aligned, especially if you will be featuring large amounts of text.

Ten Rules for Good Type Design

To sum up this discussion, I leave you with ten rules to follow to ensure that you design effectively with type. By carefully choosing your typefaces, you can make your design say whatever you want, whether it's "I'm playful," "I'm classic," or "I'm cutting-edge."

- Rule 1: Use sans serif typefaces when designing for the computer and low-resolution monitors. They are crisp, clean, and easy to read. Sans serif types include Helvetica, Arial, Avant Garde, Officina Sans, Gill Sans, and Eras. If you must use a serif typeface, stick to the tried-and-true: Times or Times New Roman, Palatino, or Garamond.

- Rule 2: Resist the urge to use too many typefaces. Just because you bought that CD or DVD with 10,000 fonts for $10 doesn't mean you have to use every one of them in your design. Limit yourself to three or four fonts per design. To achieve the most professional look, be consistent with font usage from page to page. And avoid using stylized typefaces as body copy. They are difficult to read and stress the eyes.

- Rule 3: Bigger is better. Small type is very much in vogue in print design, but it does not work for multimedia. The limitations of monitor resolutions make it almost impossible to display small body type effectively. The size you select will ultimately depend on the font you select. When it comes to display type, a large font definitely adds both visual appeal and drama.

- Rule 4: Don't create "false links" by underlining. In Web design, an underlined word or phrase indicates a link to another page. It can frustrate users when their mouse click leads nowhere. Instead, use attributes such as boldface, italics, or small caps to highlight type.

below As you can see, the first Web site, visited from a Macintosh, has slightly larger type than the second version of this same site, seen on a PC. The screen shows a difference of about 2 points. Macs display at 72 dpi, but PCs display at 96, thus the difference.

Allow yourself to loosen up. Type is supposed to be fun! This little guy was created just to demonstrate the versatility of type as a design tool.

As you can see, this good-looking page, designed by Kacey Aussner, demonstrates the best possible way to display large amounts of type. Small touches of color and neutral shades of gray make the type readable and add emphasis to important points.

This Illustrator menu shows you the options for creating outlines with your type. By completing outlines before you create a Web page, you ensure that your viewers will not have to have those typefaces installed on their computers in order to see your page designs.

When you create outlines, the computer no longer needs to have the typeface installed.

When you create outlines, the computer no longer needs to have the typeface installed.

This is what an outline looks like once it has been created. The top block of type shows what typical type looks like. The bottom type block shows what type looks like after the outlines have been created. Notice all the little "nodes," or squares, that define these new shapes.

- Rule 5: Limit the amount of text on the screen. It is considered bad design to force the viewer to scroll through pages and pages of type. Break up your text into small, easy-to-read chunks of information. And keep lines of type short.
- Rule 6: Don't use all, or full, caps. In Web e-mail, the use of full caps is considered shouting. Moreover, all caps are difficult to read and hard on the eyes.
- Rule 7: Use white, or negative, space to your advantage. Include adequate breaks between paragraphs and major areas of text. Negative space is an artistic trick to guide your reader's eyes from one point to another. Lack of it can actually cause the screen to flicker before a viewer's eyes.
- Rule 8: Minimize load times. Too many fonts that are defined as raster-based bitmaps will cause your design to take forever to load. Whenever possible, use cross-platform system fonts.
- Rule 9: Don't get carried away with font color. When it comes to type, contrast is king. It is important that your message be easy to read, so make sure that your background and type are compatible. And while we're on the subject, stay away from reversed type—white type on a black background is very difficult to read.
- Rule 10: Experiment and create your own style. Just make sure the style does what you want and never detracts from the message.

• Keep It Short and Simple

It is more difficult to read words on the screen than on a printed page, so when it comes to designing a digital interface, the rule of thumb is: Keep words to a minimum. Studies have shown that people will not spend large amounts of time reading online documents due to eyestrain. Keep your information concise, and limit the text on each page. If you feel you must include a lot of text in your digital portfolio, be sure to break it into small blocks or spread it over multiple pages. Those of you who really enjoy the process of working with type should consider kerning (adjusting the space between individual characters in a line of type). Kerning is especially important with large display type.

Typography is an art form, no doubt about it. It can support your design or even be your design, but it must always be legible. If it's not, you've defeated the purpose. Be mysterious, be engaging, be outrageous, be whatever you want to be, but be a good type designer.

Now that you know a little more about how to use color and typography effectively, we'll turn our attention in the next chapter to design and navigation issues and talk more about interface metaphors.

An Interview with Tom Kane

Tom Kane has been an advertising art director for the past 25 years, creating print ads and commercials for clients such as IBM, Liz Claiborne, Steve Madden, Yellow Tail wine, and Barnes & Noble. Tom succeeded in advertising beyond his wildest dreams. He hung with supermodels and movie stars and traveled the world doing shoots in London, Paris, Hong Kong, Amsterdam, Sydney, Auckland, and Cape Town. But secretly he was drawing and painting relentlessly during his free time. Recently, Tom decided to put together a Web site to showcase what he's been doing. The response has been overwhelming. It rekindled his desire to become an illustrator. You can see Tom Kane's work at www.tommykane.com.

1 What qualities do you look for in an applicant?

Confidence is key. Trying to get a job, especially your first, can be very nerve-racking. They must convey that they can do the job. I find now that many places freelance people first to see if they can do the work. In advertising, we like to see how people think. Ideas are king. You need to be able to come up with original ideas. It's not so easy to do. To me, design is secondary to the ideas that they show. These days, every student has a professional-looking portfolio. Some of them are downright amazing. But when you hire these people, they seem totally incapable of the work they showed you. In other words, maybe they didn't do the work in their portfolio. In advertising, you work in teams of two. Same in ad school. So maybe it was the other person in the team who was a genius and came up with all the great work in some other person's portfolio. My job is to try and weed out the fakes. That's why we freelance them first. We can tell within two days if they are for real. So what I really look for in an applicant is someone who is not trying to oversell themselves. Present a portfolio that really represents the work you do. If not, you will be found out quickly. This has become a big problem in advertising. I want someone who is punctual, hardworking, willing to learn, listens, and doesn't think they are a know-it-all.

2 In your opinion, what makes a successful interview?

The person makes a connection. They tell me something about themselves or something they are interested in that piques my interest. Something that makes me feel that this person reminds me of me when I was younger. There is a hunger to work hard. Too many people today have this sort of privileged attitude. When am I going to be made boss? I hate that. I like when people talk about things that are not related to the job. Something that happened that day, something spontaneous. That shows how you can think on your feet. Don't be preprogrammed like a robot. People should not appear desperate to get the job. You can't put all your hopes into getting that one great job. It is better to appear that other people are interested in you. So even if you are desperate and do want a job badly, keep that to yourself.

My present job is doing the advertising for Samsung electronics. It is a Korean company. My final interview was with the president of the company. In the interview, I mentioned to him that my wife happens to be Korean. He was stunned. I said she speaks perfect Korean, my in-laws cook me all sorts of Korean food. I had even traveled there. Of course, I got the job. That doesn't always happen in interviews, but to me, that was a successful interview.

3 Has the Internet had an effect on your interview process?

For me, the Internet has had no effect on the process. I can look at people's work before I interview them. But usually a headhunter sends me their book first anyway. So it doesn't matter if I see their phony ads that they didn't really do on the Internet or in person.

4 What are the five best things job candidates say that impress you during an interview? What are the five worst?

Best

1 I'm not afraid to work hard. If you hire me, I'll be the first to arrive and the last to leave each day.
2 I feel I have a lot to learn, and I am willing to listen and take direction.
3 I am not a political person. I don't care about titles or offices or any other nonsense. I just want to work hard.
4 I am a phenomenal softball player. I was recruited by every major league baseball team out of high school. I will turn the company softball team into a juggernaut.
5 I'm not afraid to work hard. If you hire me, I'll be the first to arrive and the last to leave each day.

Worst

1 What will my office look like?
2 What other opportunities are there here? Will I be able to get a title at some point?
3 It was really hard getting here today. It was such a pain.
4 How many days off will I get? How many sick days? How many personal days? How many . . . ?
5 Will I have to stay late or work on a weekend?

5 What are skills that really help all artists succeed regardless of their specialty?

In my business, it helps if you can draw. It is a fast way to show people your ideas. How you think. Today, people rely too much on the computer. They take terrible ideas and try to make them look great on the computer using great photos and type and designing the hell out of it. Then they show it to someone, and they say, "It sucks." You could have showed me a drawing in five minutes instead of spending hours on the damn computer. Some great ad agencies don't let people show their initial ideas in computer comps. They have to show drawings. The idea itself has to be strong. It can't be a gussied-up piece of junk.

People should keep up with current events and culture. Know the latest movies, music, and things about pop culture. Know art history. Be curious. Curiosity is a great skill set. Read. The world does not revolve around that dumb computer.

6 What advice would you offer to designers looking to impress you with the presentation of their work?

Make it high-quality. The work should be large enough to really get a feel for it. My book is, like, 17 × 13, or something in that neighborhood. Beautiful Epson prints are the best possible paper. Find a great binder. Something cool. Mine are made by Pina Zangaro. I'm trying to say, just spare no expense to make them look as great as can be.

You must have a Web site in this day and age. Make it look groovy. It should be easy to look at. No flash. I get to sites and they start loading, and I am out of there in two seconds. Try to look at what other people have done. Take the best bits and pieces to form what you think would work best. But try to be original. Do something to stand out if you can. You only get one chance to grab someone's attention. Last resort you could try bribery. I find that if you send someone cash, that would really impress them. It works for politicians.

Designer's Challenge 1: Using Type to Describe Oxymorons

Oxymorons are fun! You hear them all the time—jumbo shrimp, alone together, half-full. In fact, there are Web sites devoted to oxymorons. Take a look at how you might use type to express some of the more popular oxymorons.

Nothing better than a good pun with type!

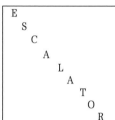

mess	mess	mess
mess	mess	mess
mess	mess	mess
mess	mess	mess

Jumbo Shrimp   Pretty Ugly

Alone Together   Half Full

Minor Disaster   Organized Mess

Down Escalator

Designer's Challenge 2: Typeface Exercise

For each of the following words, select the typeface that you think best expresses it. Enhance the meaning of the word by selecting an appropriate typeface and color.

Soft   Sad

Angry   Futuristic

Funny   Crazy

9

Maneuvering around Your Site

Navigation

Walk into any bookstore and look around at all the books. Now assume all those books are in no order whatsoever—they're not divided by category or in alphabetical order. Then suppose I ask you to find a book

about the life of Harry Houdini in that bookstore. Think how difficult it would be. Plain books everywhere . . . no departments . . . no idea where to begin! Now transfer that concept to your digital portfolio. Without clear navigational clues, someone visiting for the first time would be at a total loss as to where to go to find what he or she was looking for. It wouldn't take long for the visitor to leave—not what you want.

The home page of your Web site gives visitors the all-important first impression; the navigation system is the next most important element. Consequently, you must find a way to persuade your visitors to use the navigational devices you create so that they become entranced with your portfolio. When you make it easy for viewers to become involved with your content, they will be

more willing to explore your project thoroughly. This chapter therefore shows you how to design a clear and inviting visual interface.

Getting There from Here

I recently looked at a digital portfolio whose content was fabulous. Unfortunately, it required patience and tenacity to find the series of hidden zones that revealed work only if you happened to pass your mouse pointer over them. It was very frustrating. When asked about the confusing nature of the interface, the designer expressed the attitude that if a visitor lacked the patience to find the work, then he or she wasn't meant to see it. This is not the sort of user experience you would want to create.

You can feature every kind of cool effect you want in your project, but if your visitors can't figure out where to find them, after a while they will give up. It's as simple as that. If you employ thoughtful and professional design, your visitors will always know where they are and where to go to see more—and how to get there. You must always strive to give visitors a sense of place and a sense of context.

You need to give your viewers directions, a map of sorts, complete with landmarks for visual reference. The icons or labels you create for your interface compose the map of your project. When they are clear and unmistakable, your viewers will always know where to go and where they have been. The following subsections present guidelines for creating an effective navigational system for your digital portfolio.

Using Landmarks and Metaphors

Landmarks are easy-to-identify visual elements. Think about the times someone has given you directions for getting somewhere you've never been before. In addition to street names and numbers, he or she says things like, "Look for the building with the red roof," or "There's a McDonald's on the corner, where you turn right." You can use landmarks similarly throughout your digital portfolio to ease the user's "journey."

Likewise, you can use metaphors as guides. You're no doubt familiar with the common computer interface metaphor of a trash can to represent where to "throw" deleted files. All computer users now understand what that little trash can icon represents. You can design

metaphors that are straightforward or highly design-oriented. In the case of the former, for example, if you use the word *Home* on a page, your viewers will know that selecting or clicking that word will return them to your portfolio's home page. Or you may prefer to include a small icon of a house to represent "home." This is now a common visual metaphor for the home page. Certainly, you can choose more eclectic or personal icons as well. A photographer might, say, choose to represent his or her home page with a small roll of film or a flashbulb. A fashion designer might create an icon of a clothing button. As long as the viewer can understand the metaphor, the icons you use can be as creative as you wish.

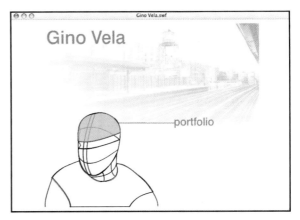

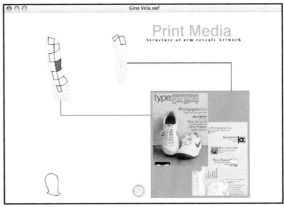

In this clever interface, created by Gino Vela, the viewer "rolls over" a darkened section of the arms with the mouse pointer, and various navigational options pop up on the screen. Uncolored areas indicate that there is nothing to find. (Gino Vela, Do 7 Grafix.)

Here is a selection of icons that can be created using the Wingdings or Webdings font. Each "letter" of the font is a different picture. Holding down the Shift key while typing gives you even more choices.

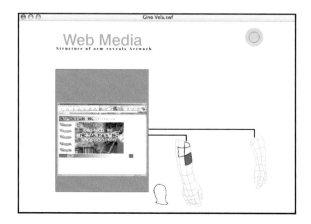

Once the viewer is in one of the sections, the option to examine individual pieces of art becomes available. (Gino Vela, Do 7 Grafix.)

Metaphors can also be thought of as extensions of the theme of your design serving to tie your project together. Some examples of metaphors you might use are an art gallery, the rooms of a house, a futuristic world—really, just about anything you can imagine.

Throughout this book, you'll see examples that illustrate this idea. You might notice icons that change when the user rolls the mouse pointer over them, such as a film canister that reveals some footage or a "brain" or "body" that changes color so as to show the visitor where the different portfolio elements are. The brain, in this case, symbolizes the artist, and each lobe represents the sections of the port. Not only is this decorative and entertaining, but it also works to help the viewer navigate the portfolio.

To help you decide on a metaphor to use, answer the following questions:

- *What structure does the metaphor offer the user?* The metaphor you develop has to make sense. Your portfolio will be divided up into a number of different sections. If, for example, you design a project that uses space-related images as the theme, they must be used consistently throughout the interface. In this case, you might design buttons as the planets of our solar system, with an icon of Earth serving to indicate "home." The metaphor you select has to make sense in the greater context of the design.
- *Is the metaphor appropriate to the site?* I recently saw an interface that featured a series of pictures of the

artist as a child. Good idea. The problem was that nothing else on the screen matched that idea. Bizarre buttons made of swirling suns and squiggly lines that morphed into odd shapes were out of place and did not support the central theme of a child and the creative process. A small series of childhood toys would have made a nice addition to the page and served to support the theme. As an example, a small plastic house from a Monopoly board would surely have pointed the way to the home page. Another site featured every possible clichéd icon representing Italy. Certainly you can reflect your cultural heritage, but it must make sense in light of your art. The cleverest idea will be a lost cause if it doesn't support the art.

- *Does the metaphor make sense?* Metaphors can represent either a series of concrete physical objects or an abstract idea. Just be sure that they don't confuse the viewer. I once looked at a portfolio that was designed with skulls and daggers. That was one scary portfolio! You can certainly personalize your design, but always keep in mind that, in your design, you are revealing bits of information (intentionally or not) about your personality and interests. If you cannot think of an appropriate theme for your design, opt instead to use just a beautiful set of colors. When in doubt, less is more.

This interface, by Robert Hough, creates a concept that carries his illustrations from the images through to the chosen type. It all works together to form a beautiful interface.

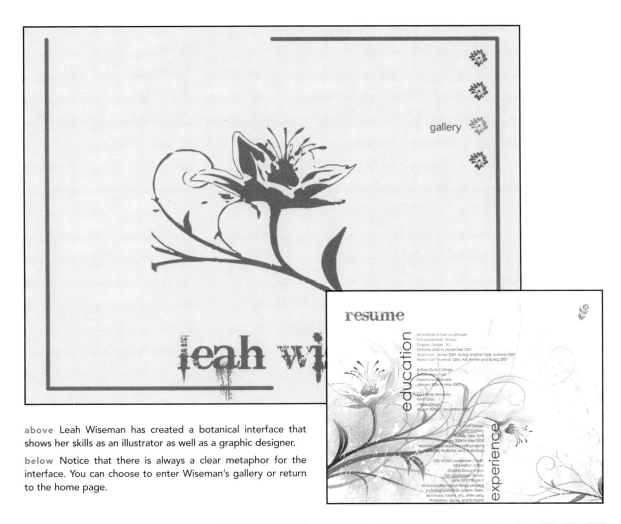

above Leah Wiseman has created a botanical interface that shows her skills as an illustrator as well as a graphic designer.

below Notice that there is always a clear metaphor for the interface. You can choose to enter Wiseman's gallery or return to the home page.

- *Is the metaphor capable of being extended, expanded?* If you need to increase the size of your interface, can your metaphor grow with it? Consider again the space theme metaphor. There are eight planets: Mercury, Venus, Earth, Mars, Jupiter, Saturn, Uranus, and Neptune. (Poor little Pluto . . . all alone!) We also have one star: the sun. If each planet represents one section of your portfolio and you have eight sections, you're in great shape! If you ever need to increase the number of sections, though, will you be able to devise additional metaphors to support the design while still being consistent? Nine sections may sound like a lot right now, but you may be surprised. Don't design yourself into a corner.
- *Can your metaphor stand up to testing?* Let's say you created an interface with icons that represent computer equipment. It makes perfect sense to you, because you're a technology whiz, but will all your viewers be able to understand them in relation to the interface? To find out, test, test, test. Ask your friends and colleagues to visit your digital portfolio. Don't assist them in any way. Watch how they work with it. Are they having any difficulties navigating the site? If they keep asking you where they should go next, you have a problem.

Navigation Techniques for Successful Interface Design

What's more important to consider in your digital portfolio? Color or a clever navigation scheme? If you said navigation, you're right. Navigating your digital portfolio should be easy and intuitive. At all times, viewers should understand where they are, where they can go,

This is an example of a hierarchical design system. Similar subject matter is grouped together under one "umbrella."

and how they can return to the home page. The most successful interface is the one that causes no confusion, raises no questions.

Your interface, essentially, will consist of three main elements: the site identity, a navigational system, and the rest of the design sections. Now, designing an interface with five or six sections is easy; designing an interface with 25 or 30 pages is much more difficult. With that much information involved, there needs to be a readily apparent way for visitors to understand and use the interface. Most digital designers agree that there are only four basic approaches to interface design:

1. Linear
2. Global
3. Hierarchical
4. Local

Linear

Linear navigation is a system that uses a set of buttons or links to enable you to navigate in a straight path. Think of a slide projector: you can advance the slide show only one picture at a time. In interface design, you can create a digital slide show that contains Previous,

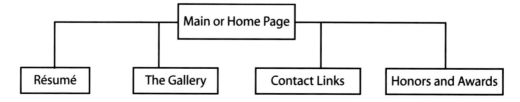

Even a basic flowchart like this one can be useful in designing your initial layout, as it helps you to visualize the navigation system.

Next, and Index links or buttons but nothing more. It is rarely used except to show art, online books, presentations, or other linear documents.

Global

Global or site-wide navigation is characterized by links or categories that appear on every page of the interface. This style of navigation features a common interface in which the same navigational elements always appear in the same location, such as the top or left side of the site. In this style of navigation, visitors can move through your site in a vertical and lateral way, which allows them to visit all parts of the site at will. For an example, take a look at Debbie Bostwick's interface. The only downside to this method is that a lot of your design space is used to display the navigational buttons or bars.

Hierarchical

A hierarchical design system groups large amounts of information into major sections or under headings. Bookstores use this system. Books are shelved according to broad-based categories such as fiction, travel, self-help, crafts, and biography. You enter the section you want and begin searching for your book. A digital interface

This artistic interface was designed by Debbie Bostwick. Notice the links at the top and bottom of this page. The pushpins indicate that the user can click to see more artwork, and the "main" text link at the top indicates how to return to the starting section of the site.

can be designed using this system as well. Divide your pages up into major site sections that represent main areas such as résumé, gallery, contact information, and home. An example of this would be a gallery area that is subdivided into logo, editorial spread, and photography areas. Within each section, include a way to return to the main gallery subsection or the home page area.

Local

Local navigation is a hybrid of the hierarchical and global systems. It is useful when you have a lot of information within broader categories. For example, say you have a major section entitled "Gallery." Within this section, there are subcategories called "Photography," "Fine Art," and "Advertising." The user navigates all of the subsections of the gallery, then back out to the main gallery area, to return to the home page.

Strategizing Navigation

Before you can decide on the layout for your digital portfolio, you must design a strategy for navigation. This normally is done by creating a flowchart. The flowchart will help you to determine how to arrange the main elements of your digital port and how to link the pages. I recommend that you sketch more than one system, to help you visualize which one will work best for your purposes. Trust me, flowcharting will save you a lot of time and frustration later on.

The basic flowchart shown here clearly demonstrates that visitors will be able to move seamlessly around the site. The connections are clear, so that, when they are implemented, content will be only a click or two away from the main page of the interface.

Once you have drawn a navigation flowchart, it's time to consider which navigation mechanisms you'll use to ensure that visitors experience your site as clear and comprehensible. The most common devices used in navigational design are:

Navigation bars, such as at Amazon.com
(www.amazon.com)
Drop-down hover navigation, such as at Adobe
(www.adobe.com)

above In this Flash project, Nicole Naierman has created this witty little fellow to lead us around her whimsical interface. The experience begins as our "guide" takes us on a journey through his world. Once we have seen the introduction, all of the interface elements are revealed as our guide runs across the screen.

below Throughout the design, all of the elements are consistently placed to offer a clear navigational system. Notice that the résumé is available as a downloadable PDF document.

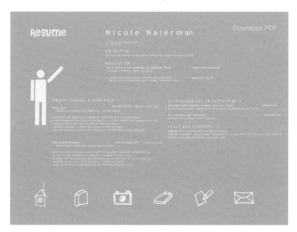

Search boxes, such as at Yahoo! (www.yahoo.com)
Short, persistent URLs, such as at Google
  (www.google.com)

Creating a common user interface strategy will ensure an easily understood portfolio experience. Most of these navigation methods are well understood by users and, as such, have become patterns of experience. A well-designed interface that follows accepted patterns makes the designer's life a lot easier; an interface that varies too much from the common experience not only makes more work for the designer but can also frustrate the visitor.

Common Navigation Elements

Your goal in designing an interface device is to convey a distinctive visual style and identity. When properly applied, a cohesive interface device will hold together a series of related, or disjointed, sections. In addition, a well-designed set of navigation elements makes a positive statement about you, the individual who designed it. Your set of navigation elements will typically consist of:

Text links
Buttons
Image maps
Navigation bars

Finding the Right Words: Using Text Links

On the Internet, a hypertext link (generated with HTML) is the most commonly used form of Web navigation. As you also know by now, a hypertext link is indicated by an underlined word or phrase in text. When the user clicks the link, it changes color, then transfers him or her to the linked content.

For digital interface design, however, a more sophisticated interface is in order. Why? Because an underlined word/phrase in a digital port would more than likely lead viewers to mistake it for an online link. Therefore, in digital design, navigational links are signified by color changes or quick animations. For example, when a user's mouse pointer passes across link text, it might turn into a drop shadow. The best advice for these links is to use labels that clearly communicate the section the viewer will be visiting next, as shown here:

| Home | Résumé | Gallery | Contact Me |

Buttons

I've already talked at some length about the importance of interface buttons. Simply put, it would be difficult to navigate even the most basic Web site without them. Buttons are created in two forms: as HTML action buttons and as graphical action buttons.

Whenever you create a home page for the Web, always suffix the file name as either **index.htm** or **index.html** to ensure that Web browsers such as Firefox, Internet Explorer, or Safari can find it. But when you want people to find you online, be aware that most search engines, such as Google, Yahoo! and Northern Light, search on title names. A title name is the information you see at the top of a Web page, such as "Welcome to Robert Samuel's Creative Portfolio."

You will typically see HTML action buttons in forms. For example, say you are asked to provide some information to sign up to receive a newsletter. After you have filled in the blanks, you commonly are asked to click on a Submit button to transmit your data. The button code is generated by HTML (or programs such as Dreamweaver). Buttons of this type are not necessarily attractive or interesting, but they are very practical.

Graphical action buttons, in contrast, are usually interesting and attractive. These are animated buttons that change in some way when the user passes the mouse pointer across them. Although more difficult to create, graphical action buttons are more interactive and give the user a clear visual clue that some action will

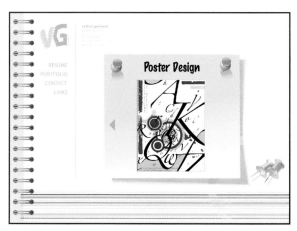

Here is a set of hypertext links in action. Notice that you can always tell where you are in the interface. The links change color to indicate when a section has already been visited. (Designed by Velina Gamova.)

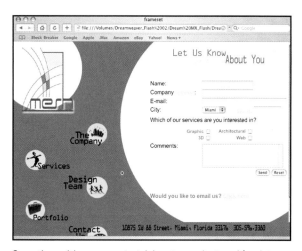

Sometimes it's more entertaining to navigate with pictures. Have some fun when you design a page—just don't forget to design for the user. (Designed by Frances Ortiz.)

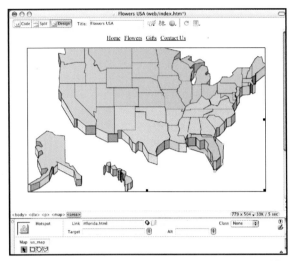

This image map shows the "hot spot" that has been created for the state of Florida. When the user rolls the mouse pointer over the state, the image of the state changes to indicate that there is a link to another part of the interface.

take place when they are clicked. The downsides to graphical action buttons are that they take up more of your limited design space and generate larger files that take longer to download. Another problem is that they can be ambiguous and thus may not communicate what you wish to every viewer. Therefore, I suggest that you never rely exclusively on such buttons for navigation.

Image Maps

I've talked about image maps before, too. Recall that an image map is a picture that has been divided into small regions, or "hot spots." When the user clicks on a hot spot, a new document begins to load. In the image map shown here, each of the links takes the user to information about a different part of the United States.

There are two types of image maps: client-side and server-side. A client-side image map is one designed using HTML. It runs directly from the user's browser, as opposed to a Web server. Server-side image maps, then, run from the server hosting the Web site. Server-side image maps speed up the Web display, but they require special software.

You can utilize image maps in interface design as well. You create hot spots on a page that produce an action when a mouse pointer rolls over them. In a port-folio, for example, you might create a series of squares. When one of the squares is touched by the mouse pointer, a piece of artwork appears.

One word of caution: image maps will not appear if the user has turned off the picture function to make his or her browser run faster.

Navigation Bars

What is the most visually effective way to let users know where they are in your interface? The navigation bar (or "nav bar," as it is sometimes called). You've no doubt seen navigation bars on the left side or perhaps at the top of the most popular Web sites. They are so common that most people understand how to use them, which makes the navigation bar an easy choice for designers. The navigation bar provides a visible link to every top-level page of your site, including the home page.

There is no hard-and-fast rule about where to place a navigation bar, though the left side is a common choice. The nav bar generally makes the major areas of the Web site readily available to the user. As a selection is made, the page changes, but the nav bar remains in the same place to ease travel through the site. Other Web sites feature nav bars on the right or even in the center. These positions are considered a little less intuitive but can work in the right design.

Navigation bars can present information in a number of different ways. Text-only links, graphical links, highlights, animations, and drop-down lists are some of the ways the nav bar can tell your story. Nav bars do have one disadvantage: they can potentially take up a lot

If you decide to use graphical buttons, be sure to include text that pops up when the mouse pointer rolls over the image. Doing so ensures that even if your visitors have turned off pictures to increase speed, they will still be able to navigate your site. Moreover, Section 508 of the Rehabilitation Act of 1973 states that every Web page must be accessible to people with disabilities. For more on this, go to www.section508.gov/index.cfm?FuseAction=Content&ID=12.

Tiina Purin has created an interface that unmistakably shows her skills as an illustrator. The metaphor of a bulletin board serves to highlight her drawings.

A quick note about frames. At some point, you may decide to put your digital portfolio online. Some designers like to embed such projects in what are called framesets. Frames are individual sections of a Web page. Each section exists as a single component of the total page. I strongly advise against this, because framesets do not work in all browsers and therefore make it impossible for search engines to index their pages. If Google or Yahoo! cannot index your site, no one will be able to find you. Frames cause other usability problems as well and make it difficult to bookmark URLs. Frames also are hard to print, take up a lot of page space, and do not make it easy to comply with Section 508 of the Rehabilitation Act of 1973 regarding accessibility for people with disabilities.

The "Bread Crumb" Approach to Navigation

The bread crumb approach to navigation is so called because it features a line of previously visited pages at the top or bottom of the page. The "crumbs" are intended to remind you of where you are in the site and how you got there as well as how you can get back to previously viewed areas. For example:

Home > Gallery > Graphic Design > Logos

Bread crumbs are thought to improve the navigation experience because they lay a path back to the main part of the interface. In the example here, the user could click on any of the links to back out of the current section. Unfortunately, this particular approach is not of much benefit in a site that has a lot of information, because it does not give the viewer a clear sense of the amount of content available; however, it will work quite nicely in tandem with other navigational systems, such as hierarchical design.

of your design space. To prevent that from happening, keep them small and simple so that they don't get in the way of your work.

Choosing the Best Navigation System for You

At this point, you may be wondering, "Which navigation system should I use?" The answer is, as long as the person visiting your portfolio can move easily from section to section, it doesn't really matter. In fact, more than one approach may work. Sometimes the best thing to do is to mix and match approaches within the same interface. In fact, the more complex the site, the greater the need for multiple ways to navigate it.

Navigation Review

The best approach to navigational system design is to follow these guidelines:

- Create a metaphor that represents you.
- Test the metaphor on people before you implement it.
- Map out your interface with a flowchart.
- Design a home page. (You must have a home page.)
- Decide on a clear system of navigation, whether linear, hierarchical, global, or local.
- Include buttons, which can be text, images, or a combination of both.
- Don't underline text unless you intend it as a link.
- Use graphics to help navigation, but include text links as well.
- Use buttons, nav bars, and/or image maps consistently.
- Provide more than one way to get to the home page.
- Use alternative labels for images (ALT=Name). An alt tag is used to help individuals with disabilities . . . the tag works in conjunction with a reader installed on the computer. The user turns the reader on and as the mouse is passed across the image, a voice reads the word to the user, thus making the user's experience much easier.
- Make sure your interface works, so test, test, test!
- Include a search box feature so that every area of your site can be located and visited.

Other review points to remember include the following:

- Your portfolio must always offer a clear, visual, and understandable navigational system.
- Pages should be broken into a home page, small section headings, and smaller subsections, as needed.
- Navigation to other parts of your site should be obvious, either through buttons, text hyperlinks, nav bars, or bread crumbs.

Remember, by the time you show your portfolio, the potential employer will probably have already seen a lot of others. This means that he or she will spend only minimal time looking at your work. So make it as easy for the employer as you can. Doing so will improve your chances of being chosen for the job.

An Interview with Roberto de Vicq de Cumptich

Roberto de Vicq de Cumptich, originally from Brazil, received his MFA in graphic design from the Pratt Institute. Mr. de Cumptich is well-known for his inventive work on the award-winning children's book and Web site Bembo's Zoo (www.bemboszoo.com). At present, Mr. de Cumptich owns and maintains his own design studio. Mr. de Cumptich designs or oversees the designs for 1,500 titles each year. He is a multiple award winner, including Webby 2005; One Show; D&DA, Silver Medal 2005; Art Directors Club, Silver Medal 2002; AIGA (50 Books/50 Covers and 365 competitions); Print magazine, Communication Arts, HOW magazine, New York Book Show, and a Literary Market Place Award.

To quote from Mr. de Vicq de Cumptich's Web site, "Design is a special combination of intelligence, inventiveness and style. From book covers to type design, from posters to website, the solution must be richly informed by the past, but should be the direction of the future." You can visit Roberto de Vicq de Cumptich's Web site at www.devicq.com.

1 **What qualities do you look for in an applicant?**

Someone who is talented and yet flexible, who has a variety of interests, and especially someone who has humor.

2 **In your opinion, what makes a successful interview?**

Normally, I conduct several interviews with each applicant. They are short, and I try to give as much information about the position as to get knowledge of the candidate.

3 **Has the Internet had an effect on your interview process?**

Yes, with portfolios online, it is much easier to see the applicant's work.

4 **What are the five best things job candidates say that impress you during an interview? What are the five worst?**

Best
- Their process that made them arrive at their design solutions.
- An edited portfolio showing only what they like to do, not what is printed or had large print runs.
- Has an idea what the company does.
- Makes allusions to things outside graphic design or to the company, relating themselves and the work to culture in general.
- Knowing how to spell my name.

Worst
- Being humorless.
- Being self-absorbed or defensive.
- Having no curiosity.
- Being too verbose or too inscrutable. Conversation needs being a listener and a talker.
- Being late.

5 **What are skills that really help all artists succeed regardless of their specialty?**

Trying to situate their work in a big picture, knowing what is going on in the world. Graphic design does not exist in a vacuum.

6 **What advice would you offer to designers looking to impress you with the presentation of their work?**

Edit the portfolio, try not to start every sentence with "I," and sell it to your audience.

Designer's Challenge 1

Create a three-ad series to advertise a new family amusement park. Consistently use all elements of page design, including:

- *Type and type color*
- *Headlines*
- *Placement of critical information*
- *Images that fully support the design*

Designer's Challenge 2

Design a sheet of wrapping paper that supports the nature of the business for which it will be utilized— for example, paper that features a logo for a high-end toy or jewelry store and can be used to wrap presents.

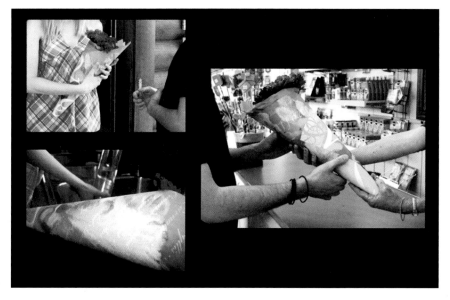

Jaime Ferguson illustrates an attractive solution to the wrapping paper challenge. The colors are well chosen and support the design. (Jaime Ferguson, graduate, Sinclair Community College.)

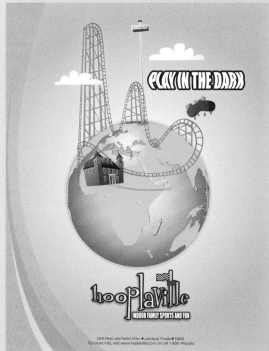

Lucia Mayela Rivas demonstrates an excellent
solution to the three-ad series challenge.

10

The Web-based Portfolio

Web Page Design

Why Web Page Design Isn't Like Page Design

I want you to design a four-page editorial spread for me, using either QuarkXPress or InDesign. "Piece of cake," I hear you say. "No problem!"

You gather your images and body copy. You write a few headlines and add a few touches here and there, and voilà—a terrific page design is created. Oh, if only it were as easy in Web design! You see, in traditional page design, the layout is not hindered by anything but your imagination. You have complete control over layout and type usage. The same is not true in Web design. Web pages are created using a language called HTML (hypertext markup language), which provides the content and structure of the pages. It also says where images, type, and other elements should be.

The good news is that programs such as Dreamweaver (or a WYSIWYG Web editor) can help you to realize your vision. The bad news is that your vision may need to be compromised a bit. Having said

that, let's see just what we need to make the Web site of your dreams.

Step 1: Start with a layout.
Step 2: Gather your assets.
Step 3: Create and code your interface.
Step 4: Publish your pages.

Step 1: Start with a Layout

You've gathered your artwork. You have all of your sketches for your design, and you're ready to begin the development of your Web site. If you've read Chapter 9, you have familiarized yourself with the basics of interface design. You have thought about the questions that

Mirtho Prepont has created an amusing interface that clearly communicates the areas of the portfolio that you can investigate. The colors are consistently used and allow the design work to shine through.

need to be answered while planning a Web page layout, such as the overall look and feel of the site, the colors you will utilize, a navigational system, and the placement of text blocks and images. You definitely need to visualize how each page will look before you actually start writing the HTML code that will create the pages. As a quick reminder, keep in mind the following design strategies:

* Your Web site should be easy to read.
* Your Web site should be easy to navigate.
* Your design should be consistent throughout your Web site.

Your Web Site Should Be Easy to Read

The typefaces you choose, the colors you select, and the way you arrange your material on the page all contribute to a well-designed Web page. Don't make the type so small that visitors have to squint to see it, and don't give them headaches by using hard-to-read colors. Dark-colored type on a light-colored background is almost always easier to read than light-colored type on a dark background. Avoid using all capital letters, and stay away from center-aligned text unless you are designing a headline or writing poetry.

Your Web Site Should Be Easy to Navigate

Whatever metaphor you choose—buttons, tabs, or rollovers—be consistent. These elements should be placed consistently on all pages. Always keep in mind that it's more important that buttons and tabs be easy to read and understand than that they have "flashy" effects. Your text links should be emphasized in some way (bold or perhaps a different color) that will indicate that they are, in fact, unique and different from the rest of the page.

Your Design Should Be Consistent throughout Your Web Site

Use all of your elements, such as color, buttons, text, and images, in a logical way that works in harmony with the rest of the pages on your site. If the design on the home page is in soft pastel colors, clicking to a page that

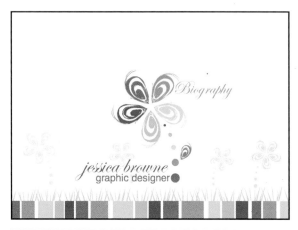

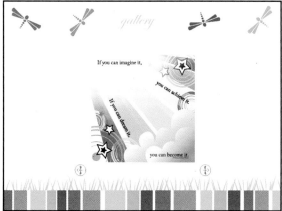

Jessica Browne uses nature as her theme for this vivid and fanciful portfolio created in Flash and Dreamweaver. The use of an Entrance button allows her to employ a set of meta tags in the HTML file in order to drive visitors to the site. Once in the portfolio, visitors are treated to an animation of dragonflies that introduces each of the areas of the site.

You will need to construct an organizational strategy for all of your assets. Most industry professionals consider this an essential part of the design process. The easiest way to approach this type of strategy is to create several folders or directories for your work. One folder should be used for all layered Photoshop files. Another folder can be used to hold your animations, sound, and video files. And finally, one more folder should be maintained for your actual Web design.

As you can see, there are four folders. The first set of two folders is for my Web site. The other set of two folders is for one of my clients.

has strong, bright colors will seem incongruous. If a sans serif type is established as the main typeface, it can be mixed with other typefaces, but you need to maintain its importance in the design. Type design that has drop shadows on the home page, italics in the gallery, and bold on the contact page will be seen as amateurish and should be avoided.

Step 2: Gather Your Assets

You have your design ideas in firmly in place, and you are just about ready to create your initial layouts. Do you have everything you need to get started? Aside from the obvious things such as a computer, scanner, digital camera, backup device, and software, you will need your images, animations, buttons, and any other graphics that will enable you to build your Web pages.

The final Web design folder is usually the one that also has one additional folder inside it, called "images." These two folders comprise the beginnings of your site. Nothing is ever placed inside these two folders other than those files that directly relate to the Web design. In other words, layers .psd files or Illustrator .ai files never get placed in these folders. They are put in backup folders safely out of harm's way.

Step 3: Create and Code Your Interface

There are a number of ways to create Web pages. Dreamweaver, WYSIWYG Web editors, Microsoft Word, Illustrator, and Photoshop can all be utilized in the process. In the world of Web design, the approach is simple: design the page and use the method you understand best to create the underlying code. There are three different ways to accomplish this:

1. HTML coding
2. Table design
3. CSS (Cascading Style Sheets)

HTML Coding

HTML is nothing more than a coding system to create structured content and the visual formatting of that content. HTML is comprised of "tags." Let's take a look at the code for a basic Web page and its parts:

```
<!DOCTYPE HTML PUBLIC "-//W3C//DTD HTML
4.01 Transitional//EN">
<html>
<head>
<title>A Terrific Restaurant!</title>
<meta http-equiv="Content-Type" con-
tent="text/html; charset=iso-8859-1">
</head>

<body>
<h3 align="center">The Green Pepper
Restaurant</h3>
<h4 align="center"><img
src="images/Peppers.jpg" width="108"
height="93"></h4>

<ul>
  <li>Drinks</li>
  <li>Appetizers</li>
  <li>Salads</li>
  <li>Main Courses</li>
  <li>Desserts</li>
</ul>
<hr width="150" size="2">
```

```
</body>
</html>
```

The first line on the top (`<!DOCTYPE HTML PUBLIC "-//W3C//DTD HTML 4.01 Transitional//EN">`) starts with a tag. A tag is a command that describes an instruction that a Web browser can interpret in order to display the content. The "less-than" sign that you see in the first line (`<!DOCTYPE . . .`) tells the browser (Internet Explorer, Firefox, or Safari) that this is an HTML document. A tag will always end with a forward slash followed by a "greater-than" sign, like this: `/>`. This ends the command.

Toward the top of the code, you will notice `<html>`, which indicates the beginning of an HTML document. At the end of a passage of Web page code appears the closing tag: `</html>`. As you might have guessed, it denotes the end of the HTML document. All other instructions are inserted between these two tags.

The next tag you will see is `<head>`. This opens a section in which you can "title" your Web page and insert special characters known as meta tags that help search engines to catalog and find your Web site. It ends with the tag `</head>`.

Within the `<head>` tag sits the `<title>` tag, which allows you to create a title for your page. When the title is defined, it appears at the top of the browser window. To end your title, use the `</title>` tag. For instance, in the example, the title is "A Terrific Restaurant!"

The `<body>` tag opens the main section that will be displayed in the Web browser. This is where most of the Web design content is created. Here is an example:

```
<h3 align="center">The Green Pepper
Restaurant</h3>
```

In this case, the tag defines the text as centered on the page and indicates that it will display as a larger typeface.

You will also see an image of different varieties of peppers. In HTML, this is seen as:

```
<h4 align="center"><img
src="file:///Macintosh
```

```
HD/Users/MySite/images/Peppers.jpg"
width="108" height="93"></h4>
```

The tag that allows some of the type to be set up as a neat indented list looks like this:

```
<li>Drinks</li>
```

That thin gray line you see at the bottom of the Web page in the accompanying illustration is created with the following code:

```
<hr width="150" size="2">
```

And finally, to end the body section, use `</body>`. When you are finished developing the page, you close the entire document with `</html>`.

I know this seems like a lot of work, but in reality, learning enough HTML to create a decent page is a fairly simple process. Don't want to write code, you say? Well, that's where Dreamweaver comes into play. Using a straightforward drag-and-drop method, you put elements on the Web page and Dreamweaver automatically writes

the code for you! The beauty of HTML editors, such as Dreamweaver, is that you don't really need to know anything about HTML coding.

Table Design

If the thought of writing HTML code makes your head spin, then it's time to think about Photoshop and Dreamweaver together as a possible solution. As you know, Photoshop is a program that lets you create in a familiar visual environment. In Photoshop, layouts can be created and converted into Web page layouts in Dreamweaver. You start with a picture, then "slice" it into segments, which are dropped into a table-based layout in Dreamweaver. The result of this conversion is a Web page, visually identical to your graphic layout. It's a bit harder to control the table and its contents once it is created, but for some right-brain types, it sure beats all that coding.

First, you create the overall look of your Web site in Photoshop. The example shown here is from the home page of my site: www.debbierosemyers.com. As I created my design, I saved many different versions until I arrived at a design solution that I was happy with. My

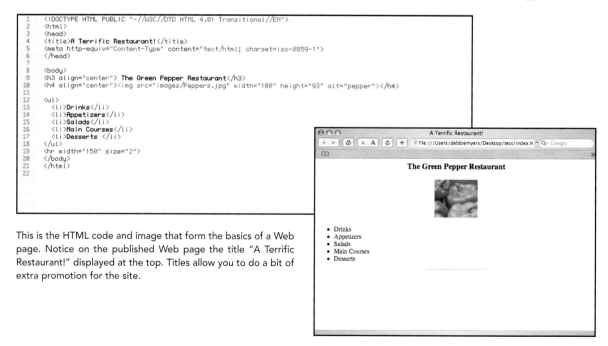

This is the HTML code and image that form the basics of a Web page. Notice on the published Web page the title "A Terrific Restaurant!" displayed at the top. Titles allow you to do a bit of extra promotion for the site.

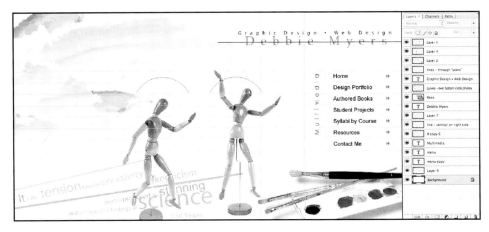

Here is the original Photoshop file with guidelines and layers. It will always be saved in its original version, so that modifications can be made as needed.

saved file contains all of the layers I used to create the design. Someday I may change the interface, and I want all elements to be available for editing. I always keep a fully editable, layered file. Once I finish my creation, I can do all of the final prep work, but always that final file is available for edits. Layers, as you may know, are a series of separate elements that sit independently of one another within a single document. Think of layers as sheets of clear plastic with pixels residing on them. Layers can be constructed one at a time to help you build up a complicated drawing. After you have achieved the desired results, you can merge and flatten them.

Once I finished creating the home page, I flattened the file.

The next step is to drag some guidelines on top of the document. These guides will be used to create the slices for the HTML tables in Dreamweaver. Take a look at the way in which I created my slices. It may look complicated, but Photoshop comes with a wonderful feature that takes care of the slicing for you: the Slice tool.

After you select the Slice tool, a menu appears above your document. (Note: Every once in a while, you will need to choose the Slice Select tool first, then the Slice tool to activate the option.) Select the Slices from Guides button, and Photoshop will create a series of numbered slices from the intersection of the guides you created. If you used a lot of guides during the creation process, you may see a ton of numbered slices. Don't let that bother you. Photoshop will allow you to "merge" some of the slices together to simplify the overall interface. The process is fairly straightforward. Using the

Slice Select tool, hold down the Shift key and select each of the individual slices you wish to merge. Then right-click (or Control-click on a Mac) and choose Combine Slices from the pop-up menu.

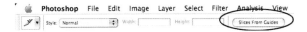

above The Slice tool and the Slices from Guides button.

below The Combine Slices option allows you to combine a lot of extra slices into a smaller number. This will make it much easier to create a table in Dreamweaver.

Here are the slices before and after they are combined.

Once you are satisfied with the newer, simplified layout, select Save for Web and Devices from the File menu. This will bring up a window to assist you as you create your final masterpiece. You will be able to choose a format: .jpg or .gif. You may wish to open the before-and-after windows by clicking the "2-Up" option at the top. This will allow you to see the state of your design before and after compression has been applied. I find that I usually select a .jpg compression preset of "High" or "Very High." It provides plenty of compression to help make for a speedy download but still keeps the images looking their best.

When you click Save, you will be presented with one last set of options. The most important of these is the Format option at the bottom. With this choice, you can tell Photoshop either to save only the images or to create the actual HTML document and put the slices directly inside it. Now, I prefer to save the images only and create my table in Dreamweaver, but that is an extra step, and not everyone wants to be bothered. My only rationale for this step is this: you will have more control over the HTML code in Dreamweaver, and I find that sometimes the HTML code that Photoshop writes is

Photoshop's Save for Web and Devices feature will allow you to create a series of small files properly prepared for the Web.

not quite as clean as it should be. Once you click Save, a folder is created called images. This named folder corresponds with the naming conventions in HTML. Open the folder once the save is complete and you will discover that Photoshop has created a series of numbered .jpg files that use your name as a beginning. How cool is that! Make sure that you move this new set of images (and the HTML document) into your Dreamweaver Web site folder.

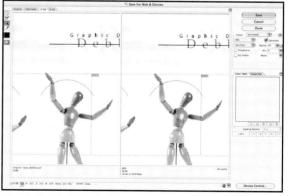

Here is the file in the before-and-after windows so that you can see the difference the compression will make. Notice that the file size difference is displayed at the bottom of the dialog box.

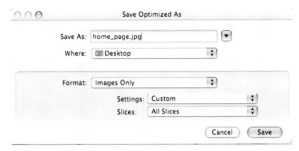

Photoshop will show you that the file will be saved as a set of .jpg images that are sequentially numbered with the name you select.

The index file that Photoshop created can now be opened in Dreamweaver. If you wish to add the image slices yourself, however, you will need to manually create an HTML document in Dreamweaver. Chances are this will be your home page, so be sure to name it index.html. It's time to create the table for the images to reside in. Go to the Insert menu, then to Table. Here's where you define how many rows and columns you are going to use. My design was based on 800 × 600, and we are using three rows and three columns. Size: 800 pixels (not percent). Zero for Border Thickness, Zero for Cell Padding, Zero for Cell Spacing, and No Header. Click OK.

Now begin the process of dragging each of your images into the table cells. (Be sure to add the Image Tag Accessibility Attributes description of the image as you do so.) Look at my example to see how the table looks as it begins to be populated with images. This small example doesn't cover the click-by-click of every step, but it should serve to give you an overview of the table design process.

CSS, or Cascading Style Sheets

Much like HTML, Cascading Style Sheets is a code-dependent language that offers a way to streamline your design process. The idea is that you create a series of styles, such as a 12-point Bold Helvetica, and then apply those styles to your Web page. In this way, you can control the layout, fonts, colors, backgrounds, and other typographical effects all at the same time in your document. In many ways, the process is similar to how you create and apply styles in QuarkXPress or InDesign. CSS has actually been around for a while. First introduced in 1996 by Bert Bos and Håkon Lie, the language was built into HTML. Why hasn't it become the standard for Web design? Because up until recently, Microsoft Internet Explorer was not very efficient at

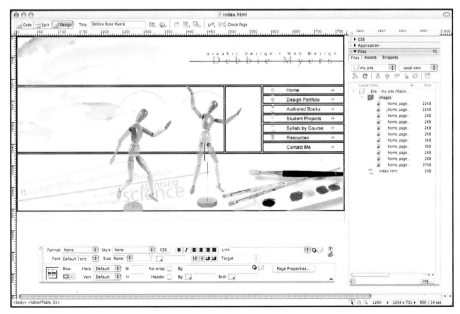

Once you are in Dreamweaver, you can create a table and drop in your images to create your interface.

dealing with CSS. Although Explorer (which has a great deal of the market share) has been revamped, it is always problematic how the browser will interpret your code. For now, pages created in CSS have to be tested a lot to ensure that they function properly.

The idea of learning a new programming language may make you want to run for the nearest door, but thankfully Dreamweaver has some helpful features to make the process a bit less intimidating. Let's revisit a slightly different version of the HTML document above and see what CSS looks like when it's applied.

```
<!DOCTYPE HTML PUBLIC "-//W3C//DTD HTML
4.01 Transitional//EN">
<html>
<head>
<title>Restaurants</title>
<meta http-equiv="Content-Type" con-
tent="text/html; charset=iso-8859-1">
<link href="menu.css" rel="stylesheet"
type="text/css">
</head>

<body>
<h3 align="center">Our Restaurants</h3>
<h4 align="center"><img
src="images/Peppers.jpg" width="108"
height="93"></h4>
<ul>
    <li>Drinks</li>
    <li>Appetizers</li>
    <li>Salads</li>
    <li>Main Courses</li>
    <li>Desserts</li>
</ul>
<hr width="150" size="2">
</body>
</html>
```

As you may have noticed, aside from minor differences in the wording of the content and the location of the image file, the main difference in this CSS code is the simple addition of this one line:

```
<link href="menu.css" rel="stylesheet"
type="text/css">
```

The style sheet information is always found at the top of the HTML document, separated from the <body> of the HTML code. If you examine the file, you will see the "rel" code. "Rel" stands for the file's "*rel*ationship" to the rest of the document. The word "type" shows that the style being defined is a text file within the CSS style sheet. Once you've created the style, you will see your pages being formatted with your defined values.

When style sheets are embedded in a Web page, the browser honors that code for the length of the HTML page. If you need to create many different styles for your

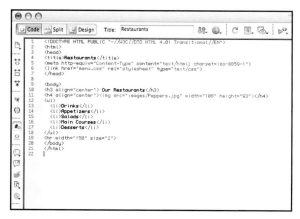

Here is the actual CSS code and the resulting image in Dreamweaver.

pages, such as headlines, subheadlines, and body copy, style sheets will prove to be a great benefit. There are a few other benefits as well. Your Web pages will download faster, sometimes by as much as 50 percent. In the long run, you'll have to type less code to create your site, your pages will ultimately be shorter and neater, and the overall look of your site will be more consistent.

With Dreamweaver, you can create a Web page using standard HTML coding, then convert the page to CSS. From the Window menu, select CSS Styles. This brings up a palette that allows you to define and apply a style sheet. Of course, you can always code the page in CSS from the beginning. There are many fine books and tutorials on CSS.

CSS has gained a lot of momentum in recent years. Although CSS is more difficult to learn than HTML, there are many who feel that this is the way Web design will be done in a few years. With that in mind, there are a number of places to find free CSS templates. You can open the file, examine it, then go into code view to see how the file was constructed. This is a great way to get started on this more advanced form of Web design. One example of a Web site that features pages and pages of professional-looking CSS templates is freeCSStemplates.org (www.freecsstemplates.org).

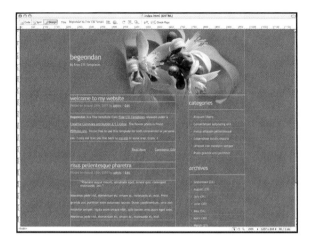

This CSS template can offer you lots of options in your design. The coding is substantial, but the results are very polished.

Step 4: Publish Your Pages

Your Web site is complete. Now you need to know how to get it online.

Once you have selected a service provider (covered in the following chapter), you are ready to get your files online for the entire world to see. Moving files from your computer to the service provider's computer is known as publishing or uploading. This process may be accomplished in a number of ways.

The easiest way to move your files is using the drag-and-drop method. Programs such as Dreamweaver offer a visual way to see both your files (called the local drive) and the remote location to which you will be moving them. You simply drag files from one side of the window to the other. This copies your Web pages to the remote site. Dreamweaver accomplishes this effortless file movement with a built-in FTP (file transfer protocol) method, which makes getting your files online very easy.

You can also transfer your files using Shareware (this is defined in the book) programs such as Fetch (for the Mac) or Classic FTP Website Maintenance Software (for Windows). They allow you to move your files in much the same way as Dreamweaver. They are not quite as intuitive as Dreamweaver, but they do the job equally well. And don't forget, the process of transferring files is a two-way street. You can download files as well as upload them. This is particularly helpful if you don't have the latest version of a Web page available to you. You can download the page from your server; make some editorial changes, say; then upload it again. I have taken on a number of Web projects in which my client no longer had access to the original files. My ability to download the entire Web site made my work a lot easier.

Final Thoughts

Your Web site should be easy to find. Now that you have created and uploaded your site, how will potential employers find you? The myth that "If I build a Web site, people will come" is still commonly believed. The reality is, employers will not find your portfolio Web site unless you promote it both online and off-line. The next chapter will show you how.

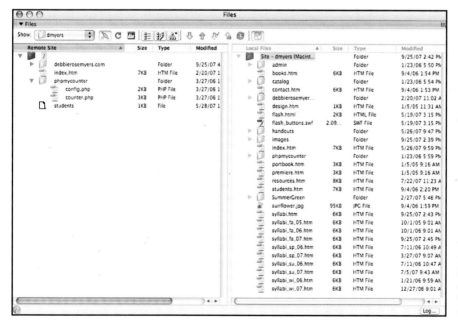

This is the easiest method to transfer your files to an online host site. You drag the files and images from the right side to the left, and Dreamweaver does the rest.

An Interview with Sigrun Eggertsdottir

Sigrun Eggertsdottir agreed to be interviewed in order to offer the unique perspective of a graduating student. Sigrun holds a bachelor's degree in graphic design from the Art Institute of Fort Lauderdale and won Best Portfolio at graduation. Visit Sigrun's Web site at http://www.bebo.com/sigruneg8.

- **When did you know you wanted to be a graphic designer?**

[*laughs*] Four months before I came here!

- **What was your background in art?**

I like to play around. . .do drawings here and there. . .I like to play with type.

- **Why did you decide to get a bachelor's degree?**

I felt I would get more in-depth art experience.

- **How much drawing have you done in your sketchbook?**

Actually, quite a lot. I am the type of person that keeps everything I have: all my notes—everything.

- **What was the hardest part of trying to decide how to begin your portfolio?**

It was really hard trying to decide what to do. I went to all my projects and tried to pick the ones I like. I know by looking at them which ones I would want to use and which I would discard.

- **How did you decide what would get rejected?**

I felt that pieces created from my early quarters couldn't really be redone effectively. The important thing is to redo a project as soon as you get your critique. You may not feel like it, but you really should. I know a lot of students who did, and the portfolio was created with less stress.

- **Did you decide to become expert in one area of graphic design or to become a generalist?**

A generalist, definitely. The field is already quite wide, and there are a lot of job possibilities.

- **What is your strength as a graphic designer?**

Layout is my strongest.

What is your weakest area?

Typography. [*laughs again*] It's getting better and better.

Talk a little bit about your experiences with real-world projects while you've been a student.

Most of my experiences have been through Artemis, our in-house ad agency, but you really have to know what you are going to be able to do for the client, and a customer is always going push you farther. You have to know whether or not you can complete the project. You have to learn how to guide the client through the process of creating the piece. You know what the solution is, and you're trying to guide the client to that correct solution if possible, without them even noticing. It's very difficult.

I know you took two classes back-to-back. How stressful were the first and second portfolio classes?

It was very stressful. I found myself keeping pieces of paper with the list of all the things that had to be done, and I was just staring at that list. It was very difficult. The press class was very hard. But the second class was really stressful! I thought I was the only one who was feeling this, and other students would feed into this, and it would get even worse.

What should people know about taking job interviews?

Go in there. Be yourself. Don't be somebody that they want you to be.

Did you take practice interviews?

Oh, yes!

This is a small sample of the self-promotion package designed by Sigrun Eggertsdottir.

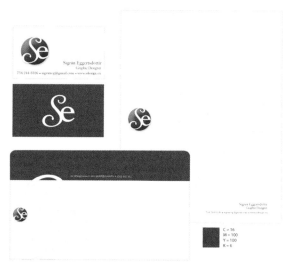

Sigrun Eggertsdottir establishes her design skills with a stunning stationery package.

Designer's Challenge

Create a magazine cover and matching table of contents page. The design should reflect the target market for the publication. It should utilize colors and type that are appropriate for the subject matter.

Sigrun Eggertsdottir presents her solution to the magazine cover design challenge. Notice how the colors are a unifying solution to hold the entire design together.

11

The Web-based Portfolio

Technical Elements

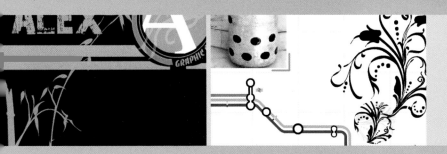

Your site is built and ready for its debut on the Web. Are you ready to send your baby out into cyberspace for all the world to see? Then this is the chapter for you. Let's turn our attention to getting your new creation online.

Do-It-Yourself Web Site Development

Chapter 10 explained how to build a Web-based portfolio. Now you need to know how to get it online. You will need the following elements:

> Domain name
> Web "host"
> Method to "publish" your pages
> Strategy to promote your site

You're familiar with the zip code in so-called snail-mail addresses. A zip code helps direct the correspondence straight to your neighborhood. Think of a

domain name as your zip code on the Internet. A domain name directs a request for a Web page or an e-mail to its final destination. It is always composed of two words or phrases, separated by periods, or dots. Here are several examples of domain names:

> www.aii.edu
> www.google.com
> www.netscape.net

All Web pages use a series of numbers (not generally visible to the user) that specify the location of the page. But so that you don't have to type a long string of numbers (such as http://64.236.24.12) every time you want to visit a Web site, domain names are used instead. A

In case you're interested, the Internet Corporation for Assigned Names and Numbers (ICANN) is the organization that maintains domain names. This nonprofit private organization ensures that all Web addresses have a unique number. ICANN was created in October 1998 by a group of people representing the business, academic, and technical communities. The organization also coordinates IP address numbers.

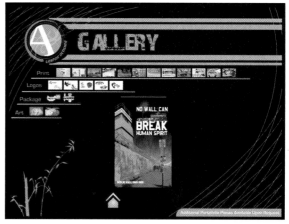

Alex Pretelt presents this Asian-inspired interface with hanging vines that act as the links to the other areas of the interface.

domain name directs your request for a Web page to the appropriate host or IP (Internet protocol) address. A more complete explanation is provided in the sidebar.

Selecting a domain name is a little like grocery shopping. If I tell you to buy a can of tomato soup, you'll head to the soup aisle of the supermarket, not the juice section. Picking out a domain name should use a similar logic. Your domain name should always reflect the service you provide.

The problem is that many good domain names are already taken. So it's advisable to make a list of domain names you like and then do some research online to find out if they're still available. Almost any Web site that offers to host your Web site has a search feature that will enable you to see if the name you want is available. Here are a few sites you can use for this purpose:

Register.com: www.register.com
GoDaddy.com:
    www.godaddy.com/gdshop/default.asp
Yahoo! Small Business:
    smallbusiness.yahoo.com/webhosting
OurInternet.Us: www.ourinternet.us

Be aware that you might not be able to "own" your domain name. If the name you want has already been registered by someone, known as the "registrant," you may have to "rent" the name. You can research the owner of a domain name on the Internet using Whois.net (www.whois.net). You pay a monthly fee for the right to use the name.

If you already have a design or company name, you may encounter some difficulties acquiring the rights to a related domain name. The cost to secure the rights to a domain name is usually based on the popularity or ease of use of the name. You may find that the price is simply too high for someone just starting out.

Deleted Domains (www.deleteddomains.com) is a great place to find domain names that have reappeared on the market. If you're fast (and lucky), you might just find the domain name of your dreams!

• Domain Names

Here is a more complete explanation of domain names, using the following imaginary Web site: www.mywebsite.thehost.com.

The domain name breaks up into three parts:

1. Top-level domain
2. Second-level domain
3. Third-level domain

The letters in the domain name identify the Internet protocol address and point you at the correct address of the site (like a zip code). They represent a series of numbers that identify a computer running on a network. Every computer connected to the Internet is assigned a unique number, known as the IP address. (For example, if you typed http://64.236.24.12, you would arrive at www.cnn.com.)

Every Web site has a top-level domain name (or suffix) that identifies the category of the site. Sites are broadly defined as either generic or by country. For www.mywebsite.thehost.com, the top-level domain (or TLD) is .com, located at the right end of a Web address. www.mywebsite.thehost.com should be www.thehost.com/ mywebsite. Here is an example . . . http://www.members.tripod.com/dg_myers/.

Generic domain names are used to classify many different types of environments, such as commercial business, educational institutions, and personal Web pages.

Their suffixes are as follows:

com: commercial businesses
gov: government agencies
edu: educational institutions
org: nonprofit organizations
mil: military
net: network organizations

Country domain names specify the Web page's country of origin—for example:

uk: United Kingdom/Great Britain
th: Thailand
fr: France
dk: Denmark

The second part (or second level) of the domain name (in our example name, "my website" is the unique name that identifies the site. The two parts together make up the overall domain name. Second-level domain names are what you submit to register your Web site. Domain names can be registered through many different companies (known as "registrars"), which compete with one another. A listing of these companies can be found at the ICANN Web site (www.icann.org).

To continue with the zip code analogy, as you know, zip codes now come with a second set of four numbers (known as the delivery point numbers), such as the "1234" in 33316-1234. These add-on numbers identify a particular area within a larger geographic region (such as a city block or a large building complex). Web names may have secondary addresses as well. Third-level domain names include both the first- and second-level portion of the domain, plus a third part, to further define where a file may be found on the server. The most popular is "www" (the abbreviation for "World Wide Web"), but it can also stand for other areas of a Web site. For example, our fictitious Web site, www.thehost.com/mywebsite might have greatart.thehost.com or, in our example, www.thehost.com/mywebsite. should be www.thehost.com/mywebsite/greatart.html. "Greatart" and "mywebsite" are the third-level names.

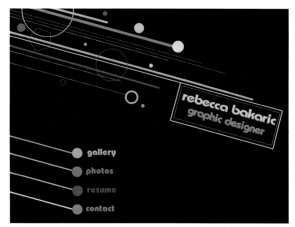

In Valentin Miloje's design, the words "Balancing Business and Art" are revealed as the tightrope walker makes his way across the screen. Blue is the linking color that helps to hold the interface together.

Rebecca Bakaric creates a strong diagonal composition for her interface. The intense colors really pop out against the black background.

If you want to create a domain name from scratch, you have lots of options and lots of things to consider. First, think about how you will be marketing your site. (We will discuss this more later in the chapter.) Printed materials such as brochures and business cards will have your Web address on them. Users will then have to type the Web address in order to visit your site. A long name makes it more likely they will make typing mistakes, so keep the address short and simple. Stay away from characters such as dashes and underscores. Avoid having double letters in the name, such as www.design-nexis.com. And if you find yourself having to spell the name over and over for your clients and in interviews, you should rethink your domain name and modify it as soon as possible.

Here are a few suggestions to assist you as you choose your domain name:

- Use words that represent your design services.
- Choose words that imply quality and value.
- Stay away from cutesy names that pun but are impossible to spell, such as www.I-luv-2design.com.
- Make the name memorable.
- Use words that are short and easy to type.
- Refrain from including words that can be easily misspelled.
- Stay away from hyphenated words.
- Don't use an abbreviation for your domain name. No one will remember it.
- Use the plural form of a word if it seems natural.

There's been a lot of buzz recently about a new incarnation of the Internet—coined Web 2.0. But just what is it, and what does it mean to you? Look for a definition and you will discover a lot of references to second-generation Web-based communities, such as YouTube and MySpace.

Think of Web 2.0 as a more powerful way to facilitate creativity, collaboration, and sharing among users. If Britannica Online was the way to conduct traditional research using Web 1.0 technology, then Wikipedia and the ability to create historical references in real time is Web 2.0. In Web 1.0, you created Web pages; in Web 2.0, you create user experiences and participation. Ever participate in a game in real time on the Internet? Then you've experienced the Web 2.0 environment. There are free sites that let you create holiday cards to send to your friends. Sites such as Google have fully embraced Web 2.0 with created applications, such as Google maps, that allow you to see the world virtually, one building at a time. The up-and-coming Second Life features a 3-D virtual world entirely created by you and millions of other residents globally. Visit Central Park, or go shopping—it's up to you. Even large companies, such as Carnival Cruise Lines, have created a rich user experience in which you can upload pictures and write reviews of your trip.

Alejandro Haydar uses the colors gray and yellow to create a very dynamic and technical feel for his interface. The yellow acts as a unifying element throughout the design.

- If the domain name you want is taken, consider using the plural form if that option is offered—for example, instead of www.mydesign.com, www.mydesigns.com.
- Be careful not to infringe on trademarks.

Finding a Web Host

Once you have designed and named your Web site, you will have to decide where it will reside or, as it is known in the Internet community, be hosted. Your files must be placed on a Web server (which you can think of as a giant hard drive) that is connected to the Internet 24 hours a day. The server might actually be a dedicated computer located in your home or office. Most designers, however, prefer to use a Web hosting service, which provides the server where your Web pages reside. When you register your domain name, you point it to the host server. The hosting service takes care of all the technical details, allowing you to concentrate on designing your beautiful site. There are two types of hosting services: free and fee-based. Before you get all excited about the free service, remember the famous cliché "You get what you pay for." Let's examine the pros and cons of both.

Free Hosting

There are many Web hosting services available that will host your personal site for free. But you don't actually get something for nothing. What they frequently ask for in return is the right to run advertisements on your site. If you feel that your carefully designed and constructed site will be marred by ads (over which you have no control) that appear at the top and sides of your pages, then this is not the option for you.

Free services are generally used by people who have small Web sites. So if you can get by with less than 100 megabytes of space and a relatively slow speed, and you don't mind the ads, then check out one of the following hosting sites. This is a small selection of free-service sites. New ones become available all the time.

Great Now: www.greatnow.com
1ASPHost.com: www.1asphost.com
Angelfire: http://angelfire.lycos.com
Fortune City: http://www.fortunecity.com/
    free-web-hosting.shtml
eSmartStart.com: www.esmartstart.com
Yahoo! GeoCities: http://geocities.yahoo.com/home
totalfreehost.com: http://totalfreehost.com
Tripod: www.tripod.lycos.com
Bravenet: www.bravenet.com

These sites are particularly great for artists:

creativeshake.com: www.creativeshake.com
Art Industri: www.artistportfolio.net
Sunstreams:
    www.sunstreams.com/web_hosting.htm
AmbitiousLemon: www.ambitiouslemon.com
BestCatalog.net: www.bestcatalog.net/free_
    hosting_cpanel.php

There are even Web sites to help you find free Web sites! These sites evaluate the potential free host sites and offer some feedback on their overall quality. Here is one for you to visit:

FreeWebspace.net: www.freewebspace.net

If you connect to the Internet with a provider such as BellSouth, AOL, or CompuServe, chances are very good that you are entitled to free (albeit limited) server space. (In truth, the host service is not free. You are already paying Internet access fees.) Still, if you do not need a lot of space, this is an excellent option. Best of all, generally no ads will be posted on your site. Check with your service provider for details about space allocation.

Paid Hosting

With a paid service, you get all the bells and whistles—fast Internet access and the ability to upload huge amounts of files. Web hosting prices range from ridiculously low to extremely high, depending on your requirements. It is possible to get a complete Web hosting package for as little as $3.59 per month. Web sites

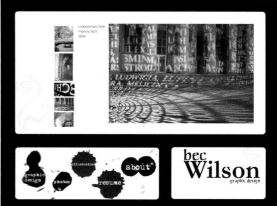

Rebecca Wilson creates an interface that clearly communicates the navigational strategy. It's easy to find all the places to visit, and the artwork always enjoys center stage.

such as OurInternet.Us (www.ourinternet.us) offer plans for every budget. (It hosts my Web site: www.debbierosemyers.com.) For this small sum, you have as much as 5 gigabytes of storage space, free e-mail, a blog where you can offer your thoughts to the world, and even e-commerce options to sell your freelance business. You may also have at your disposal statistical resources to track visitors to your site and gather information on its popularity. Paid services offer additional perks, such as promotional tools to help you announce to the world that your site has arrived.

It is important to do your research before deciding on a paid service. Quality can vary from one provider to the next. Here are some questions to think about before you select a host company: How long has the company

A restaurant site, designed by Vincent Pirozzi, uses a wonderful amount of white space to convey a sense of elegance. Clicking on the logo (bottom right) will return the visitor to the home page.

been in business? You don't want to be the guinea pig for a start-up company. Make sure that the provider offers 24-7 service and support. (For any paid service, this uptime should be 99.5 percent or higher.) Having problems uploading your files at 3:00 in the morning is one thing; not being able to reach someone to find out the cause is another. Make sure that the support staff is made up of professional programmers or network specialists. For emergencies such as this, the host should be able to respond within the hour to get your site up and running again. The availability of a support ticket system is key. You log in your request and receive a reply when the message has been received, when the problem is addressed, and when it has been resolved.

As a Web designer, you may encounter additional problems with conflicts between the program code you write and the server that is hosting the site. Sometimes these problems occur in the middle of the night. You wake up the next morning and check your site, only to find it's down. How fast can you get it back online? (Don't scoff; it recently happened when I changed a shopping cart function for one of my clients. Her site was down for two days, and she wasn't happy!) That's when you want a reliable company in charge. Establish that the provider has the facilities to keep its server running on full backup systems.

Are you thinking of running a freelance business? You are going to need a transaction system to accept payment. Does the hosting service offer e-commerce options? PayPal is a good basic service that allows payments to be made, but at some point, you may need something a bit more sophisticated. If you want to accept credit-card payments directly, you will need an individual SSL certificate (short for Secure Sockets Layer—a system for transmitting private documents via the Internet) or a shared SSL on your host's server. This feature provides a safe way to conduct financial transactions. Check to make sure or ask if your host has scripts for e-commerce such as osCommerce or Miva Merchant with the payment extensions to PayPal or 2Checkout. These are important features that offer security to your potential clients.

Finally, determine whether security issues have been addressed. You need to be reassured that your site information will be safe and secure. Ask whether the host company has a security expert on staff. There is no such thing as perfect security on the Internet, but if the company is not forthcoming about its ability to protect your files, then it is not for you. Inquire about the methods it uses to keep hackers (malicious computer experts) from invading the site.

Find a service provider that offers at least 2 gigabytes of storage space (especially if you are thinking of running a business). Those Flash files you are going to create will be large, so you may want to purchase a plan that has 50 gigabytes of storage space. Ask what extra charges there are for using more than the allotted space. High-volume sites need a lot of speed. Does the provider offer high-speed Internet access?

What kind of domain names will the host company offer you? First-level or second-level? You want to buy your domain name and have it as a top-level domain. The Web address www.mywebsite.com looks professional; www.thehost.com/mywebsite does not. It is too long to type and way too long to fit on a business card. Some service providers do not want to spend the money necessary to create full path names for their clients. The /mywebsite naming system does not take as much time to create.

Does the company provide a way for you to upload and test your pages? Will you have full file transfer protocol (FTP) access? (We'll discussed this in more detail in Chapter 14.) Does the company offer support for advanced languages such as Common Gateway Interface (CGI) so you can use forms, database searches, and image maps? Does it support Dreamweaver, PHP, MySQL, and ColdFusion? Larger hosting services do.

If you really are serious about starting a business as well as getting that first job, consider a host company that offers you some free advertising. One type of promotion perk may be credits for advertising with companies such as Google AdWords, Microsoft adCenter, and Yahoo! These ads will get your company noticed fast and may jump-start your new business.

There are now a number of independent review Web sites that evaluate the top-ten Web hosting providers. Sites are ranked according to expense and overall hosting plans. Here are some examples of sites that offer evaluations:

Best-WebHosting-2008.com: www.best-
   webhosting-2008.com
RateItAll.com: www.rateitall.com/t-87-
   webhosting-sites.aspx
Web Hosting Geeks:
   http://webhostinggeeks.com/?PHPSES-
   SID=2614c60e48388951c46cafd509a86bcb

Dreamweaver makes it easy to connect to a remote server. Once you have all your information assembled, you simply type the information into the appropriate boxes within the program's manage sites area. When the Web design is done, you drag the files from your computer to the host computer.

Promoting Your Site

Your Web site is finally online! Now you have to make sure people can find you. It's time to discuss marketing techniques. Your domain name is the starting point of Web promotion. Place your domain name on your business cards, letterhead, and résumé. If you have developed any promotional materials, be sure to include it there as well.

Make sure you have your Web site listed as part of your signature at the bottom of every e-mail you send. E-mail potential employers and announce your site. Don't just e-mail your résumé; e-mail your Web site address as well. Here is a sample letter to show you how:

Dear Mr. Thompson,

Are you presently looking for a creative designer? I am seeking a position with an up-and-coming design house such as yours. I am including my résumé for your consideration. I have also just created a Web site to manage and promote my career, and I'd like you to be one of the first to see it, at http://designsthatwork.com. I hope you will take a moment to visit my site. I would really appreciate your critique or any comments you might offer.

Sincerely,
[your name]

Let's take a look at some other ways to promote yourself.

Include Some Web Pages in Your Portfolio

Print out some of your best Web pages for inclusion in your portfolio. Carry printed samples of the Web site, just as you would your résumé. If you are marketing yourself using postcards as promotional material, be sure to include your Web address on the postcards. If your school has job boards, be sure to include your Web address on any applications you fill out. Also incorporate it in any bios you create for professional organizations, clubs, museum shows, volunteer work, or workshops you attend. If you do anything for your local community, send a press release to the local newspaper and include your Web site address. The business desk of your local newspaper will provide you with some guidelines on the proper procedure. You can also use a Web news release service such as PRWeb (www.prweb.com) free of charge—but don't post a press release unless you have something to say.

Let All Your Contacts Know about Your Site

Don't forget to show your Web site to your current employer. Tell all your friends and coworkers. Personalize the subject line of your e-mail to attract their attention. It will serve to remind them how talented you are. And don't forget any companies you do freelance work for. You never know to whom they might mention your site.

Network Effectively

Join professional organizations and start attending meetings. Join the local chapter of the American Advertising Federation. If there isn't one in your area, start one. The local chamber of commerce is a great place to network. Offer to help the group with its Web site or ads. You'll make friends and contacts fast!

Consider Wearable Advertising

Advertise yourself on your clothing. Put your logo and Web site address on a T-shirt, tote bag, or baseball cap and wear them everywhere you go.

Join an Online Newsgroup

Never overlook the power of online newsgroups. Find a newsgroup that interests you and jump in. Let's say you enjoy sports. Find the newsgroup for your favorite team

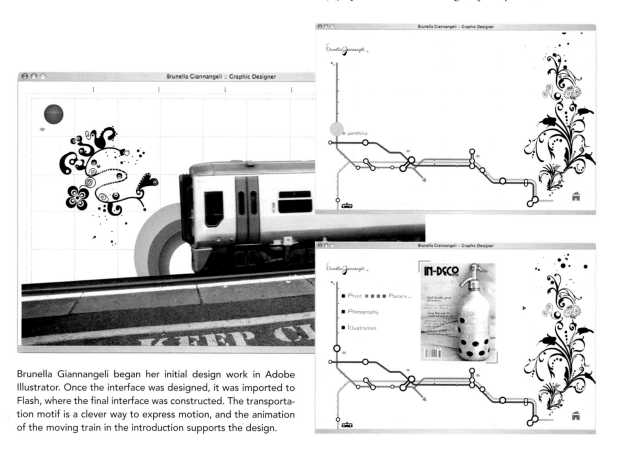

Brunella Giannangeli began her initial design work in Adobe Illustrator. Once the interface was designed, it was imported to Flash, where the final interface was constructed. The transportation motif is a clever way to express motion, and the animation of the moving train in the introduction supports the design.

• Start Blogging

You have something you want to share with the graphic design world. Don't just sit there—start blogging! Blogs have been part of the World Wide Web since its creation. The term *Weblog* was first coined by Jorn Barger in December 1997. A blog is a set of Web pages made up of text and images. A blog is usually chronologically arranged by date, with the newest entries placed at the top of the page. The person creating the page is called a blogger.

You can create a blog to share information about virtually anything, from your favorite musician to your philosophy of art. Your readers also can leave comments, and this makes the blog interactive and can lead to even richer experiences for your visitors.

You don't need to know very much about programming to create a blog. The service is generally available to you via your host site. The most popular blogs are powered by WordPress.org (http://wordpress.org), Blogger (www.blogger.com/start), TypePad (www.typepad.com), and Movable Type (www.movabletype.com/download/personal-use. html). There are thousands of premade templates available for each of these platforms, and armed with a bit of knowledge, you can create a template of your own.

The most popular blogs are updated on a regular basis. You can get good visibility on the Internet by writing entries in your blog weekly. If you can write entries daily, your chances of getting noticed are even better.

The Website created by Technorati (http://technorati.com) is one of the definitive places to locate the top blogs. So how do you get your blog listed at the site? Here are ten ideas to get you started:

1 Interview someone important in the industry. Locate a prominent art director from your community and ask for an interview. Most designers love to learn about the thoughts of a professional in the design world.

2 Spark a debate. "Should Comic Sans be banned as a typeface?" is sure to generate some feedback.

3 Design a tutorial. Who doesn't want to learn a few tricks in Flash or Dreamweaver?

4 Create a comprehensive list. What are the best colors for global package design?

5 Ask a question and generate some responses. What are the top ten news sites in the world? Who are the top art directors or agencies?

6 Write an "advantages/disadvantages" post. The use or abuse of stock photography can serve as a starting point for online conversation.

7 Write about how to use a product in an unconventional way. "Don't throw away your computer monitor. Turn it into a cool planter!" or "I went on vacation without my camera tripod. What can I use to stabilize the camera?"

8 Transcribe a live event. Have you attended a design conference? This is an opportunity to offer a valuable service to everyone who couldn't attend.

9 Generate a post that is motivating. "How I generate my best ideas" is a theme sure to be of interest to all designers.

10 Cite some statistics and write social commentary regarding them. What are the top Web ad campaigns? What age groups use the Internet the most?

and become a member. Contribute to the discussion, and when you "sign off," include your Web site address under your name in a "signature" at the bottom of your message. This is a subtle way to announce the availability of your site without offending anyone.

Promote Yourself on a Social or Professional Network Web Site

MySpace, Facebook, and LinkedIn all offer you the opportunity to promote your graphic design work. You may need to visit several different sites before you find the one that best serves your needs, and you certainly can promote your business and work on more than one site. Here are a few of these sites:

LinkedIn: www.linkedin.com
XING: www.xing.com
Flickr: http://flickr.com
MySpace: http://home.myspace.com
Facebook: www.facebook.com
WorldWIT: www.imakenews.com/worldwit

Maintain Your Own Blog

Start and write an instructive or amusing blog. A blog is a first-rate technique to share your creative or technical expertise. It can help to build Web traffic and connect you with potential customers. So what are you good at? Photoshop? InDesign? Design a cool tutorial and post it at your blog. Show off your design examples as part of the tutorial. Add your blog to blog directories such as BlogCatalog.com (www.blogcatalog.com) and blogarama.com (www.blogarama.com), and be sure to link your blog to other blogs. Add your blog to search engines such as Google and Yahoo! A blog is one of the most effective forms of self-promotion.

My blog is created as a way for my students to offer their thoughts on design. There are thousands of templates to choose from, and it is easy to get a blog up and running.

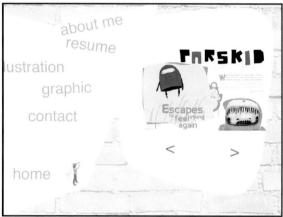

Idil Gozde is an illustrator as well as a graphic designer. She decided to design this amazing and creative interface to reflect that background.

Design a Video Tutorial

If you have something clever to show or say, YouTube (www.youtube.com) is a great way to market yourself. That Photoshop tutorial idea mentioned above created with video will surely attract attention. You'll know very quickly if your video is a success!

Create a Video Résumé

If you're not shy, you can make a video of yourself discussing your thoughts on design or your background as a designer and post it on your Web site. A well-made video will demonstrate to potential employers your poise and ability to think under pressure.

Create a Podcast

An intelligent, well-developed podcast will show the world that you are articulate, educated, and ready to enter the job market. Use a podcast to create content for your Web page or blog that will educate as well as entertain. Maybe you know a cool InDesign shortcut, or perhaps you want to share your ideas about creativity. Podcasts offer you a way to express yourself orally when the idea of sitting in front of a camera is too daunting.

Write a Newsletter Article

If you know anyone who creates newsletters in your area of expertise, offer to write an article. If you include your name and Web address at the bottom, you will effectively get your name out there for others to see.

Redesign an Unsuccessful Web Site for Free

Select an unsuccessful Web site and offer free redesign services. Contact the site's owner and offer to do an upgrade. You can barter by asking to place your own Web site listing at the bottom of the home page and possibly drive some traffic over to your site. This also helps with the search engines' ranking of your site.

Become an Expert

People have lots of questions on just about every imaginable topic, and you can provide the answers and get noticed while you're doing it. Sites such as Yahoo! Answers (http://advision.webevents.yahoo.com/answersnetwork/landing.html), Answers.com (www.answers.com), and AllExperts Questions & Answers (www.allexperts .com) give you the opportunity to be smart and network at the same time.

Use Search Engines to Attract Potential Employers

You will also want to attract potential employers to your site via search engines. There's nothing quite so thrilling as typing your name (or the name of your company) into a search engine such as Google, Dogpile, Ask, MSN, AltaVista, or AOL Search and seeing your Web site appear on the very first page of "hits." How do you make that happen? The trick is to have your Web pages

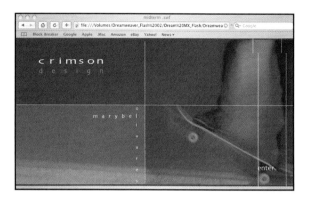

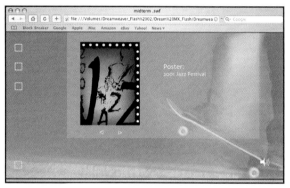

Marybel Olivares's stylish creation shows that even strong colors such as red can be used to create a stunning, rich design interface.

examined by the different search engines. It need not cost a dime, but it is a little complicated. First, you have to announce to the various companies that you wish to be included in their pages. It may take four to six weeks (or longer) before you see yourself listed. So many Web sites are now being added on a daily basis that the search companies are behind in their evaluation schedules. You may even have to resubmit several times before you get results. Be patient. You can also pay a service to list your site for you, but if you are persistent, you can do it yourself.

All the search engines will list you for free, although for a fee, they will "express" list you. This is a fast-track process designed to get your site out there more quickly. It's not cheap ($49 at Yahoo!), but it may be worth it if you are in a hurry to get your site noticed. You can also purchase what is known as a "cost-per-click" (CPC) ad. Your business gets listed with a search engine, and

A meta tag is a set of key words or phrases that people might use if they were looking for your site. These key words are placed at the top of the Web page, between the <head> and </head> tags. In a meta tag in this format, that looks like this:

```
<Meta name= "your name, artist, designer,
    freelance" content= If you're looking
    for a great artist with a proven track
    record, then I'm your designer.">
```

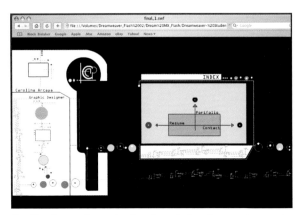

Carolina Arcaya shows that interface design does not have to be boring. This interface features a high-tech look but is easy to understand and navigate.

each time someone clicks on the link, you are charged a small fee.

The best strategy is to explore directly at your Web site. Insert special words that will help the search engines locate you more easily. These words, called meta tags, are embedded in your Web page coding. Your software package will offer helpful information on how and where to place meta tags. Also write a short descriptive title that will appear at the top of every one of your Web pages. Once your site is online, the search engines will send out special robots (called spiders) to evaluate your site. The spiders will look at your meta tags in order to index the content on your site. This, in part, determines your site's ranking when someone tries to find you using a search engine.

How does a Web site get ranked in the number one position in a search engine? No one really knows all of the formulas that are used to select the first site from a search. Some think that it is a combination of meta tags, content tags, title descriptions, relevancy of Web pages to the aforementioned items, and just plain good luck. There are products designed to help you better position your Web pages. One such product is SubmitWizard Professional <http://submitwizard.superstats.com/learn_more.html>. It analyzes your existing Web pages and gives advice on how to improve them. It comes with a simple HTML editor and even submits your pages to the major search engines.

Link Your Site to Other Sites

Another way to get people to your site is by linking it to others. Not only does this help your traffic, but it has the added benefit of making your site look more attractive to the search engines and will help raise your overall ranking. The first step in doing this is to contact Open Directory Project (www.dmoz.com), a dedicated forum of individuals committed to helping you get your site out to the major search engines. A volunteer group of people associated with the project provides directory services for the most popular search engines and portals, including Netscape Search, AOL, Google, Lycos, HotBot, DirectHit, and hundreds of others.

Do you belong to any professional organizations that maintain Web sites? Ask for a link to your site from their main page. Does your local community have a Web site? How about your local chamber of commerce? Ask if you might include a link in its pages as well.

Final Thoughts

Designing an interface is certainly the starting point, but as you can see, there's a lot of work ahead to create, publish, and promote your site. Still, armed with the information in this chapter, you're well on your way to getting your name out there. It's only a matter of time before the real search for your dream job commences.

An Interview with Etni Estrella

Etni Estrella is a recent graduate of the Art Institute of Fort Lauderdale. Etni would be the first to tell you that the road to graduation was filled with innumerable projects that he pushed aside as "not good enough." When he finally arrived at his portfolio class, he had to remake the port from scratch, and that was an interesting process. Etni ultimately graduated with Best Portfolio. Etni Estrella would like to share his insights with you.

left The ADDY Award is one of the most prestigious awards in advertising today. Here is Etni Estrella with his Gold ADDY Award.

• How long have you known you were going to be a graphic designer?

I think the first time I suspected that I was a designer was when my friend in high school used Photoshop in front of me for the first time. I had never used these types of programs before, and my friend started doing things that I thought were supercool. That was in ninth grade. So I signed up for the graphic design course that they offered at my high school.

• Did you do design work prior to that?

I was in this class where we had to draw. I could draw things that were already there. That's when I first realized I had an artistic talent.

• Do you use your rough book a lot?

I use it a good amount but not as much as I should. Sometimes as I am working on a project, I realize that if I had just sat down and done some thumbs and some roughs, I would have been a lot farther along. But I get very eager, and I want to hurry up and open a page in the program and start working, but obviously, all of my better pieces are the ones that were created when I did the legwork up front—so, lesson learned.

• What was portfolio class like?

I never really liked anything that I did prior to coming to my portfolio class, so in essence, I started from scratch. I had the great hard drive failure of '04 and the great motherboard crash of '05, so basically, I lost all my work and had to start from scratch anyway. The thing is, if I had it to do all over, I would have kept everything that I did, so I would have something to look at in portfolio class. There would have been less work, and it would have been easier all around. Wouldn't have had to search through the depths of my hard drive for pieces that could be adapted.

• What's the best piece of advice for anyone enrolled in his or her last quarter of study?

Think of every project and every class assignment as if it's going to be in your portfolio and ask yourself how you want to come across. If I had done that from the beginning, I would have had even stronger concepts than I have now.

What motivates you?

I'm not really motivated by money. I was at the beginning, but eventually, my motivation morphed into how I can make a difference. I don't want to be compared to anybody else. I want to be my own designer. I know I probably won't start the next big art movement, but I sure want to influence the design business. Advertising shapes everything, and I want to be the voice that speaks for everyone—the person that tells everyone what to think and what to buy.

What's your strength? What's your weakness?

Logos are my weakness, no question about it. Concept is my strength. I come up with some weird ideas. I also learned that a great concept can be ruined by poor choice of type, that Helvetica isn't the answer for everything. I used to think that Myriad was the only type I could use. Now I know better.

Are you a generalist or a specialist?

I've proven to be a specialist, but on the whole, I don't ever want to be in a position where I am given an assignment and can't do the job. So I think at the end of the day, I really am more of a generalist. I have a unique style to my work, but I try to make myself available for the project. That's why I know as many computer programs as I do. If I want to design a billboard, I need to know the software necessary to do that job. In my opinion, you can't afford to be an elitist.

Have you practiced taking job interviews before?

I'm familiar with the interviewing process. I've had jobs prior to going to school. I don't want to go into an interview and just tell them what they want to hear. It's about coexisting with your employer. Just tell them what your strong points are, and tell them what your weak points are. You'll find the person you just mesh with, and that's the person you are going to want to work for. Eventually, you will work your way up the ladder and become the art director.

What's the one thing you want freshman students entering design school to know?

Design is not really that hard if you're in love with it. It's no more than your hand or another finger—it's an extension of who you are. It may seem overwhelming at first, but, eventually, you may create one of the greatest pieces ever. Here's my advice: (a) breathe, and (b) just be real with your design. Don't try to emulate some other designer or design company; just be yourself.

This is one of Etni's editorial spreads. As you can see, he uses images as an important support visual for the overall concept of the design.

Etni builds a corporate ID package for a gardening business. The stylized letter *S* is used effectively as both the first letter of the word and a visual indicator of the nature of the business.

Designer's Challenge 1

Create a CD jacket. Using graphics and type as appropriate, design a CD cover for a music group. The images must support the genre of the music, and all critical information must be included.

Frances Gonzalez produces an outstanding answer to the designer's challenge.

Designer's Challenge 2

Create a catalog. Select a company and design a series of layouts using its products. You can find a wide selection of ideas in office supply stores, crafts stores, or gardening stores. Each layout should consistently display elements that hold the entire design together.

This catalog page, designed by Fernando Velasquez, contains lots of different items displayed using an inviting arrangement.

12

Multimedia and Your Interface

With your interface goals, structure, and content worked out, you have all the information you need to start building your site. But before you click to open your authoring program, there's still one more vital question

to answer: What exactly is this thing going to look like? To answer that question, consider another: What attracts you to a Web site or digital interface? The color scheme? The layout? The music? The animation? You may add any or all of these components to your portfolio interface, but to do so effectively, you must understand both the positive impact and inherent limitations of each.

Each extra component you include in your interface will either add to the user experience or subtract from it. Too many bells and whistles will overwhelm the project. Too basic an interface will be boring. Your goal is to impress viewers, so that they will spend quality time with your portfolio. The digital experience you create isn't just about readability and navigation but about

style. In short, your portfolio should encompass all facets of interface design. To that end, in this chapter, we'll examine a number of multimedia techniques for producing a successful interface.

Multimedia and the Digital Portfolio

The term *multimedia* means, simply, using or including several types of media. These media may contain or transmit many kinds of material—text, graphics, drawings, video, animation, and audio. In the early days of the Internet, it was a "static" medium, capable only of displaying text to present information. Today, thanks to

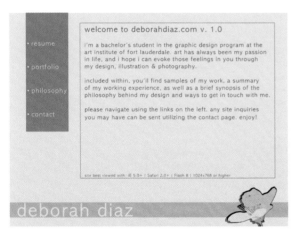

Deborah Diaz takes her viewers into account. As you can see, she indicates that you will need to use Flash and a minimum size screen to best enjoy her interface.

advances in technology, information of all types and in larger amounts can be transmitted in a matter of seconds, depending on the kind and speed of your connection to the online community.

You will most certainly want to include some form of multimedia as part of your project. A plain interface without a little pizzazz is not really going to attract much attention. What you choose to include will depend largely on the projected final output. For the purposes of this discussion, we're going to assume you will produce a project that is intended both for the Web and for CD/DVD. And because the Internet has more limitations than CD or DVD output, we will consider lower specifications as we make our multimedia selections.

It's important to learn some techniques for optimizing the quality of the final product when you plan to include the more labor- and time-intensive audio and video components in your digital portfolio.

I don't recommend using any of the popular multimedia editing programs that come with sample sounds and music. Too many others will have access to the same software and therefore the same sounds and effects. Remember, your objective is to demonstrate your originality, your creativity.

Adding Audio to Your Portfolio

In conjunction with other design elements, well-chosen audio can make your digital portfolio really stand out. Yet too many people treat music as an afterthought rather than a focal point. Music should, in fact, be one of the first things you think about in the process of laying out your portfolio. Just as animation used well improves the narrative flow, the right music can enhance the story you are trying to tell. Think about how scary music adds to the experience of a horror movie. And what good is a chase scene without intense, throbbing music designed to keep you on the edge of your seat?

Never assume that any music is out of copyright. Always double-check with the composer or lyricist or the current owner of the content. The last thing you want is to be sued for copyright infringement. The U.S. government clearly specifies what constitutes copyright, so take some time to find out the specifics of the law. Here are a couple of Web sites that will help you learn more about copyright laws and music: "Copyright Primer on Computer Music Files" (www.reach.net/~scherer/p/copyrit1.htm) and the United States Copyright Office's page (www.copyright.gov) at the Library of Congress Web site. In brief, you may use up to but not more than four measures of any piece of copyright-protected music without being in violation. If you figure that there are 4 beats in a measure, that equals 16 beats of music.

Audio files are used for digital design in several different ways: sound effects, music playing throughout, and voice files all can be embedded in digital projects. Music is probably the most common use of audio, although sound effects and speech are quite popular as well. Online instructors, for example, frequently use sound files to "speak" to their students in the same way they would in a lecture hall. And sound effects used to accompany button clicks can give effective clues as to the purpose of this navigational tool. Music can be used in the form of anything from a short recorded piece to an entire musical composition or album available for downloading. Pop music groups have been using the Web for several years to promote their work. Even the music industry is discovering the Web as a promotion device.

Preparing Sound for Multimedia

Adding sound to your site involves these basic steps:

1. Locate and acquire the audio.
2. Capture the audio.
3. Edit the audio.
4. Compress and encode the audio.
5. Add the audio file to your multimedia project.
6. Inform users that appropriate players or plug-ins may be needed.

Let's take a look at each of these steps.

Locate and Acquire the Audio

Do you need audio? Would you have been as scared without the theme from *Jaws*? It's no longer a question of whether you should add music to your project but, rather, what's the best way to accomplish it. However, before you can place anything on your Web page, you must first consider how you will obtain it. Although you can, if you're talented musically, create your own music, most people have to obtain it from a secondary source. I'll tell you about four ways here.

There are literally thousands of places on the Web to obtain free (or almost free) music. Sites such as Partners in Rhyme (www.partnersinrhyme.com/pir/free_music_loops.shtml) and Flying Hands (www.flyinghands.com/cat-free_music_clips.html) offer both free music and low-cost music for almost every type of project imaginable. These sites feature every conceivable form of sounds and music (as well as textures and video). The quality can vary quite a bit, so take your time and shop around. Check out your local computer store as well, and consult the appendix for a couple of places to start your search.

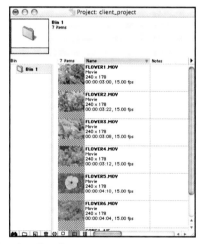

Adobe Premiere Pro allows you to import various types of audio and video files for use in your digital interface, and you can edit the music.

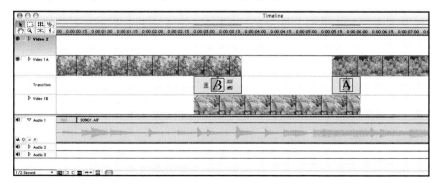

Once the music has been imported, you can edit it to delete unwanted sound that may cause your files to become too large.

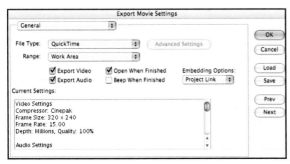

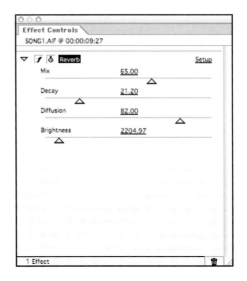

In this Adobe Premiere Pro project window, the compressor is set to "uncompressed." The audio file will be adjusted first. The final compression system will be added as the file is exported to its final destination.

You can also purchase, usually for a onetime license fee, CDs or DVDs that come with special sound effects and all sorts of interesting sound tracks. These CDs and DVDs can be purchased at popular computer stores and online. To locate lots of music, type "free looped audio tracks" into your favorite Internet search engine. You'll be amazed at the number of Web sites that offer inexpensive or free music. You make one small payment, usually about $30, and you can use these professional music recordings as many times as you like for any multimedia project you create. In addition, you can use this royalty-free music for other projects, such as video, broadcast, stage, or live presentations. The only limitation is that you may not distribute the music to anyone else. Only you have the right to use the music, since only you paid for it.

A third source of music is that which has reverted to the "public domain." All music produced by an American composer or lyricist before 1922 is now out of copyright and can be used without payment. No one can claim ownership of any music that has reverted to the public domain, and so these songs and/or compositions may be used without paying royalties to anyone. You never know, you just might find something that fits the look and feel of your project. Public domain music can be easily located by typing "free public domain music" into your Internet search engine of choice.

You can also hire a musician. And it may not be as expensive as you think. Why not barter for it? There are many fine musicians around who would be more than happy to cut some tracks for you in exchange for, say,

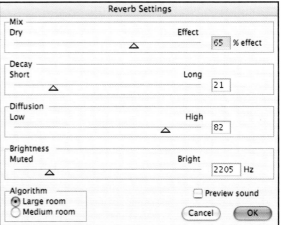

Most video-editing programs, such as Adobe Premiere Pro, come with a sound mixer. Although not quite as complex as the professional mixers, these "mini"-mixers offer a wide range of enhancement features for your sound files.

your design skills to produce a poster announcing their upcoming gig. Or they may be willing to do it in exchange for receiving credit (accompanied by a contact number) somewhere in your project. Leave flyers in your school, neighborhood music store, coffee shop, or place of worship. Don't forget to check online forums. Chances are you'll find a few up-and-coming artists who would welcome the opportunity to have an audience to hear their work in a digital environment.

As long as you save your sound files in a compatible format, most multimedia programs will be able to import them.

Capture the Audio

Once you have selected the audio you plan to include in your digital portfolio, you are ready to capture it into your computer. Capturing an audio file from a CD or DVD is a fairly simple process. Just open the audio editor you are using (such as GarageBand, included in iLife on a Mac, or Windows Media Player with a sound input card on the PC) and hit Record while the CD or DVD is playing in the CD-ROM or DVD drive. Some editors allow you to capture the file directly off the CD or DVD. (Note: If your editor can't "find" the audio, you may have to configure your computer to receive the audio signal. To do this, locate the internal sound manager and change its settings so that it knows to receive its audio input from the CD-ROM or DVD drive.)

Edit the Audio

Music editing is a challenging and complicated task. Fortunately, there are dozens of programs on the market to help you with this, as well as several inexpensive shareware audio editors available online. Windows users can use SoundEdit Pro or Audio Editor Pro. Macintosh users have many choices as well, including Sound

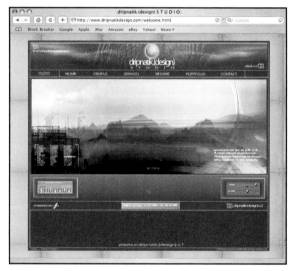

This awesome Web site, by Jair Acevedo, recognizes that the visitor may not have the latest Flash viewer. The visitor is informed that a new player may be needed and then is given the Web address from which the player can be downloaded. Thoughtful and practical.

Studio and Wave Editor, both shareware programs with many of the features of high-end editors. Audacity, which is one of the leading audio editors, is available for Windows, Mac OS 9, and Mac OS X.

All offer good, reliable ways to capture and edit sound. Full-blown audio editors, such as Adobe Audition (once known as Cool Edit Pro) or Sony's Sound Forge, can be quite pricey, but they offer every conceivable effect and filter.

As you begin to think about the music you will use in your production, remember that music says as much about you as your art. Soft jazz, tension-driven trance beats, and classical pieces all offer clues as to who you are. But think of your listeners, too. Rhythms that repeat over and over, for example, may be annoying to them. Remember, there's a subliminal message in everything you include as part of your production, so choose wisely— express yourself, yes, but include your audience in your decision-making process.

Compress and Encode the Audio

After you edit your sound, you will need to prepare it for the multimedia project. A number of settings that affect the quality and size of your audio files can be adjusted. Digital audio files are large (the better the sound quality, the larger the file). Your favorite song, for example (44.1 kilohertz, 16-bit stereo), takes up about 10 megabytes per minute. Even with the fastest digital subscriber line (DSL) connection, it will take a while to download enough of the clip so that it can even begin to play. To speed up this process in your project (so as not to "lose" your viewers), save the audio clip in a format such as WAV, AIFF, or MP3. AIFF is the standard for Mac computers; WAV files can play on both Windows and Mac platforms. For more compression, use MP3, which is great for reducing file size while maintaining acceptable standards of quality. Just keep in mind that music is generally enhanced and edited while still in an uncompressed format. Compression is usually done after the editing is complete.

The rule of thumb where audio compression is concerned is, use the lowest possible setting to reduce file size without significantly reducing sound quality. As I have mentioned before, projects designed to go on the Web will be much smaller than those created for CD/DVD because the needs of the two platforms are so different. Most audio-editing programs have a preview mode that allows you to hear the compressed music before you complete your final save. Experiment and find the audio level that is acceptable for your project. Here are some settings that can apply to both Web and CD/DVD audio usage:

- 22,050 hertz sample rate (also called sampling frequency)
- 16 or 32 kilobits per second
- 11 kilohertz mono channel setting

Amazingly enough, the average listener thinks that this lower quality actually sounds better than a 32-kilobits-per-second stereo file. It's also half the size. The other file size can be from 96 to 192 kilobits per second. Any higher is higher than CD or DVD quality. You can always prepare a file to play at both lower and higher levels, then offer the visitor a choice of which file to load.

DVD-Audio offers many possible configurations of audio channels, ranging from single-channel mono to 5.1-channel surround sound, at various sampling frequencies and sample rates.[1] (The ".1" denotes a Low-frequency effects channel (LFE) for bass and/or special audio effects.)

Compared to the compact disc, the much higher capacity DVD format enables the inclusion of either:

- Considerably more music (with respect to total running time and quantity of songs) or
- Far higher audio quality, reflected by higher linear sampling rates and higher bit-per-sample resolution, and/or
- Additional channels for spatial sound reproduction.

http://en.wikipedia.org/wiki/DVD-Audio

You will want to compress your sound files at some point in the editing process, although it is generally best

below Audio can be opened and previewed in Flash after it is added to the time line.

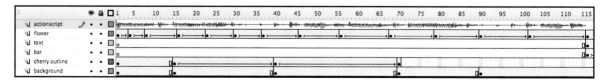

to leave your sound uncompressed as you work with it. You never want to compress a file twice. It makes the sound muddy. So complete every little special effect first, then compress at the very end.

Here are some additional guidelines on creating quality sound:

- Normalize your files. Most audio editors have a "normalize" command, which lets you equalize your sound files. This keeps the files from being too loud or too soft in certain spots, by creating a steady, stable signal.
- Purchase and use a good set of headphones or speakers. How can you tell whether the sound quality is good if it's coming from that $3^{1}/_{2}$-inch computer speaker? You don't have to spend a fortune to be able to filter out the ambient noise in your room.
- Test your audio on different computers. Run sound files on different platforms just as you do text files. Play them through the big speakers (if available) and on the built-in computer speaker. Make sure the sound quality is acceptable to you in both environments.
- Never work on the original file. Experiment, play around, make changes, go crazy, but don't accidentally mess up or erase your original file! Save frequently under different file names.
- Keep it simple. Just because you can add major sound effects and bizarre sounds doesn't mean you should. A good piece of music always stands alone.

Add the Audio Files to Your Multimedia Project

The type of multimedia program (CD/DVD or Web) you intend to produce will determine the method of audio you select. Generally, audio files are imported to the authoring program, where they are added at key points during the production. As an example, theme music might play throughout the project, and sound effects might be added to buttons. Audio files can be set up to play using two systems: nonstreaming and streaming.

Nonstreaming, or static, audio files are fully embedded in the project. These files (and all other parts of the

below Randy Gossman conceptualized this entertaining storyboard. Notice that the descriptions clearly indicate the movement of the actors within each frame. The camera action (such as a zoom-in or a pan) is indicated as well. A good storyboard leaves nothing to chance.

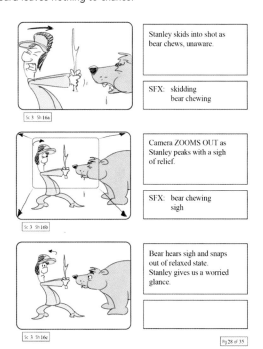

production) must be fully loaded before they can begin to play or be heard. And, again, audio files can be quite large, meaning that download times on the Web and spin-up times on a CD or DVD can be lengthy, so you need to make these files as small as possible.

Streaming audio files are not attached to the project file. They are *referenced* via programming scripts. Once "called," the audio file is downloaded to a player, where it begins to play. Probably you figured out that the main disadvantage to using streaming audio files is that you need to know some programming to use the technology. Also, the visitor may need to have a special player to hear the audio. But your file will load very fast, and this will vastly improve the visitor's experience.

Inform Users That Players or Plug-ins May Be Needed

The final step in this process is to inform your users if they will need an additional program to hear your audio. Nothing is more frustrating than waiting for a file to load only to have nothing happen once the file is on the screen. If you created a Web site, supply a link to download the missing player. If you are offering your project on CD or DVD, include the file on the disc. You won't be sorry.

The Effect of Sound Effects

Sound effects enhance a visual or textual experience. Think about the following text example: "It was a dark and stormy evening. The wind was howling through the trees. Occasionally, a branch would whip against my window, and I could hear the distant sound of thunder. I knew a storm was coming." How many sounds would it take to create the audio track for this little scene? Would the scene be effective without them? Doubtful.

Even special-effects button sounds can really add to your production. They're kind of like sprinkles on top of ice cream: they're not essential, but they certainly contribute a lot. Just be sure you select sounds that will enhance the button and not "overstay their welcome." For instance, the famous Homer Simpson "Duh!" sound was used in one production I viewed. It was funny the first time, but after about 20 clicks, it became really annoying.

Meeting the Video Challenge

What's your favorite type of television show? News? Reality? Talk? Drama? Sitcom? Do you know why? Because they inform or entertain you. When it comes to making a decision regarding the use of video in your digital portfolio, you must do the same—either inform or entertain. And what better way to inform visitors about your qualifications for the job market than with a video that explains your ideas and business savvy?

We live in a video-oriented society, so it's only natural that you would want to include video in your multimedia project. Unfortunately, video is the most challenging of all forms of multimedia content to deliver digitally. One second of uncompressed video requires 27 megabytes of disk space—a huge amount. Needless to say, this takes careful preparation, which I'll explain in this section.

Preparing Video for Multimedia

Let's say that you have decided to make a short video to display one of your 3-D sculptures or perhaps to explain your thoughts on design. Here are the five basic steps involved in producing video files for your multimedia project:

1. Shoot and capture the video.
2. Edit the video.
3. Compress the video.
4. Add the video file to your multimedia project.
5. Inform users that appropriate players or plug-ins may be necessary.

Shoot and Capture the Video

You may think of yourself as a budding Stanley Kubrick or Francis Ford Coppola, and you may want to produce the next great video masterpiece, but that takes time and lots of money, so for the purposes of your digital portfolio, let's discuss a more practical (and cost-effective) approach to video production. We'll start with a good, basic production recommendation: use a tripod for your camera. You want your camera to be as stable as possible. This will really improve the quality of your video footage. In addition, minimizing the differences between frames (and by that I mean, stand still!) contributes to better overall video compression. A shaky

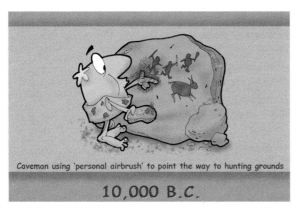

Caveman using 'personal airbrush' to point the way to hunting grounds

10,000 B.C.

"Eat Ox" Sign Chiseled in Stone Using Early Aramaic Alphabet

200 A.D.

Scribe, Paul Lindbourg, illustrating pastoral scene for Les Tres Riches.

1413–1416 A.D.

The first adventure romance novel was introduced

1517 A.D.

above In this witty and well-made cartoon video, Sue vanHamersveld demonstrates the power of QuickTime movies to tell a story. In this video, we are introduced to the history of graphic design.

camera doesn't allow the video program compression algorithms to effectively reduce the size of the file. More movement equals more information, and more information makes the file larger.

Because the size of your final video will be small (most Web-based videos are no larger than 320 × 240 pixels), you need to be aware of a number of basic shooting strategies:

- When shooting a close-up, leave a little breathing room around your subject. With a small format, a large group of people will look like ants, so close-up shots are very important. But be careful. An extreme close-up will look like an image from a horror movie!
- Keep backgrounds simple and neutral. A video camera will try to compensate for too-white or black-saturated colors. And be on the alert for possible distractions.

An example would be shooting outside with cars driving by at close range. Move the camera slowly and steadily. On a tiny screen, even the smallest movements become exaggerated.

- Don't forget to turn off the time-code function on your camera. Tape one shot, rewind the camera, and review the shot in the viewfinder. An extra ten minutes here might save you an entire day of reshooting.
- Create a storyboard and use it. The clear mark of a video amateur is someone who shoots and shoots with no concept in mind.
- Avoid starting and stopping the camera dozens of times. This will result in a lot of jump cuts or shots that have no continuity. The overall look of the shots should be clean and simple. And remember, sometimes a still shot can tell your story as effectively as a moving shot. Again, the screen is small, so a busy shot will be difficult to focus on.
- Leave a little extra time at the beginning and end of each shot. It usually takes a couple of seconds before

the action occurs, so give yourself a bit of extra time. If, for example, you want to catch the image of a dog running in the camera's view screen, turn the camera on early. It's difficult to control exactly when the pup will decide to take off, so you want to be ready and have the camera rolling. Believe me, this will make your editing a lot easier.

- Follow your storyboard and keep track of your shots. There's nothing worse than completing your shoot only to discover that you forgot one shot and have to go back out and shoot again.
- Avoid excessive adjustments to the camera. Zooming in and out or panning left and right can make low-frame-rate movies difficult to view.
- Don't forget lighting. The camera sets the iris in the lens according to the brightest light in the environment. It's important to play back the video and look closely at the quality of the shots.
- Consider all the angles. A creative videographer examines the various visual elements in the viewfinder frame and determines the best possible shot. For example, an unbalanced asymmetrical composition can give a sense of motion. Even a lamp can look visually exciting under the right conditions.
- Create the illusion of depth. We see the world in three dimensions, but video flattens out any subject

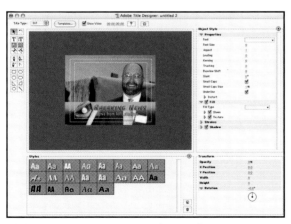

Adobe Premiere Pro's unique titling window gives you the ability to create professional overlays to enhance your video. Here is our "newscaster," Robert Goodwin, reporting a breaking news story.

• Lights, Camera, Action! The Résumé Video

One of the new trends in job hunting is using online sites such as YouTube, MySpace, and Jobster to promote yourself with a video résumé. A video résumé certainly gives you an opportunity to distinguish yourself from everyone else. If you can chat comfortably and be articulate in front of a camera, you increase your job possibilities. The ability to inject a bit of humor will show you in a way that a paper résumé can never do. Not everyone, however, is enthusiastic about video résumés, although some employers feel that they are one way to weed out those who are not "right" for the job. Individual characteristics such as hair color or tattoos could count against you, so before you start the process of creating the video, make sure that you will be successful. Do a trial video and have your friends or coworkers critique you.

Here's what you need to get started:

- Wear a professional outfit just as if you were going on a live interview.
- Look around your house and find a solid background such as an off-white wall.
- Create good lighting that will show you at your very best.
- Don't forget to use a stable tripod to keep the camera steady.
- Position yourself so you're centered in the camera's view screen from the waist up.
- Introduce yourself.
- Make eye contact with the camera.
- Don't fidget or look down at notes.
- Thank the viewer for his or her time.
- Keep the video short. One to three minutes is more than enough.

matter. To minimize this effect, always place your camera at an angle so you can see at least two sides of the person or object in your viewfinder.

Once the shooting is completed, you are ready to capture the video. This may mean capturing it directly from a digital format, but it may also mean converting

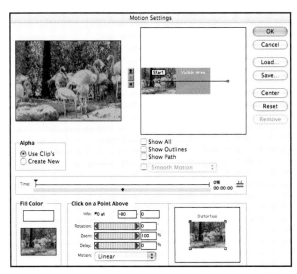

Adobe Premiere Pro comes with all sorts of special effects. Video can zoom in or slide across the screen. This gives another dimension to your video.

it into digital from an analog format. If you are converting video from an analog device, such as a VCR, you will need to purchase a video-capture card (a different type of card from the one you use for gaming). If you own one of the newer digital camcorders, you will not need the card, as the incoming signal is already digital. You will also need a program that captures video, along with the necessary cables to connect the camera to the computer. In most cases, you then simply hit Play on your VCR or video camera and select Record in the video-capture software program. Video footage appears in a viewing area and, once saved, becomes available to be edited.

You'll have two options for capturing video. The first is to simply record the uncompressed video as is—that is, with no compression. The video is compressed at the end, after it has been edited. This is a good plan, as long as you're aware that the uncompressed video will take up huge amounts of space on your hard drive. The second is to encode "on the fly" (for example, to MPEG—a standardized compression system). The disadvantage of this method is that there is a gap in the processing between the time the video comes into the computer and the time it takes to compress it. This sometimes leads to dropped frames and a "jerky" video. So, if you

have enough space on your hard drive, I recommend that you capture your video without compression.

Here are a few more video-capture suggestions:

- Give your computer as much available RAM as possible. If 1 gigabyte is good, 2 gigabytes are better.
- While capturing video, don't run any other programs. They take up valuable computer resources.
- Record only what you need, unless you have extra hard drives.
- Select a low frame rate for the capture. Use 12 to 15 frames per second. You may need to tinker around with this one. The lower the frame rate, the faster the load, but at a cost. You don't want to totally forgo the illusion of motion. Try to find a happy medium. Remember that the quality of each frame is more important than the number of frames per second.
- Make sure the video window size is no larger than 320 × 240 pixels. Currently, this is a standard size for the Web. You can use other sizes (480 × 360, for example), but the decision is based mostly on your target audience and how long you think they will be willing to wait. Many people have DSL, but some providers have the speeds set lower than nationwide standards, so it's best to take a conservative approach when deciding on physical size.
- It's a good idea to offer your video at several different sizes that take into account the various Internet configurations of your many visitors.
- Purchase a good video-capture board. And remember the adage "You get what you pay for." A $199 board does not have the capability to capture full-motion, full-frame video.
- Experiment with your capture settings before doing the actual work. Get the settings right now and you won't have so much work to do later.

Edit the Video

If you want to add a movie to your digital portfolio, a video editor is essential. Several video editors are available for both PCs and Macs, but all are somewhat feature-limited. That said, the leading products are Adobe's Premiere Pro and Apple's iLife and Final Cut Pro. Adobe's Premiere Pro and Apple's Final Cut Pro aren't cheap, but they are the best and are both excellent pro-

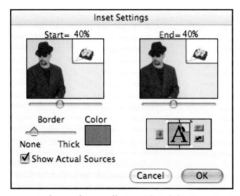

You can create freeze-frame effects with Adobe Premiere Pro. In a portfolio video, you could discuss your art and display each piece in a corner of the screen as you are talking about it.

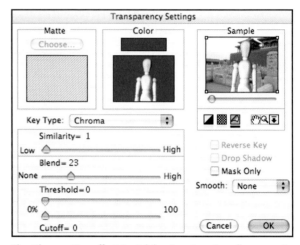

The Chroma Key effect in Adobe Premiere Pro allows you to place your actor in front of a blue screen. The color is stripped out, allowing your actor to be in any location you wish.

grams. Apple's iLife certainly edits work well for basic needs, but the high-end video programs offer tons of special features and special effects. Both products allow you to take all of your movie clips and assemble them on a time line. You can add audio and innumerable special effects. And, if you can afford it, Adobe's After Effects is another excellent addition to your multimedia toolbox. It can animate your titles and move objects along motion paths; plus, it offers many filters and effects, such as scaling, color enhancements, and masks.

Here are my guidelines on editing:

- Don't clutter the screen with too many words. Remember, content rules.
- When in doubt, use a basic transition, such as a "cut," the quick change from one shot to another. A cut is the cleanest form of editing.

Once upon a time, video was shot in sequence, and the clips were edited in the order in which they were shot. This was known as "linear editing," because the finished product was built as edit decisions were made. That meant if a mistake was made in the early part of the edit, the entire video had to be rebuilt. Today, with digital "nonlinear" editing, all edit decisions can made as the project is built. Nonlinear editing allows you to test edits and preview the finished product before exporting to more permanent media.

- Don't use transitional effects such as slow dissolves. Leave that for mushy, sentimental movies. Too many dissolves will put your viewer to sleep.
- Pass by wipes as passé. Remember *Batman* or *Charlie's Angels*? Wipes were fun back then but are considered old hat today.
- Always fade in from black at the beginning of your production. Always fade out to black at the end.
- Review the video. This is the most important guideline. You don't want to overlook a misspelled word, for example, which will jeopardize the impression your port makes on viewers. People always remember the errors.

Compress the Video

After you have edited your movie clips, you're ready to convert your video project into its final form, as a movie that can be played on a CD/DVD or Web site. This involves the process of compression, which, as you know from earlier discussions, reduces the size of your video while maintaining acceptable quality. There are many different compression systems, or codecs (compression/decompression), on the market today. Codecs work their magic on your video by constantly deleting repeated and unneeded information. This happens as the codec looks at what it perceives as "key frames," or important places inside the video. As each frame is

- Don't shoot a minute of video until you have a clear concept of the project. A storyboard of the shots will help you to determine how many shots you will need and the length of each shot.
- Shoot three to five times the amount of video you think you will need for the project.
- Negotiate permission for any audio or video material shot by others that you will include in your portfolio.
- Obtain releases from every person who gives you material to use in your project. This includes video, images, and audio material.
- Consider using a commercial "voice" if you need a "voice-over" (a narrator). Strong regional accents will detract from the professional effect you are trying to achieve. If you can't afford a professional voice, ask your friends to audition for the job. You might be surprised! Just make sure your audio talent knows how to pronounce difficult or technical words and acronyms.
- Listen carefully to the ambient sounds during a recording session. Do you hear planes flying by or cars honking? Such sounds will detract from the professionalism of your production.
- Don't overwhelm the viewer with sound effects just because they are available. Remember what I said earlier: they get old fast.

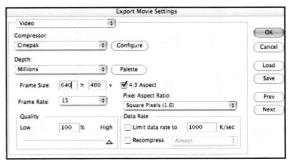

The compression feature in Adobe Premiere Pro gives you a variety of options from which to choose.

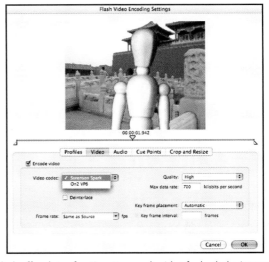

Flash offers lots of options to encode video for both the Internet and CD/DVD.

repeatedly improved and old frames are deleted, the video plays, or "streams."

There are two ways to compress your video files. You can use a program that has a compression system built into it (such as Adobe Premiere Pro or Flash), or you can use an independent program (such as Sorenson Squish or DivX Codec) that performs a single function—getting your file down to its lowest acceptable size.

Digital video means a lot of data. So whether it is viewed streaming over the Web or viewed from a CD or DVD, it is imperative that the quality be worth the wait. Although video compression is much improved, your success in giving the visitor a rich visual experience

essentially comes down to basic plumbing: the size of the pipes (bandwidth) and the amount of flow (file sizes). Let's begin by examining some of the basics.

It starts with the resolution. The standard digital video size on a DVD, on a DV camcorder tape, or on digital television is 720 × 480 pixels. Video designed to stream over the Web is usually limited to 320 × 240, or quarter-screen resolution. This makes sense. If you limit the resolution, you limit the wait time.

Full-motion video is generally recorded at about 30 frames per second (actually, 29.97). Reduce the number of frames per second and you increase the speed of the download. The downside to this is that the more the frame rate is reduced, the more jerky the picture looks.

It's All about the Compression

There are many compression techniques to try in order to achieve an acceptable video. No one method is perfect, so you have to tinker a bit to find a solution that shows your video at its best production value without causing too much wait time. Image compression is at the core of digital video. There are basically two compression methods: intraframe and interframe techniques. Intra means "within," so intraframe compression is done within a single video frame. Inter means "between two," so interframe compression occurs between consecutive video frames.

The more widely accepted system is intraframe. Most video-editing programs use this method. And it makes sense. Since each frame is self-contained, intraframe compression makes it easier for the program to edit and to add titling graphics and effects to the project during the creation process. This method of compression is also popular because it keeps the footage from degrading as the compression is applied.

There are two types of compression:

1. Lossless, in which all the data is preserved. Typically, this will compress images 2:1.
2. Lossy, in which the data is degraded, the more so the greater the compression ratio used.

Some popular codecs for computer video include MPEG, Indeo and Cinepak, and Sorenson Video 3 Pro codec or Sorenson Squeeze 5. Probably the most widely used formats for delivering video over the Internet are MPEG-4 and Windows Media. Which you'll choose is driven primarily by platform. Sorenson is most widely used by Macintosh software, although Cinepak is available for both Macs and PCs. Cinepak is widely used on both digital video and CD-ROMs/ DVDs. It has decent output quality and is included free with the QuickTime software. Its only drawback is that it requires a very lengthy compression time.

It's All about the Format

An understanding of codecs and players is essential to the creation of video for multimedia. Regardless of which format you choose, recognize that delivery will not be instantaneous, but by using the appropriate codecs and players, you'll deliver high-quality video that

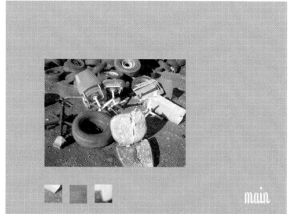

Sasha Kobrynich presents this elegant digital portfolio. As you can see, there are a couple of video clips embedded in the site.

your audience won't mind waiting for. For most video projects, QuickTime is probably your best choice. QuickTime works on PCs and Macs and makes videos that play in iTunes Music Store and on Apple TV. It is an industry standard, and most computers have the necessary plug-in.

Once the file is compressed, it can be saved and exported in one of several different formats. The thing to remember is that the most common reason a video file will not play is that the video codec used by the file is not installed on the system being used to attempt to play the file. So with that in mind, let's take a look at the most common players:

- QuickTime MOV for Mac and Windows
- Windows Media Player for Windows and Mac

- MPEG (Moving Pictures Experts Group) for all platforms (including UNIX)
- RealNetworks' RealOne for Mac and Windows
- Flash Video

Apple QuickTime is the multiplatform industry standard to create and deliver graphics, sound, video, text, and music. It is one of the most widely used formats on the Internet. QuickTime movies (movies saved with a .MOV file extension) can be created and compressed using software packages such as Adobe Premiere Pro. This product has been around for quite a while, in many versions. On newer versions, the video starts playing before the entire file downloads. And one important consideration is that QuickTime is free, which naturally makes it very attractive. No other application currently allows you to view a movie without first loading drivers. QuickTime offers high-quality video and audio/video.

Microsoft Windows Media Player comes free with Windows (and a special Mac version can be downloaded). It is a universal player that supports more than 20 different file formats, including WAV, AVI, MPEG-1, MPEG-2, MIDI, MOV, MP3, QuickTime, and RealVideo. The player also supports Web-based streaming media, which enables users to play back audio and video content without having to download the file from the Web. Once viewers are at the Web site, Windows Media Player instantaneously plays back the content that they want to see or hear.

Motion JPEG (MJPEG, Joint Photographic Experts Group standard) or MPEG (Moving Pictures Experts Group standard) was introduced in QuickTime 2.5. It is considered a lossy (which, remember, means it degrades the information if the file is used and resaved repeatedly) compression system codec. It produces bulky file sizes at 100 percent quality but creates smaller file sizes than Cinepak. MPEG is a decent choice for files intended for the Internet. MPEG compresses individual frames, which can then be played back. Compressing large amounts of video is a daunting task, so video-capture boards that use the MJPEG technique usually rely on dedicated encoder chips. The MPEG codec is included in most popular digital camcorders.

RealNetworks' RealPlayer is a program that can transmit audio, video, text, and animation directly to

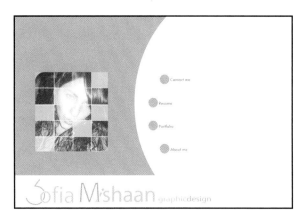

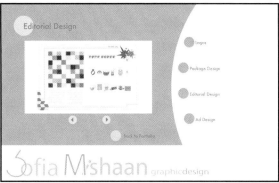

Sofia Mishaan's interface is clean and easily understood. Even in her gallery area, the visitor can find all of her art and follow a clear path to her home page.

your desktop. It uses streaming technology, which requires special server software, although some versions of the player are free. The user selects a file based on the connection speed, and the program optimizes the file for that speed. RealPlayer offers full-screen video capacity and enhanced sound quality.

Flash Video is a great choice when it comes to streaming video. Flash Video now has two default codecs: Sorenson Spark and On2. What makes Flash so popular is the amount of compression the program can accomplish. With a bit of tinkering, a 5.4-megabyte video file can be compressed down to around 40 kilobytes. It is the format of choice for two of the most popular sites on the Web: YouTube and MySpace.

The latest statistics show that Flash Player is on 97.3 percent of all of the Internet-enabled computers in use today. Microsoft's Windows Media Player is on 83 percent of computers, QuickTime is on about 66 percent, and RealPlayer is hovering at 56 percent.

Recommended Settings

Here are some settings for you to consider as you decide how best to compress your video files.

QuickTime

- Extension: .mov.
- Size: depends on the aspect ratio. 4:3 (640 × 480 or 320 × 240) or 16:9 = 640 × 360. (16:9 is rapidly becoming an industry standard.)
- Codec: h.264.
- Data rate: 1500 to 2000 megabits per second. (The higher, the better.)
- Audio: AAC audio.
- Render settings: best.
- Target bit rate: 128+.
- Key frame interval: auto. (Lower is better, so start experimenting now!)
- Fast Start: on. If you don't select Fast Start, QuickTime movies won't play until the entire file downloads.
- Frame rate: current.
- Frame Controls: off.

Flash

- Frames per second (fps): 15 frames per second.
- Data rate: 400 kilobits per second video.
- Audio: 64 kilobits per second mono.
- Source resolution based on initial settings during the shooting session
- Frames per second: Start with 16 frames per second. (Film uses 24 frames per second. TV uses 30 frames per second.)

- Data rate (kilobits per second): Start with 1000, then experiment a bit.
- Audio: 128 kilobits per second.

Add the Video File to Your Multimedia Project

Once you have edited and compressed your video, it is ready to be placed in its final application. If you created the video for a CD or DVD, it will be transferred to a multimedia program such as PowerPoint or Flash. You can create a button that loads the video for the user's enjoyment. If the movie is being uploaded to the Web, you will embed it in an HTML document. On the Web page, you'll put an invitation to the user to play the video; if the invitation is accepted, the file will be streamed to the user's computer.

Inform Users That Appropriate Players or Plug-Ins May Be Necessary

You'll note that informing users about any necessary players or plug-ins is the final step in all the procedures described in this chapter. It's important, so don't overlook it. In this case, offer users more than one way to watch your video. For example, make the movie available in both QuickTime and Flash Video. You never know what software viewers will have, so cover your bases. Also, as a courtesy, offer your visitors the opportunity to load any plug-ins necessary to play the video by supplying links to the sites that have the required software players.

As CD/DVD and Web technologies continue to evolve, there will be new ways to bring multimedia to life. As a multimedia developer, your goal is to familiarize yourself with the most popular types of players in order to attract the widest possible audience.

An Interview with Christine David

An award-winning graphic designer and program chair for advertising and graphic design at the Art Institute of Fort Lauderdale, Christine David continuously and energetically inspires students in pursuit of their creative passions and dream careers. Christine is a nationally recognized and published designer, fine artist, and public speaker. She is the creative/art director for Artemis Design Group, a full-service advertising agency that employs students and graduates of the Art Institute of Fort Lauderdale. Her clients have included Coca-Cola, Toyota, Truly Nolen, Zippo Manufacturing Company, and Harley-Davidson. Christine is also a member of numerous professional organizations, including the American Advertising Federation, AIGA, and the National Association of University Women.

"I will always be a part of the advertising design industry," reflects Christine; "however, my true path and love in life is found in teaching. I decided to get into education to make a difference in the world. What we do is all about communication. We have the ability to entice humans to do the 'right thing' via our words and images. The more I am able to share this insight with students, to teach them that they have the power to affect the outcome of the way we as humans live and treat each other and the world, the more likely they are to go into the world and make a difference for the greater good."

Christine is a Native American who is devoted to causes that protect the Earth, nature, and children. "Within each of us there lies a creative spirit capable of unimagined things. It is my goal to bring all that cross my path into the light of the creative spirit and back to knowing that universally we are all interconnected."

1 What qualities do you look for in an applicant?

First, creative personality. If they have that, they can accomplish nearly anything. The applicant should be able to talk about every aspect of their work and while doing so be excited about what they have created. The second aspect I look for is dependability. I need to know they will show up for work, for a meeting, meet a deadline, and complete a job right the first time.

2 In your opinion, what makes a successful interview?

Well, a person who demonstrates the above qualities, someone who I connect with on a creative-spiritual plane. When I say that, I am referring to someone who is passionate about what they create: it is not just about the money but rather making a difference with what they communicate. Again, able to talk about their work, knowledge about my business and my clients, and a reason to want to work with me.

3 Has the Internet had an effect on your interview process?

Yes, if I am able to see an applicant's work from the comfort of my laptop (which is anywhere), the interview process speeds up. I know right away if the applicant's work style is something I can use or not. I am also able to bookmark that site so I can use them at a later date if need be. Once I see great creative work, I like to follow up with a face-to-face interview.

4 What are the five best things job candidates say that impress you during an interview?

- I can do that!
- Able to speak about work.
- I really want to work with you because _____.
- Can tell me what book they just read.
- Truly anything that is stated well.
- Able to talk about other jobs they have done (if they have any).

What are the five worst?

- I don't know. I'm not sure.
- I know I could do this better, but . . .
- Because it is cool.
- I'm sorry.
- I just did it on the computer; there was no research or thumbs.

5 What are skills that really help all artists succeed regardless of their specialty?

- People skills
- Ability to think quick on your feet (yes, BS)
- Extra skills like Web or interactive design
- Photography, ability to make comps
- A true passion for creation
- Copywriting/concepting

6 What advice would you offer to designers looking to impress you with the presentation of their work?

Be original in your presentation. Make sure your work is crafted well and presented well. Be able to talk about every aspect of your work from color and type to layout and style. Make sure you have a Web page of any type.

I want to be able to look at your work right away. Have continuity to your look, the résumé, site, portfolio, et cetera. Lastly, follow up with a letter of thanks and/or a self-promo piece that is clever.

A couple of the many advertisements created by Christine David.

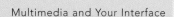

Designer's Challenge 1

Create a series of mailers that advertise an event. Using a limited color set, design a set of four different mailers that all have a similar look and feel. They should reflect the event using images that target the recipients' demographics.

Thomas Slonaker has created an excellent, well-designed set of mailers as an answer to this designer's challenge. (Thomas Slonaker, Sinclair Community College Design Department, 2007.)

Designer's Challenge 2

Create a nontraditional invitation. Design an invitation to a museum opening or concert that uses an unusual method of construction. It should be constructed in such a way that it can be mailed or delivered.

This outstanding "paint can" was created by Thomas Slonaker. It promotes an opening at a contemporary museum. (Thomas Slonaker, Sinclair Community College Design Department, 2007.)

13

Designer Checklists

Before we move on to the final topic in this book, presenting your portfolio, I want to review the many factors we've discussed that go into the design of a successful digital portfolio. In this chapter, you'll find lists of

questions that you can use as checklists, to ensure you have covered all that you need to before you put your portfolio "out there." Before we begin, though, I want you to recognize that your first (and probably second or third) multimedia design project will not be perfect. No one's is. Expect to make mistakes. Expect crazy things to happen. That's how you learn. Eventually, you will get it right.

Designer Checklist for Digital Portfolios

○ *Did you define specific objectives for your project?* Quick! In 100 words or less, describe your design philosophy for your project interface. If you can't,

then you're not ready to begin. This project is intended as a reflection of your design sensibilities and conception skills. To be seen as a cutting-edge designer, you must have a concept.

○ *Is your project innovative?* What sets you apart from everyone else? What do you offer that is different from every other job applicant? Maybe it's your sense of humor. Or perhaps you use a clever animated character to introduce your work. Whatever style of interface you develop, try to bring something new and unique to the project. (Take a look at the fantastic student examples throughout this book.)

○ *Do your pages have a consistent look and feel?* Most people do not navigate projects in a linear way.

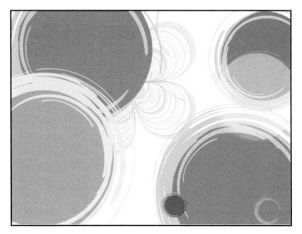

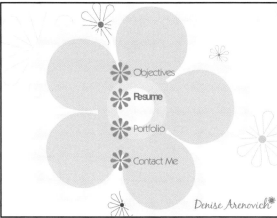

This playful, fun interface was developed by Denise Arenovich. It has a clear navigation system and reveals her witty side.

That is to say, you can't control the way your project will be viewed. Therefore, it is very important that all of your pages reflect a cohesive look. Potential employers should always be aware of who you are and where they are while viewing the project. You can achieve this by using logos, colors, or design elements, but use them consistently. A lack of consistency in the interface communicates an unprofessional image.

○ Have you included all the necessary information in your interface? Does your interface have the following elements?

   ○ A statement of philosophy or career objective

   ○ A "gallery" of your work

   ○ Enough pieces (at least 10–15) to give a complete picture of you as an artist

   ○ A "where to contact me" page

○ *Did you give credit to contributors, such as musical talent?* Include a credits page in your presentation, if necessary. This both demonstrates that you understand copyright laws and protects you against lawsuits.

○ *Are your pages designed so they are easy to read?* Create a menu so the reader does not have to scroll down the page to locate important information. Start with a clever animated opening, but keep your home page simple. You want to engage the viewer right off the bat. A well-organized, easy-to-comprehend home page will encourage the user to explore your site further.

Are your links clearly labeled? Don't make the user guess what a button does. Go ahead and use a cute icon in place of a word; just make sure it clearly represents that section of the port. The same goes for text links: make them clearly descriptive, such as Objectives, Résumé, Gallery, Personal Philosophy, Technical Skills, Contact Me. Links should always reflect the skills you are marketing and the field in which you are seeking employment.

Did you showcase your best work? If you have 25 pieces of art, determine which are the weakest and pull them out. There are two related reasons for this: first, if you include too many pieces, chances are viewers won't take the time to go through them all; second, that means they might miss your best selections—which, in turn, means that you might miss out on being the candidate of choice. Include only your most pertinent work in the port.

Did you use text in a creative way? Vary your text styles to emphasize the most important parts of your interface. Utilize different sizes, different fonts, and different attributes (italics, color, and bold) to highlight information and create a site that is pleasing to the eye.

Did you include thumbnails of your work? One of the best ways to display a digital gallery is to use small thumbnails as links to larger versions of your art. Thumbnails can be created as either rollovers (where the image pops up on the screen) or links (where a mouse click opens the image in a separate window). This is especially effective if you have six or more images.

Did you exercise restraint in your use of sound and animation? Don't clutter up your beautiful interface with a lot of pointless distractions. If an image, animation, or sound doesn't enhance your design, don't use it. Aside from slowing download times, not all animations will work in all browsers.

Have you tested your site to ensure it works properly before posting it? Take the time necessary to test your links. Use more than one browser. Just

Etni Estrella has designed a project based on nature's moody fall sky. The red is a consistent color used throughout the interface.

• Link Lookup

There are a number of online companies that will check your site links for free. (But if you like the result, the companies ask you to purchase the service.) Here are a few sites to check out for this purpose:

2bone: www.2bone.com/links/linkchecker.shtml
Link Alarm: www.linkalarm.com
Link Validation Spider: www.dead-links.com
Web Page Purifier:
    www.delorie.com/web/purify.html
AnyBrowser.com:
    www.anybrowser.com/linkchecker.html
LinkTiger: http://www.linktiger.com/

Although there is a lot of information on this Web page, Jair Acevedo shows us how a clean interface can make it easy to see everything. The links are clearly labeled, and the icons act as additional references.

because you use Firefox doesn't mean everyone else does. Do it often; occasionally, links get lost or damaged, so verify they are in working order. And don't forget to update address, telephone, and e-mail changes when they occur.

○ *Do you maintain a flowchart that represents where the project links are located?* Fancy or simple, in a computer file or on a napkin, it doesn't really matter as long as you keep a well-developed mapping of your interface. Nonlinear programs allow you to adjust if you change your mind along the way, but linear programs can be very unforgiving, so the more completely you track your interface, the less likely you will experience problems.

○ *Do the icons and images artistically and logically reflect the look and feel of the project?* Let's say you decide to create an interface around a travel theme. While designing your buttons, you choose an image map of the United States to act as your Gallery button. Will that make sense to the user? Probably not. Again, test your ideas on several people to get feedback.

○ *Do you provide regular visual guidance?* Do you give viewers visual clues that they are where they meant to be? For example, after they click the Gallery button, will it be clear that they are indeed in the gallery area? Does text or graphics indicate that the transition has been successful? Would a sound clip help?

○ *Have you decided between vector- or raster-based graphics as the primary element of the interface?* If you want to increase your project's speed (and download time), always use vector-based graphics. But if you have lots of pictures that must be displayed, using raster-based images is your only option.

Design Elements Checklist

○ *Do you have (or need) a grid?* Grids help to organize your material into a logical sequence. Design one and try placing your objects on the page. Do you like the results?

○ *Have you made good color choices?* You've made the home page background color a deep emerald green. Should the gallery section be vivid yellow? Number one, that's not a very uniform color system, but more important, yellow may not be the best choice to feature your designs. Is there adequate contrast between the type, images, and background? Unusual colors may be fine for certain projects, but good design is the name of the game where your art is concerned. Is the on-screen text readable?

○ *Is text laid out effectively?* Can the viewer tell the difference between body text and text that acts as links to other areas of the portfolio? Did you check for spelling errors?

Sasha Kobrynich creates a very artistic interface. Each of the "drips" at the bottom leads to a section of the interface.

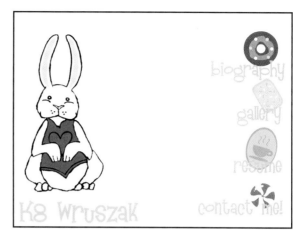

Kate Wruszak leads us down the rabbit hole with this charming design. Even the buttons have a whimsical feel to them.

- *Is there an understandable navigational menu?* Don't leave your viewers wondering how to get there from here.
- *Do your gallery buttons support your gallery?* The gallery can feature a self-timed art show, a pair of forward and back buttons that allow the viewer to navigate through the work, or a series of clever rollovers. Whatever method you use, make sure it shows the work to its best advantage.
- *Are interface buttons logical and in good working order?* Most people understand that a button with an arrow pointing to the right means forward and that a button with a little house on it usually indicates the home page. The point is, make your interface buttons intuitive. Never make the user guess what they signify. Do all of your buttons work? When's the last time you checked?
- *Are common interface design elements used consistently?* Rules, borders, dots, and type all contribute to the overall look and feel of your design. Make sure that any elements you use support your message.

Technical Design Checklist

- *Did you test the project on multiple platforms?* Will the project play on both PCs and Macs? In the Macintosh world alone, there is the iMac, the Mac Pro, the Mac mini, the MacBook, the MacBook Pro, and the MacBook Air. All work at different speeds and may cause your project to run at unusual speeds. Will it play on multiple operating systems? There's more than one version of Windows on the market today, and Apple has at least four operating systems. Will your project work on all of them?
- *Will the project open on multiple Web browsers?* Safari, Internet Explorer, and others will each treat your files somewhat differently. Make sure the project works with at least the most popular browsers.
- *Are loading times reasonable?* No one is going to wait more than several seconds for your project to load. Keep your visitors in mind and don't try their patience.

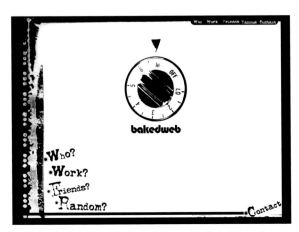

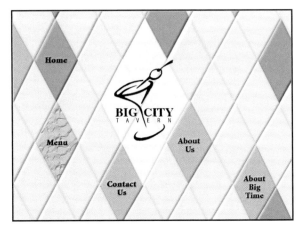

Bellatrix Martinez uses black to its fullest advantage. The color acts as a neutral background to showcase the designs on the Web site.

○ *Did you have someone "beta test" the project for you?* Before a play opens to the public, the actors always rehearse their scenes. Think of the beta test as your project's rehearsal. You certainly don't want to go on a job interview and find out then that your file refuses to open.

○ *Have you prepared for the worst?* Never underestimate the power of the computer gods to trip you up. Do you have a backup file? Better yet, have two. Do you have a battery-backup UPS (uninterruptible power supply) unit?

Valerie Dziedzic creates this stylish interface as her final project for a class in Web design. The links are clear and unambiguous. The menu is created using iFrames—a nested system to put Web pages inside of Web pages.

Miscellaneous Designer Checklist

○ *Do you keep a record of all your ideas and designs?* Don't discard any of your ideas. Even if they're not appropriate for the project at hand, they may be right for another somewhere down the road. Keep all of your thumbnail sketches—you never know . . . .

○ *Do you have a support system in place?* Things always seem to go wrong when you least expect it. Where will you go for help? Books? The Internet? Friends and colleagues? Know in advance where to turn if you need assistance. And don't be embarrassed to ask questions.

○ *Have you allotted enough time to produce the project?* Never underestimate how long it's going to take to construct the digital portfolio. No matter how long

you think it's going to take, it will always take longer. There will always be some little problem that stops you in your tracks as you near the deadline. Once, without realizing it, I used a program that contained corrupt data. After several frustrating hours of watching the program randomly crash, I decided to reinstall it. As it turned out, I had to install an early version first, then reinstall each incremental upgrade until I had the program running again at its current version. Three hours later, everything was fine (except my nerves).

○ *Do you make it easy on your viewers?* I've said this before, but it bears repeating: offer links in your

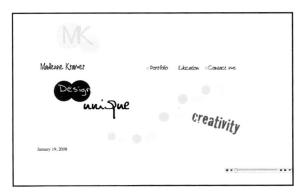

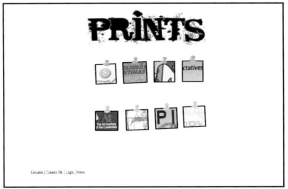

Madlenne Kramer creates her own Web site with a clean design to best showcase the artwork. The interface for the images teases the visitor with a small cropped image that opens to reveal a larger complete design.

project to places where software players can be downloaded, if they're necessary to experience your site. Make it as easy as possible for your viewers to experience your project; this is a simple act of consideration—and one that will pay big dividends for you.

○ *Do you stretch your limits?* I say, always bite off more than you can chew! You'll never grow as an artist if you don't push beyond what you already know. Just don't do it when you're on a tight deadline.

Final Thoughts

Let me close this chapter with some suggestions about what to do when things go wrong—as they inevitably will. First, don't panic; don't lose your cool. Don't become so frustrated that you behave in a way you'll regret later. I witnessed one student yank a keyboard from its cable and hurl it across the room, where it slammed into a wall. Aside from the embarrassment factor, the incident earned him a suspension and cost him the price of a replacement keyboard. If you feel yourself getting that worked up, leave your desk, walk around, clear your mind, get something to drink, breathe some fresh air—in short, chill out. Then sit down again when you feel up to it and have another go. It will do you no good to try to work when you are not up to the task. I know I don't have to tell you that creativity comes in spurts. When you are truly in the mood, the project will come together in a meaningful way.

And keep in mind, as I mentioned at the start of the chapter, probably you won't be happy with your first effort. You wouldn't be a true artist if you were. Besides, you never want to tell yourself, "It's good enough." You want to keep improving. So make that second or third effort. You'll get there.

Don't forget to have fun! The process of building a portfolio is supposed to be enjoyable as well as hard work. So relax and savor the experience. When you need inspiration, explore Web sites devoted to digital portfolios. Ask yourself what works and what doesn't.

Finally, be creative, but be practical. Make sure your portfolio is professional, but don't be afraid to cut loose. Here are some Web sites to help you in your creative quest:

- Creativeshake.com: www.creativeshake.com
- Artspan: www.artspan.com/become_mbr.php

- a2z Web Designer Resources: www.a2zwebdesignsource.com/Graphic_Design_Artists
- Adobe's Site of the day: http://www.adobe.com/cfusion/showcase/index.cfm> Design Directory: www.dexigner.com/directory/cat/Graphic_Design/Portfolios/19.html
- DesignersTalk: www.designerstalk.com/forums/great-designs/31042-ikea-ads.html

An Interview with Nancy Karamarkos

Nancy Karamarkos has more than 13 years of professional art direction, page-layout, and graphic design experience in the publishing and marketing fields. She is a detail-oriented individual who is creative while working under tight deadlines. Ms. Karamarkos is a conceptual thinker who has worked closely with photographers, illustrators, stock agencies, and printers and has won numerous awards, including Design Merit / Cover for the Society of Publication Designers' December 2006, September 2003, November 2002, and July–August 2002 issues. Ms. Karamarkos also received the Golden Ink Award, Silver Medal, in 2000 and 2001 for her work in the Society of Publication Designers.

Nancy Karamarkos's clients include Food Arts magazine, Bristol-Myers Squibb, Prudential, and the National Audubon Society. Ms. Karamarkos holds a bachelor of arts degree in communications from Rowan University, Glassboro, New Jersey. You can visit her Web site at www.nancykaramarkos.com.

1 **What qualities do you look for in an applicant?**

Other than a strong portfolio, someone who can problem-solve and seems capable of fitting in with the preexisting design style of the magazine/project. They should also bring new creative ideas to the table—that aren't too much of a departure from what's already being done—and a certain level of confidence in their own design abilities. They should be pleasant and capable of handling stressful situations.

2 **In your opinion, what makes a successful interview?**

When interviewing a potential new employee, I like to see a certain amount of interest from the candidate. They are responding positively to the job description that I'm giving and are able to suggest how they might handle some of the responsibilities. They might explain how a past experience would be helpful to how they approach this new job. I should have an easy rapport with this person and not feel as if our personalities would clash down the road. I have to feel that I can work with this person day in and day out and that they will fit in with the rest of the staff.

3 Has the Internet had an effect on your interview process?

The Internet has changed the way we post jobs and also search for new employees. I can post a job opening, and the résumés start pouring in immediately. If the applicant has their work online, I can view it within minutes and decide right away if that person could be a potential employee, without the hassle of calling in a large number of portfolios. On the other hand, if you're not prepared for the influx of résumés, it can clog your e-mail account. Also, because of the ease of sending your résumé over e-mail, I find that I get twice as many applicants and the majority of them are either over- or underqualified—applying because they have nothing to lose by sending their credentials. Also, candidates tend to get sloppy over e-mail. Grammar, spelling, and punctuation should be treated the same as a printed letter. If I see these kinds of mistakes, I delete that applicant's material. It shows me that they're not serious about the position.

4 What are the five best things job candidates say that impress you during an interview? What are the five worst?

Best: That they're exited about the job and don't act like it's a stepping-stone to the next job. That they are anxious to learn. They say something that shows me they can relate to the style of the magazine—either by a previous design experience they've had or by connecting with something they saw in the magazine. They say something that shows me they can handle the workload. They say something that shows me they'll be making a contribution to the existing style with either their sense of design or a creative imagination.

Worst: When asked, they don't really know what they want professionally. They don't relate with the magazine's content or the existing design style. They argue with me on a design point (really happened). They don't seem interested in the magazine—don't ask any questions or can't elaborate on any answers when questioned by me. They seem on the fence about how interested they are in the job.

5 What are skills that really help all artists succeed regardless of their specialty?

Ask questions. The writers/editors know you're not an expert on the topic to be designed. The designer should understand the product or service, get a sense of his or her audience, and then design accordingly.

You should explain why you decided on a certain style or layout. Whether you're selling it to a client or presenting it to an editorial staff, it's important for them to understand the thought process behind your work—especially if it's conceptual.

Offer more than one solution to a design problem. Sometimes sketching it out with the client helps with the brainstorming process. If they feel like they are involved with the design, you're more likely to have a successful outcome.

6 What advice would you offer to designers looking to impress you with the presentation of their work?

The presentation should be clean and neat. Don't put everything you've ever done in it, just the best. It should also have flow. Arrange them in an order that makes sense visually. Don't put all your best work up front. Your book should be strong from start to finish.

Add your own personal touch to your portfolio. Maybe you've designed interesting invitations for a personal occasion or you have a serious hobby in photography. These elements could be incorporated to show that you have broad design skills. But be careful. If you overdo it, it could create a negative effect. I once called in a beautiful portfolio that came in a gorgeous wooden box and all the design examples were reduced down to fit on small note cards. It was lovely, but the style was all wrong for what I was looking for. You should show a variety of styles in your work, but keep the overall look of your book interesting but neutral. You want the employer to imagine how your design talents will work for them.

Designer's Challenge 1

Create a menu design and support material for a restaurant. Craft the drink and dinner menus as well as the ads and business cards.

Kryztina Spence designs a series of collateral pieces for a restaurant called the Wild East Asian Bistro.

Designer's Challenge 2

Fashion a unique T-shirt design to promote yourself. It's time to advertise your design abilities. Utilize your logo or start from scratch and create an exceptional T-shirt.

Jamie Johnson shows off his unique self-promotional T-shirt creation.

14

Taking Interviews and Presenting Your Portfolio

The telephone rings. Someone from the human resources department at a company you're interested in working for is calling to set up a job interview. You've done it! You've landed the interview of your dreams.

Your résumé has done its work; now it's up to you, to the first impression you make personally, and to your portfolio. Showing your port is your big chance to demonstrate your accomplishments. But before you take that all-important interview, you must prepare. This chapter tells you how.

Preparing for a Job Interview

Preparation is the key to a successful job search. The more information you have about the potential employer, the better you can articulate your message. In addition, your knowledge of the company demonstrates that you are resourceful and have a genuine interest in the position.

Research the Company

No doubt about it, being called on an interview is cause for celebration. You're one of a select few to "make the first cut." But now you must distinguish yourself further. The first way to do this is to conduct research, to obtain knowledge that places you ahead of the pack. You want to find out as much about the company as you possibly can, about its goals and fiscal outlook. Here are some recommendations for successfully researching your potential employer.

Visit the Library

Everything you need to know about the company is in the library. Research librarians can help you to find all the relevant information. They can direct you to busi-

Kwesi Williams exhibits a superb package he has designed.

Gaby Menesses produces a memorable way for you to remember her. The unusual business card and painterly approach to her design are sure to catch an employer's attention.

ness providers such as Hoover's reports, which provide valuable business information on the top 750 companies, both public and private, in this country as well as on more than 40,000 of the world's top business enterprises. In addition, they detail events, strategies, and people that have impacted each company. Other business providers, such as Moody's Company Data and Morningstar, also are available to help you in your information quest.

Visit the Company's Web Site

Most advertising and design companies have a strong Web presence these days. Go online and check out the potential employer's site. What is the look of the company? Can you learn a bit about its style from its ads and layouts? Is your art compatible with what the company might be looking for? Can you tailor your port to feature pieces that your potential employer might be interested in? Don't just sit there. Start surfing!

Request a Copy of the Company's Annual Report

Larger companies will provide an annual report upon request, free of charge. Get it for the company you're interested in and read it. The report provides information about the company's direction and any current media coverage. It also gives details about the company's

financial condition and offers insight into its management philosophy.

You may be able to find the annual report online, typically in PDF format. These Web sites are a great place to start your research:

AnnualReports.com: www.annualreports.com
Annual Report Service:
    www.annualreportservice.com
The Public Register's Annual Report Service:
    www.prars.com

Iliena Popow explains that a trip to a dollar store led to the creation of this colorful self-promotional piece. The colors of the business card were designed to match the fish.

When an employer receives this self-promotional package from Bellatrix Martinez, the effect will be striking and immediate.

Financial Times (for European companies):
  http://ft.ar.wilink.com/asp/P003_search_ENG.asp
The Annual Reports Library: www.zpub.com/sf/arl

Visit Standard & Poor's Online

The Standard & Poor's Web site (www.standardand-poors.com) is a valuable research tool, especially for checking out private businesses, those that are not publicly traded on the open market. You'll also find biographies of thousands of corporate executives and directors, to help you identify the movers and shakers (and, if you're lucky, your eventual boss). There may even be additional information available on the company's customers and vendors.

Tailor Your Portfolio for Each Interview

I don't need to tell you that every job you apply for is different. So each item you place in your portfolio should reflect the requirements of the job at hand. If the position calls for someone with Web design skills, arriving with a selection of printed brochures will not impress the potential employer.

Turn a critical eye toward your work. Don't forget what I said earlier in the book: you will always be remembered by the weakest piece in your case, so pull

How badly do you want that interview, that job? Taking an unconventional approach might just do the trick. You want to stand out from the crowd, right? One student I know volunteered to work for a company for no pay for two weeks. She told her potential employers that if they didn't like her, then they didn't have to hire her. She got the job! Don't be afraid to offer something a little off-the-wall when applying for the job. Send a small box of paint and brushes when applying for that gallery position. Include a miniature floor plan or a toy house when applying for an interior design position.

I won a job using this approach myself once. While I was on a job interview, the prospective employer informed me that he wouldn't be making a decision for some time because he intended to interview other applicants. I informed him that there would be no additional applicants because I had removed the job ad from the wall in the employment office at my college. He hired me the next day!

For other ideas, check out books on self-promotion. You can find them in both the business and art sections of your local bookstore.

The job is his once this package from Philip A. Wolters is opened. The little duck holds his computer and is ready to start working!

People take summer vacations; you need a job. Sounds like a match to me! Merely because you've finished school for the academic year doesn't mean you should simply sit around. Find a summer job. There's a chance that your summer employment will contribute to your success in getting a real job later on. "What?" I hear you say. "I don't want to just stock shelves." Think of your employment opportunity with a store as product merchandising. You learned how to direct inventory and work with department heads. I once demonstrated crêpe makers at a local department store. Product demonstration shows that you can work with many different kinds of people in stressful situations. Even doing handiwork and dog-walking jobs around the neighborhood shows you have initiative. Here are some Web sites to get you started:

SummerJobs.com (www.summerjobs.com): Lists jobs with camps, amusement parks, resorts, national parks, hotels, and even environmental organizations by region.

SnagAJob.com (www.snagajob.com): Lists companies looking for summer employees so you can see at a glance what's out there.

GrooveJob.com (www.groovejob.com): Offers part-time jobs, student jobs, teen jobs, and hourly jobs. The information is arranged by zip code so you can find a job in your area. There's some good additional information on job skills, interviewing, and so forth.

Cool Works (www.coolworks.com): Helps you to find a seasonal job in such diverse areas as ski resorts, ranches, theme parks, tour companies, and camps.

studentjobs.gov (www.studentjobs.gov): Helps the federal government attract the best and brightest students who may later seek a government job.

jobsonline.net—a wonderful site that cross references by location and job description. You enter the information and the site lists what's available.

• Finding Your Way

If you are unsure of the address of the interviewing firm, go online to MapQuest (www.mapquest.com). Here you will find exact directions to any location in any city. Then take a test drive to the location ahead of time. Getting lost on the day of the interview will make you late, not to mention very nervous and anxious—neither of which will help you make that important good first impression. You want to be calm, cool, collected, and on time.

anything that you think won't "carry its weight" for the upcoming interview. Seriously outdated work may cast doubt on your current talents and skills, and this is no time to be sentimental about an old favorite piece. A polished and current portfolio is what you want. The more pieces you have to choose from, the more you can customize your port to make an impact on the interviewer.

How to Take a Successful Interview

Start with a positive attitude. Don't forget, you were chosen from a pool of many applicants. The job is yours to win. The secret to your success lies in careful preparation and effective communication. Believe in yourself and your abilities. Try to relax. An interview is an opportunity to present yourself and your work, not an interrogation. In this section, I'll walk you through a plan to help you get that great job.

Dress Appropriately

It is said that a job is won in the first six minutes of the interview. The point is, impressions are formed almost immediately. Therefore, your choice of clothing can make the difference. Always dress appropriately for the organization. You want to convey an image of professionalism, confidence, and ability. I have heard job candidates comment, "Why should I dress up? They're all artists, and everyone wears jeans." True, but they already have a job! Dress correctly now, and later, after you have the job, you may dress casually if that's accepted in the

Be prepared to talk about your work. You will be asked why you created a piece. This package was designed by Blanca Sanchez, who can clearly articulate her creative vision.

Joel Morales offers this graphic designer's survival kit. It comes equipped with markers and paint, and you won't soon forget his creative self-promotional.

company. In general, "correctly" means conservatively. Men should wear a jacket and tie, or a suit. Women should wear a skirt or pants suit, or a dress, or some other well-coordinated outfit. Neutral colors are the safest. And, ladies, take off wild nail polish, and leave the trendy shoes in the closet. Be conservative with accessories, your fragrance, and cosmetics. Don't wear jewelry that makes noise. It's distracting during an interview.

Lay out what you plan to wear the night before. Make sure your portfolio is ready to go. Then get a good night's rest.

Put Yourself in a Positive Frame of Mind

Plan your journey so that you can be sure to arrive 10 to 15 minutes before the interview. This gives you time to gather your thoughts, check out your surroundings, and relax. Look around for any literature available that might provide a little more information about the company.

Greet the receptionist with courtesy and respect. You never know, he or she may report your behavior to the employer. This is where you make your first impression.

While you are waiting, paint a positive mental picture, or play a mental movie, in which the interview goes perfectly. Imagine the interviewer asking questions that you answer with clarity and insight. For the ending of your "movie," imagine the interviewer telling you that you are the perfect person for the job. These are the types of visual images that you want going through your mind before the interview.

Make a Good First Impression

The employer reaches out to shake your hand. Stand up straight and offer a firm, full-handed handshake to men and women alike. Don't go to either extreme: neither

Over and over, I've heard my young designers lament, "I have no job experience. I've never had a job in design. Who will hire me?" I say, "You have more job background than you think!" Let's take a moment to consider your "other" skills. Are you a good multitasker? I bet you are! It's 3:00 a.m. Are you writing a paper and researching your topic on the Internet? Listening to your MP3 player and text-messaging your fellow students? Then you will be great at juggling multiple projects at work. Your ability to work full-time and take a full load of classes demonstrates that you know how to manage your time efficiently. Spend any time on Facebook and MySpace? This illustrates your social networking, not to mention communication skills. Have you ever collaborated on a school project? My college offers a campaign advertising class that prepares you to work in a group environment. Each group of five prepares a marketing campaign for a new product. The ability to work on a complex project proves that you are a team player who can work effectively in a large company. Sleep much? If you're a student with a full-time job, I'm guessing not. Even this shows that you will forgo the "nine-to-five-job" scenario in order to make deadlines. So the next time someone wonders whether you have the right skills, let him or her know that you are more than ready to take on the job!

Danielle D'Achille mixes it up with a combination of pink and black to create this outrageous promo piece.

In addition to your portfolio, bring extra résumés, business cards, and letters of reference with you to the interview. Include extra CDs or DVDs of your digital port to give out. You may wish to carry a notebook with your questions written in advance (more on your questions later in the chapter). This adds to your professional demeanor.

Interviews often begin with what's called an "open-ended icebreaker" question, such as "Tell me about yourself." Anticipate this and have an answer at the ready. Don't ramble on about your childhood. Practice an appropriate answer that, ideally, reveals your intelligence and sense of humor. Once you get past the first question, you'll find yourself beginning to relax.

Types of Interviews

Most interviews are either directive (structured) or nondirective (unstructured). In a directive interview, the employer asks a predetermined set of situational questions designed to gather specific information about your ability to handle the job. Nondirective interviews use probing, open-ended questions designed to allow you to do most of the talking. You will generally be exposed to a mixture of both types of questions in an interview. Both types are designed to help the interviewer learn more about your skills and personality.

Other interview methods include the stress-style interaction, used to determine how you react under

light and demure handshakes nor overpowering, knuckle-cracking handshakes are appropriate. The interviewer knows you are nervous, but you want to give the impression that you aren't.

Address the interviewer by title (Ms., Mr., Dr.) and last name. If you are unsure of the pronunciation, ask the receptionist how to pronounce the interviewer's name before going into the interview. (Better yet, you should call in advance of your interview date to find out.) Do not sit down until you are offered a chair. Sit up straight and make and maintain eye contact with the interviewer throughout.

Crystal Thomas presents this very organic and attractive way for you to remember her. Created completely from scratch, this package features her work, résumé, and business card.

pressure. You may, for example, be asked to role-play a client conflict or to take a timed test. Or you may find yourself in a group interview, which pits you against your competition. This type is often used to determine how you interact as a team member and thus can be very intimidating. A third type, the team interview, involves more than one interviewer questioning you. In this case, you will have to find a way to establish a connection with each person, so in this style of interview, direct eye contact is especially important.

Be aware that not all employers are adept at conducting interviews; sometimes, they are quite inexperienced at it or are just as uncomfortable as you are. When you find yourself in this situation, maintain your professionalism and practice effective interviewing techniques. You'll be rewarded with positive feedback and a good job offer.

Long before the interview begins, think of three factors that make you the best candidate for the job you're applying for. Somehow during the interview find a skillful way to inject those positive attributes—even if they don't directly answer a question asked.

With all that in mind, here are a few more insights on interviewing successfully:

- Smile. Banish negative thoughts. Don't let the phrase "What if they don't like me?" enter your mind.
- Take time to think before answering a question.
- Exude confidence.
- Avoid single-word responses such as "Yes" or "No."
- Acknowledge that you understand the questions you are being asked.
- Show enthusiasm.
- Don't use slang expressions. You are in the business of communication. Use professional language—not, "like, you know" or "uh."
- Don't fidget.
- Refrain from nervous habits such as playing with your hair or cracking your knuckles.
- Say nothing negative about past jobs, employers, or coworkers.
- Always present yourself in the best possible light.
- Never offer personal information.
- If you don't understand a question, say so. Ask the employer to please rephrase the question.

Presenting Your Portfolio

You'll probably start to wonder when is the best time to present your portfolio. Most likely, the opportunity will

Joana Lopez uses a box created from scratch to present her credentials. The materials were printed first; then the box was constructed to take full advantage of the design space.

arise naturally during the course of the interview. You might, for instance, be asked, "What did you do at your last job?" You could answer by saying, "Let me show you some of the projects I worked on while I was at XYZ Company." Or the potential employer might ask you directly to show your work, by saying, for example, "Have you brought work along today to show me?" or "Show me a sample of the projects you've worked on." Now's your chance! Open your case and begin explaining some of the pieces. If you have heeded the advice in this book, you are prepared with a detailed explanation for each of your pieces.

In other situations, the opportunity to display your work may come in a more subtle way. The interviewer may start discussing some of the company's current projects. At this point, you can say, "I have a couple of similar projects that I was involved in that I'd like to show you," or "I solved similar problems at my firm, and I'd like to show you how." And while you are showing your work, pay attention to the interviewer's body language. If he or she seems uninterested or shifts around a lot, it's time to move on to another piece. Do not feel that you must show every piece in the case.

One of the keys to negotiating a successful interview is to listen very carefully to the questions you are asked. If queried as to how you arrived at a solution for a piece, don't explain how it was made. That's not what you were asked. You may be asked whether the piece was

successful and satisfied the client. You might be questioned as to why you selected the colors you used. Whatever the question, answer it appropriately.

A word of warning: you won't be asked in every interview to show your portfolio. When this happens, don't take it personally. Some employers would rather hear you talk about your ideas or what you can do for the company.

Preventing Portfolio Presentation Problems—and Dealing with the Inevitable Glitches

You are so ready for this interview! You are appropriately dressed and are standing tall and confident; your design portfolio is in hand, and you feel ready to meet the challenge. The interview begins. Everything is going splendidly when you are asked to open your portfolio. You lift the case up onto the employer's desk, and as you unzip it, several of the pieces slip out of their sleeves and slide (in slow motion) to the floor. You are mortified.

Think this can't happen to you? Think again! An important aspect of preparing for the interview is to anticipate what can go wrong. You never know what kind of situation you will face when you step into an employer's office, so let's take a few minutes to design a game plan for handling possible problems.

If you have put your artwork in a sleeve-style portfolio, make sure the pieces are securely bound. Use small strips of tape to keep them from sliding around in their sleeves. Don't use big strips of tape or heavy-duty adhesive. You want to be able to replace older pieces with newer pieces to freshen up the work as necessary. If you

Marisabel Santana Castejon demonstrates her love of color in this piece, which clearly communicates her many interests.

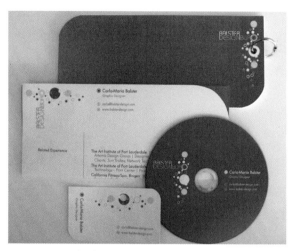

Every piece in this beautiful promotional package shows Carla-Maria Balster's attention to detail. Notice the clever way she holds the booklet together with a ring. This allows the observer to rotate the art freely.

have pieces that must be removed during the interview (such as slides or folders), create sleeves or pockets that will hold the work in place until needed.

If any of your work is mounted on boards and placed in a portfolio box, you face additional challenges. Ideally, you hope to be provided with a fairly large table on which to display the work to the interviewer. But what you may find instead is that the interviewer asks you to show the work on top of his or her desk, which is already overflowing with papers and materials. So practice in advance handling the boards under such awkward conditions, so you don't fumble around. In addition to looking unprofessional, you risk damaging your work. (In any case, you should plan to reprint and remount your work occasionally to keep it looking fresh.)

What about an electronic portfolio? What equipment should you bring to an interview for display purposes? In theory, you need only the CD or DVD; in actuality, that may not be the case. As I explained in Chapter 6, there are many issues to consider—monitor size, computer speed and memory, spin-up time of the CD or DVD, fonts, and colors. Some or all of these things may contribute to the success—or failure—of your presentation. Another problem to consider is software compatibility. You may have created your project in the latest version of the software, but will it run if the

interviewer's computer has an earlier version or doesn't have the same software at all?

It's a good idea to save the project in a backward-compatible version that is designed to play on older systems, especially if you employ a program not in widespread use. I once created for an interview a neat little multimedia show to describe my philosophy of education. To save money, I had used a shareware program. The project contained about 50 slides, which took quite a lot of time to run because the program embedded the slides in a way that consumed a great deal of computer memory. When I arrived at the interview (early, to make sure my program would run), I discovered that the machine the committee had set up for me to use was too old to work at all. I had to ask them to locate another computer. This delayed my interview as well as all subsequent interviews that day.

Even when you believe you've thought of everything, you may still run into problems. For example, a presentation designed to be backward-compatible can do weird things to your files (e.g., presentation created in the newest version of Flash may not open at all in a previous version of the same program). In some cases, files may open, but formatting problems may occur (such as strange-looking bullets or misaligned paragraphs or

Rebecca Molder makes use of a clear plastic carrying case to display her self-promotional piece. There's even a small side pouch to hold a pen with her name imprinted on it.

tabs); program scripts may not run; fonts may not appear—you get the idea.

Should you decide to bring a laptop computer with you to the interview, you can't be careful enough. Test your project on the machine well in advance, especially if it's not your computer. There may not be enough memory, or fonts may be missing. Don't take any chances. And don't forget about power. I once left for an interview, grabbed my laptop, and forgot to check the battery, only to discover that the computer had no power when I arrived at the interview. Worse yet, I had forgotten to bring along my power cord and had to ask the interviewer to find one for me. Not the best way to begin an interview.

Length and Breakdown of Interviews

First interviews normally take about an hour, although they can last much longer. Generally, you can expect approximately 30 percent of the interview to be spent discussing you and your qualifications and 70 percent discussing the company and the vacant position. Though this breakdown may seem unbalanced, studies bear it out. The first interview is generally regarded as a screening process, and your objective should be to leave the interviewer with the unmistakable impression that you want and can do the job.

Assuming you were successful at the first interview and are invited back for a second, in this one, you can expect to spend 50 percent of the time discussing yourself and your qualifications and 50 percent on the vacant position. This session will be clearly focused on you. Generally, the second interview is the final step before a job offer is (or is not) made and is generally conducted with the person you will be working for directly—your immediate supervisor.

The second interview frequently lasts longer, sometimes as much as an entire day. You may be given a tour of the work environment. You may also have an opportunity to talk with future fellow workers. Be very careful when speaking to these people—you never know who has the ear of your potential boss. More on the mechanics of the second interview later in this chapter.

Listen closely, and indicate by gestures and facial expressions that you understand each of the interviewer's remarks and questions. Questions at this stage are asked for very specific reasons. So think about why each question is being asked before you respond. If you have trouble formulating an answer, try a second approach. And make sure your message has been understood. It's perfectly acceptable to refer to your notes (or even take notes) in answering questions.

How would you describe your pieces during an interview? What would you say about the color choices and typography? Have your answers ready. Tiffany Braguta presents a lively color set to support these designs.

• Know Your Type!

If you are showing art pieces that feature type, be sure you know the names of the typefaces you used and be prepared to explain why you chose them. I once asked a student why he selected a particular typeface in the design. His reply was, "It's a new computer, and it only came with a couple of fonts, and I haven't had time to get any others." Not the answer a professional designer would give.

The employer will set the tone of the interview, but you should never miss an opportunity to sell yourself. It is your responsibility to make sure that everything important about your qualifications is covered during the interview.

• Reading Your Interviewer's Body Language

Is your interview going well? You may get some clues from your potential employer's body language. Eye contact and body position are just two of the telltale signs that things may not be going quite as well as you had hoped. If an interviewer is shuffling through papers or constantly checking the computer, then you may not be taking the best interview. It may be time for you to dial up your enthusiasm.

When you observe the interviewer leaning forward in the chair or you are making direct eye contact, the interviewer is fully engaged and things are looking up! A furrowed brow can signal displeasure, a slightly tilted head can indicate curiosity or interest. Arms folded across the chest is a defensive posture; stroking the chin can indicate a decision being made. A head resting in the hand, eyes downcast, may point toward boredom, and a hand stroking the cheek may signify evaluation and thinking. Learning to read your interviewer is just one more way you can lay claim to a successful interview.

• Do Some Role-playing

If you tend to get nervous in interview situations, a day or two before the meeting, ask a friend or family member to play the role of the prospective employer, using the list of questions provided later in this chapter. Practice your answers. Present your portfolio as part of this mock interview. The more you practice your answers, the more easily they will come during the actual interview. Experiment with different scenarios (disinterested interviewer, aggressive interviewer, etc.) to gain confidence as you discuss your work. Don't, however, try to memorize answers to possible questions. You will end up sounding stiff, and you will forget to listen.

Your Turn to Ask

At some point during the interview (generally, near the end), you will be asked if you have any questions. Be ready. This is your chance to show that you've done your homework. You want to sound intelligent, sincere, and interested. It is important that you have prepared some well-thought-out questions. The questions you ask can reveal as much about you as those asked by the interviewer. You may, of course, ask about salary and benefits during this time, but never make it your first question. Never ask about money issues early in the interview. Be careful not to ask a question the interviewer answered earlier. This will indicate you weren't paying attention during the interview; that said, don't hesitate to request clarification on anything you're not sure you understood earlier.

This is your last chance to point out any of your strengths not covered earlier or to stress important qualifications mentioned earlier. But don't go on and on. Make your points once and clearly; then state again that you are very interested in the job. Find a way to turn negatives into positives. If asked how you'll get up in the morning for an 8:00 a.m. job, explain how you learned to get to an early morning class on time—thus turning a potential negative into a positive. Finally, ask when you can contact the interviewer to follow up.

Here's a list of questions you may want to ask when given the opportunity in an interview. Also, use this list to trigger ideas for other questions you may want to ask.

- Why is this position open? Is it an existing post or a newly created position?
- Can you describe your company's corporate culture? Please describe a typical workday.
- What would you like done differently by the next person who fills this position?
- If I'm chosen to fill this job, what kind of projects can I expect to be involved in during the next three to six months?
- What gives your company the competitive edge over other firms in this field?
- What promotional opportunities are available within your company?
- Do you provide professional development and continuing education programs?

Always dress appropriately for an interview. When you dress up, you show respect for the potential employer.

- Would I be working independently or as part of a team?
- How many more candidates do you expect to interview?
- When would you need me to start work?
- Why did you come to work here?
- What particular computer equipment and software will be made available for my use?

Close the Interview and Follow Up

It's time for your big finish. If it hasn't already come up in the question-and-answer period of the interview, ask when the employer expects to make his or her decision. Then, as the interview concludes, make one last positive statement about your future with the company, such as one of the following:

- "I am really looking forward to working here."
- "May I contact you, or would you prefer to call me?"
- "Your company offers the kind of creative environment I would very much like to work in."

Be upbeat; never sound desperate. Stand, shake the interviewer's hand, and make your exit. Don't forget to thank the secretary or assistant on your way out.

Send a Thank-you Letter—Promptly

You had a great interview! To expand on that success, take the time to say thank-you and remind the interviewer that you're the perfect person for the job. As soon as possible, sit down and make some notes about the interview. These first few thoughts will become the basis for your thank-you letter. This letter is one more way to promote yourself to the company. It's also another opportunity to add any important information that you might have forgotten to mention. If you were interviewed by a team, send individual letters to each member. The letters can be essentially the same, but personalize them in some small way. If you do not hear from the company in a week or so, call the firm and ask about the status of your application.

Here are a few more interview follow-up tips:

- Don't procrastinate. Send your thank-you letter within one day.
- Print the letter on matching paper and envelope.
- Verify the correct spellings of names and titles of each person who interviewed you.
- Express your appreciation for the opportunity to meet with people from the company, but don't gush.
- Tailor the letter to the company. Don't send a generic letter. If you noticed something that was particularly interesting about the company during your visit, point it out.

Here is a sample thank-you letter. Notice that it has been created in a standard business format, with name, address, and date at the top and the addressee's name and address on the left just above the salutation.

Cory Gershberg creates a dynamic display. Notice the way the art is mounted on black boards to stand up in the background.

Alan Courtland
2710 3rd Court
Glenwood, FL 32722
(305) 555-1234
Courtland@yahoo.com
May 18, 2009

Mr. Robert Samuels
All Design, Inc.
3720 SW 12th Street
Altamonte Springs, FL 32716

Dear Mr. Samuels,

Thank you for taking the time to meet with me to discuss the graphic designer position at All Design, Inc. I was very impressed by the quality of service your company provides and am convinced that my design abilities would fit well with your current needs.

I appreciate that you spent so much of your time with me. Now that I have met you and some of your colleagues, and know more about the activities of All Design, Inc., I am even more excited about the possibility of working with you and your team of designers. The high level of creative energy among your artists, as well as their personal pride in the company, was evident in all of them. I feel that I would definitely be a worthwhile addition to your company.

Again, thank you for your time and consideration. I look forward to hearing from you.

Sincerely,
Alan Courtland

Second-interview Structure

If you have been invited for a second interview, it's a clear indication that the employer believes you have all the skills and credentials necessary to fill the open position. The second interview is conducted to determine more specifically how good a "fit" you are on a more personal basis. You can expect the second interview to last significantly longer than the first. During this time, you may be introduced to many of the upper-management people and other coworkers and be given a tour of the premises. This is a great opportunity to ask any questions that you didn't raise the first time or that occurred to you after you left.

As during the first interview, you want to be relaxed during the second one, but keep your energy level high and your attention focused for the duration. And be prepared to discuss salary during the second interview if it was not discussed during your first visit.

Bring extra résumés and business cards with you for the second interview, in case you are asked to give them to other management-level staff you meet. (Hand them out only when asked, however.) Probably your résumé has already been given to the key staff, but it's always a good idea to come prepared. You will look professional and considerate.

Interviewing: A Two-way Street

Getting a job is a lot like getting married. You and your new company want to be productive, work well together, and grow together. So before you take that "walk down the aisle," it is critical that both of you find out as much as possible about each other. In a personal relationship, nothing is off-limits when it comes to the kinds of questions people ask each other; in a professional environment, however, there are restrictions as to what an employer can ask a job candidate, and you need to be aware of those.

Handling Inappropriate Questions

The interview is going so smoothly that you are starting to think that the job may be yours. Then, in the middle of the process, comes the question "Are you planning on getting pregnant anytime soon?" or "Will your religion prevent you from working weekends or holidays?" These types of questions, and many others, though perhaps asked innocently enough, are prohibited by law in interview situations. These restrictions are spelled out in the Equal Employment Opportunity Commission (EEOC) guidelines, which you can learn about online at www.eeoc.gov/abouteeo/overview_practices.html.

If this happens to you, be aware that illegal questions are usually asked in ignorance—that is, the person isn't aware he or she has ventured into "protected areas." In this case, probably the best approach is to change the subject as delicately as you can, perhaps by saying something along the lines of, "I'd like to review the subject of office hours." This is not the time to assert your constitutional rights. By changing the subject, you give the interviewer the chance to realize that he or she said something incorrect and will let the matter drop.

If, however, you feel that the question was asked intentionally (unfortunately, as we all know, discrimination still exists), you have every right to terminate the interview. Here are examples of topics that, if asked about, might be interpreted as discriminatory:

- Race, creed, color, religion, sexual orientation, or national origin
- Marital status
- Disabilities of any kind
- Health or medical history
- Age or date of birth (unless you are under 16)
- Date and type of military service
- Pregnancy, birth control, and child care
- Psychiatric treatment, drug addiction, or alcoholism
- Arrest record (You may, however, be asked about a conviction if the question is accompanied by a statement saying that a conviction will not necessarily disqualify you for employment.)

Questions You Must Be Prepared to Answer

Your résumé offers information, and your portfolio speaks volumes, about your professional qualifications, but the bottom-line reason a company conducts personal interviews is to find out which candidate is a good match for the company. To determine that, employers typically ask a number of similar questions, some serious and others that might seem quirky to you. But when you know the intent behind these questions, you can better prepare your answers.

Here you'll find a sampling of questions in this arena, along with possible responses. The point is not to memorize these answers but to jump-start your thoughts as to how you might respond during your interview.

Tell me about yourself. Take a couple of minutes to discuss your education, work experience, and recent accomplishments. Don't ramble on about unrelated topics.

Where do you want to be five years from now? When I was asked this during an interview, my response was, "I want to be president of NBC." This is a question that begs a more unconventional response. Resist the temptation to say, "I want your job," which will not be taken well.

What are your weaknesses? For this tough question, it is always best to turn a negative into a positive, responding, for example, "I sometimes expect too much of myself" or "I am too hardworking."

What did you dislike about your last job? Under no circumstances complain about former bosses or coworkers. Rather, say something along the lines of, "The job was not challenging enough," or "There wasn't enough opportunity for advancement."

What was the last book you read? What was the last movie you saw? The point here is to demonstrate that you know the importance of striking a balance between your professional and personal life. Don't be afraid to reveal that you like scary movies or mushy romantic novels.

Why do you want to work for this company? "Because I want to work for the best company. I've done my research, and yours is the best!" Then describe the positive attributes of the firm. (You have done your research, right?)

What can you offer us that no one else can? This is no time to be modest. Tell the employer about your successful projects, your triumphs, and your leadership roles. Make it clear to the employer that you have healthy self-esteem and confidence in your abilities.

What kind of working environment are you looking for? Your answer should reflect your research on the company. If the company is a small one, your answer might be, "I prefer to work for smaller companies where my skills can really impact the company directly." A larger company requires a different answer, such as, "I want to work for a

Fernando Velasquez uses a set of Lucite stands to display his business cards and self-promotional pieces.

larger company where I have plenty of opportunities for advancement."

What other companies have you interviewed with? Be aware that you do not have to divulge any specifics about your job search. You can say that you have been on several other interviews and are still waiting to hear the results. If you have been offered a job and didn't accept it, you can reveal this as well, but be prepared to say why you turned it down. Don't be critical; just say that you believe that this company would be much better for you. By the way, if you have been on a lot of interviews, do not divulge that, as it might give the impression that no one is interested in you.

If you could start over, what would you do differently? This is a trick question. Do not answer with a negative comment such as, "I would never have gone to work at ABC Graphics if I had known they were going to fire me." Focus on some minor event that will not reflect adversely on the job you are applying for, such as "I wish I had decided to study art earlier," or "Actually, I'm pretty happy with my decisions so far."

Other Questions You Should Know How to Answer

Many common interview questions are designed to get you to reveal aspects of yourself or your personality that you might not be expecting. Here is a list of some very

Lucite stands are normally used to hold miniature paintings. These small stands from the local craft store provide a great way to support these three-dimensional pieces created by Maribelle Romero.

popular questions that might come up and that you should be prepared to answer:

- What are your goals in life?
- What are you good at? What are you bad at?
- What kind of person are you?
- Why did you leave your last job?
- How do you work with others?
- Do you prefer to work in teams or alone?
- What motivates you?
- How have you changed as an artist in the last couple of years?
- How do you deal with stress?
- What would you do if a coworker didn't like you?
- What would your friends say about you?
- What would your coworkers say about you?
- What, to you, constitutes the ideal work environment?
- What has been your biggest problem at work, and how have you handled it?
- What would you like to make as a salary?
- If you weren't doing this, what you like to do?
- How are you at dealing with people?
- What additional training would you like to receive?
- What do you most look forward to in a job?
- What makes you think you can succeed in this job?
- Why should we employ you instead of someone else?
- We sometimes have difficult deadlines. Are you available to work after hours?
- Do you have any hobbies?

- Are you currently a member of any clubs or charitable organizations?
- What do you do when you're not working?
- How would you describe your management skills?
- Do you consider yourself a leader or a follower?
- Where else have you applied for a job? (You don't have to answer this.)
- Have you taken any other interviews?
- If we offer you this job, how much notice would you have to give your current employer?
- Have you ever traveled outside this country?
- What other languages do you speak?
- Do you have any questions at this time?
- How would you describe yourself?
- What subjects did you like best (or least) in college?
- What do you know about our company?
- What three things are most important to you in your job?
- What is your philosophy of design?
- How would you describe success?

Responding to a Job Offer

The phone rings. You pick it up and say, "Hello." The voice at the other end says, "Ms. Radford, we'd like to offer you the position at Creative Design." Now the job is yours—if you want it. Not all offers are made over the telephone, however; some are made in writing or during the second interview. By this time, you should

Here is a lovely self-promo piece designed by Julisa Henriquez, using colors, circles, and leaves as a theme. Notice that even the jelly beans are color-coordinated to match.

know whether this is the job you want. Unless you are waiting to hear about another (possibly better) job, it's time to make a commitment. If you are holding out for another job you prefer over this one, don't act in haste or you may regret it later. It's perfectly acceptable to ask for time to think about the offer—in which case, ask when you need to get back to the company with your answer.

If you decide you want the job, and salary was not discussed in a previous meeting, now is the time to express your desire to negotiate your salary. Whatever you decide to do, respond in writing to the offer as soon as possible. If you accept the offer over the telephone, a letter of acceptance is still in order. If you are no longer interested in the job, say so. Don't say, "I'll get back to you," and not do it. Not only is this very rude, but it may also come back to "bite" you, as you might want to work for this firm in the future.

An Interview with Rick Tuckerman

Rick Tuckerman graduated with a BBA from Temple University. Mr. Tuckerman served as vice president of marketing for a large financial institution in Miami before opening his agency in 1989. He currently acts as owner/creative director of his agency and is working on accounts in gaming, entertainment, health care, real estate, finance, and retail. You can visit the Web site of Rick Tuckerman's company at www.zoomIQ.com.

1 What qualities do you look for in an applicant?

The obvious answer would be a good portfolio. After all, this is a job where your work takes precedence over *almost* everything else. However, while many students think the job is all about sitting in front of a computer, many creative jobs entail interacting with clients and vendors, and in that case, the ideal candidate will have other qualities that range from a professional demeanor to presentation skills (being able to articulate their ideas in a compelling fashion, having a certain amount of presence, conveying knowledge and trust, etc.). In addition to creating great work, the ability to sell your ideas will ultimately determine whether you can succeed in this business.

2 In your opinion, what makes a successful interview?

First and foremost, being professional about the process. Prior to the interview, I like to see the applicant confirm the appointment. Then, of course, show up on time. (Sounds obvious, but many applicants do not.) Most employers are looking for a designer who wants to cut right to the chase and see the work. There is a fine line between letting the work speak for itself and going overboard on describing the rationale behind it. I have interviewed students who present the rationale nicely, and then the end product is disappointing. The opposite situation (the work is great, but the communication skills are light) offers much more potential to me because I feel we can develop their presentation skills, not their creative skills. My feeling is that they either have it, or they don't. They either get it, or they don't. And if it's the latter, they may never get it. Finally, in the interview, I think it's important to show attributes every employer wants to see, regardless of the position. These include enthusiasm, asking interesting questions, asking to see some of the work of the agency, having some knowledge of the firm beforehand, conveying your commitment to the firm, responding truthfully to questions about your level of knowledge. (No one expects a student to have all the answers, but I would like to see the applicant show that they have the initiative to find the answers.)

3 Has the Internet had an effect on your interview process?

It has had an impact on sourcing out applicants—via Monster.com, for example. You can quickly see whether an applicant has what you are looking for. Unfortunately, though, as mentioned earlier, what we'd really like to see is their work before inviting them in for an interview. We suggest the student include a link to their online portfolio, which helps us determine whether it's a good fit.

4 What are the five best things job candidates say that impress you during an interview? What are the five worst?

Best

1 I appreciate your allowing me to come in for an interview.
2 My passion is creative.
3 I have a great work ethic. I am very meticulous when it comes to my work.
4 I understand that this is a deadline-oriented business, and when the pressure's on, I rise to the occasion.
5 I want the job. (Sounds obvious, but a lot of students are not bold enough to be that direct.)

Worst

1 What are your working hours? (They are probably looking for a nine-to-five job, and it doesn't exist in this business.)
2 Asking almost no questions of the interviewer.
3 Spending too much time talking about personal issues. (Read: They'll bring a lot of drama with them to the job.)
4 I have another job offer, but before I took it, I thought I'd hear what you have to say. ("Good-bye" is what I'd say.)
5 Not shaking my hand at the conclusion.

5 What are skills that really help all artists succeed regardless of their specialty?

- Enthusiasm, presence, communication skills.
- Being fast with your work. Computers have given clients the misconception that everything happens by just pressing a few buttons.

6 What advice would you offer to designers looking to impress you with the presentation of their work?

Practice. Don't just flip pages in your portfolio; take a moment to describe why you like the work you've done. Remove anything in your portfolio that you don't feel is representative of your best work. Be organized and neat.

Designer's Challenge 1

Design a poster that teaches a lesson about color. Include one famous quote on the subject. Be sure to include the name of the author of the quote and any other critical information such as the sponsoring organization.

Abbey Fortney presents an entertaining and colorful solution to the designer's challenge to design a poster.

Designer's Challenge 2

Sketch and design a complicated package for a "client." The package should feature a unique set of folds and be sturdy enough to hold the product contained within. All appropriate information must be included on the package.

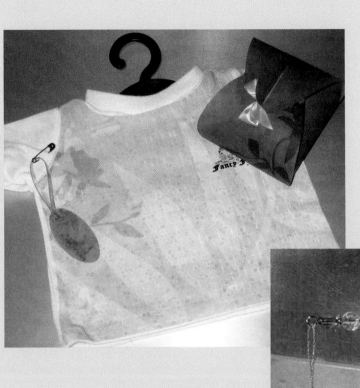

Iliena Popow shows her advanced skills in designing packages. Notice the added elements, such as the "jewelry" and the key chain.

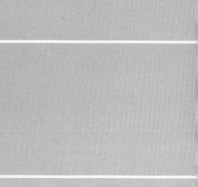

glossary

24-bit: Describes a scanned file or preview image made up of RGB color information. An 8-bit-per-pixel card can generate 256 colors; 24 bits per pixel yields 16.8 million colors.

Accomplishments: Your achievements. The job duties or responsibilities that set you apart from everyone else. Always highlight your accomplishments in your cover letter and résumé.

ActionScript: An object-oriented programming language developed for use in its Flash animation program. The language is designed to work most effectively with vector-based graphics, but it can also work with raster-based files.

Action verbs: Descriptive verbs used to express talents, experience, or accomplishments. Choose action verbs when you are describing your outstanding skills.

Address: In this context, the series of letters and numbers by which the Internet identifies you or the location where information is stored. Examples include your e-mail and Web addresses.

Adobe Type 1 fonts: Developed by Adobe in the early 1980s, Type 1 technology uses the PostScript page description language (PDL) to render fonts on the screen and in print. Type 1 fonts have two parts: the screen font and the printer font. Both must be present on the computer in order for a file to render (print) properly.

Alignment: The shape of the text block in relation to the page margins. Type can be set to left alignment (sometimes called flush left), right alignment (sometimes called flush right), center alignment, justified alignment, and force-justified alignment.

Analog signal: A signal based on an alternating current. The current is then modified in some way, usually by varying the frequency, in order to add information. Broadcast and telephone transmissions have conventionally used analog technology.

Analogous colors: Any three colors next to one another on the color wheel. An example of analogous colors would be red, red-orange, and orange.

Annual report: A corporate document that provides important information to the stockholders about a company. This information includes details about the company's financial status and offers insight into its management philosophy.

Application: A program or software that tells the computer to do what you want it to do. Examples include Safari, FireFox Navigator, Microsoft Internet Explorer, HTML editors, Flash, and QuickTime.

Artist's statement: A short essay written to help potential employers understand what you believe to be the most important aspects of your art. It may also discuss techniques and artistic influences.

Ascender: The part of a lowercase letter that rises above the main body of the letter, such as on the letters b, f, and h.

Background check: A procedure used by companies to verify the information provided by an applicant on his or her application form. The information verified can include employment, educational background, and references.

Bandwidth: The amount of data that can be sent from one computer to another through a particular connection in a certain amount of time. The higher the bandwidth, the faster your page will load.

Benefits: Your compensation package. The medical benefits, life insurance, sick leave, holidays, vacation, stock options, and retirement plan are all part of your salary negotiation. A good benefits package can add up to 40 percent of your salary.

Bindery equipment: A machine used to fasten paper together. There are many different types of bindery machines on the market. They vary by price and features.

Binding: The methods used to hold various amounts of paper together. These include:

- *Saddle-stitch binding:* One or more staples are inserted in the center of a page.
- *Side-stitch binding:* One or more staples are placed on the side of the page. Not as professional-looking as saddle stitching.
- *Perfect binding:* All pages are pressed together on one side. Once the pages are flat, glue is applied on the outside edge.
- *Case binding:* All pages are glued to a gauze strip, then glued again to endpapers. The endpapers are attached to a hard cover. Books are produced using this technique.
- *Plastic comb binding:* Plastic teeth are inserted into a series of tiny holes (square or round) in a stack of paper. The spines can be removed easily as needed. Very inexpensive, but not as professional as perfect binding.

- *Three-ring binder:* The standard binder that comes with three metal rings. Used primarily for reports and found in most stores.

Bit: The smallest unit of computer information. The value of a bit is 1 or 0.

Bitmap: A digital graphic image that consists of a map of dots or squares. Each square has a color value represented by either 1 bit (simple black and white) or up to 32 bits (high-definition color). Bitmaps include GIF, JPEG, and other file formats, which can be read by such programs as Adobe Photoshop and Corel Painter.

Bookmark: In this context, a method of saving a Web site location to an electronic "address book." Creating bookmarks allows you to return to previously visited Web addresses.

Broken link: A link or hyperlink that doesn't work when the user clicks on it. This generally occurs because the designer didn't properly establish the link. Broken links can also occur if the Web site is temporarily unavailable.

Browser: A program that allows users to visit and access information on the World Wide Web. Popular browsers include FireFox, Safari, and Internet Explorer.

Buffer size: The access time or the speed by which data is made available to your computer for processing from a CD or DVD.

Bug: A programming code error that causes a program or computer system to perform unpredictably or, in some extreme cases, crash.

Cache: The area of your computer's memory where temporary data is stored. The information stays as long as the computer is turned on. Cache memory allows you to hit the Back button to return to previously visited sites.

Capture video: To convert video from a standard analog signal into digital format.

Career change: Progressing from one area of specialization to another. The act of gathering information in order to synthesize, gain competencies, make decisions, set goals, and take action. Most experts agree that the average person will change careers three to five times during his or her lifetime, for a wide variety of reasons, including boredom, downsizing, and relocating.

Career fairs: Special events in which employers from many different companies come to interview candidates and fill positions. There are many types of job and career fairs, from generalized ones that a city might hold to industry-specific ones for professionals.

Career objective/job objective: A concise statement about your accomplishments or job goals. This is not a required part of the résumé, but used wisely, it can direct the employer's attention to the specifics of your focus.

Career planning: The process of appraising your skills, personality, and career path in order to make informed decisions about future employment.

Cascading Style Sheets (CSS): A system complementary to HTML that allows style features (color, font size, spacing, and page layering) to be specified for certain elements. CSS is excellent for making a global change to multiple Web pages.

CD-ROM: Abbreviation for "compact disc read-only memory." An optical digital storage device, capable of holding about 650 megabytes of information.

CD-ROM read/write speed: The maximum rate at which a CD drive records data to a disc. The read (or transfer) rate is how fast the drive reads data off a disc. The speed of the drive is historically compared to music CDs, where 1X, or 1 speed, gives a data-transfer rate of 150 kilobytes per second.

CD-RW (rewritable compact disk): Similar to a CD, except that a CD-RW disc can be written and erased up to 1000 times.

Chronological résumé: See Résumé.

Clip art: Royalty-free images that can be brought into art programs and presentation applications. Clip art can be edited or used as is. Additional images, including some in bitmap format, are available from commercial suppliers and online.

CMYK: The four process colors used in printing: cyan, magenta, yellow, and black. When printed, these four colors appear to the naked eye as full color.

Cold call: Contacting a potential employer without first sending a cover letter and/or a résumé. This is one way of uncovering jobs that might not otherwise be advertised.

Color space: The range, or gamut, of colors available to a viewer. The color space for a graphic designer is CMYK (cyan, magenta, yellow, and black).

Compact disc (CD): A relatively small optical disc on which text, data, sounds, and visual images can be recorded with laser technology. The discs themselves can be "burned" only once.

Complementary colors: Two colors directly opposite each other on the color wheel. Red and green are complements of each other.

Compression: A system that reduces the size of multimedia files while attempting to maintain acceptable quality. There are many different compression systems, or codecs (compression/decompression), on the market; the most widely used are Sorenson and Cinepak.

Copyright: The rights to an original literary, artistic, or musical work held by an individual or a corporation. Additional rights may be gained in such areas as film, broadcasting, computer programs, trademarks, and many other forms. Unauthorized use of copyrighted materials is punishable by law, and the punishments can include fines and/or imprisonment.

Corporate culture: The behaviors, routines, and regulations dictated by company policy and adhered to by employees. Corporate culture can refer to both formal and informal company policies concerning everything from dress code and employee relationships to breaks, social interactions, and professional hierarchy. It is important to learn about a company's culture before you accept a position, to make sure you will fit in and be happy.

Cost per click (CPC): In Web advertising, the amount an advertiser will pay each time a visitor clicks on an ad.

Counteroffer/counterproposal: An offer made by a potential employer that counters an offer you have proposed. The negotiations begin with the employer's first offer. If you wish, you may make a counteroffer in hopes of securing a higher salary or more benefits. The employer then counters that to make yet one more offer. This is generally used to arrive at a compromise when the employer and employee are far apart in salary range. It can involve money, benefits, or special job perks (such as a company car).

Cover letter: An introductory document in which you briefly tell the employer about your interest in the job and highlight important reasons why you would be the most qualified candidate. A cover letter should always accompany your résumé.

Cover sheet: A piece of paper used to add short comments about a work. The cover sheet generally provides a brief explanation of the purpose or artistic style of the work or the scope of a project.

CSS (Cascading Style Sheets): A language used to describe how HTML documents should be formatted. The term *cascading* derives from the fact that multiple style sheets can be applied to the same Web page. CSS was developed by the World Wide Web Consortium.

Cut: A quick shift from one video shot to another.

Declining letter: A letter sent to an employer to turn down a job offer. It is considered a courtesy to submit a formal refusal when a job is offered that you are not accepting. You never know when you might want to work for that company in the future!

Degrees and certifications: Official recognition bestowed upon a student upon completion of a program of study. These may come from workshops, trade schools, colleges, and universities.

Descender: The part of a lowercase letter (such as g, j, or p) that descends below the main body of the letter.

Dial-up connection: The capability to connect to the Internet through a land-based telephone line. It is the most common form of Internet connection.

Directive (or structured) interview: Interview in which a predetermined set of situational questions is asked. These questions are designed to gather specific information about your ability to handle the job.

Display type: Large, bold, or special fonts typically used to command attention, also called novelty or decorative type. Display type is designed to imitate brushstrokes or handwriting techniques. Decorative initial capital letters also fall into this category.

Dissolve: A slow transition from one video shot to another. Both shots are blended together for a brief period of time.

Document source: The HTML code created to generate a Web page. Many Web sites allow you to "view the source code" of the pages, although sometimes the code is hidden to protect the designer's copyright.

Domain name: The "zip code" in a Web address. A domain name directs a request for a Web site or an e-mail to its final destination. A domain name is always composed of two words or phrases, separated by dots—for example, yahoo.com.

Dots per inch (dpi): A measure of resolution for printers, scanners, and displays. Magazines are typically printed at 300 dots per inch. Large-scale commercial typesetters (e.g., for fancy catalogs) can print at about 1200 dpi.

Download: The transfer of files from one computer to another or from the Web to your own computer.

Dress for success: The idea that what you wear should reflect a professional attention to detail. Dressing properly will give you a competitive edge by making a positive first impression.

DVD: Abbreviation for "digital video disc." An optical digital storage device, capable of holding about 4.7 gigabytes of information. Whereas CDs use only one side, DVDs can be recorded on both sides as well as in dual layers. DVD drives/players read most CD media as well.

E-commerce: Conducting commercial transactions on the Internet, where goods, information, or services are bought and then paid for.

E-mail address: An electronic postal address. An e-mail address consists of a series of characters, such as gail@yahoo.net, that uniquely identifies the mailbox of a person who can send and receive electronic mail.

Electronic or digital résumé: A résumé that is created on a computer with the intent of transmitting it electronically. It is traditional in format but is generally sent to the employer via e-mail or is posted at a Web site.

Em dash: Dash that is the same width as the point size of a particular font.

Employment gaps: Periods of time when you can show no employment. Whatever the reason—illness, pregnancy, or other circumstances—it is important to be able to account for these gaps in your work history.

An interviewer will notice them and ask for an explanation. You should have an answer.

En dash: Dash that is half the width of an em dash.

Encode audio: To compress and prepare audio for the final output.

Extensible markup language (XML): A variation of HTML that is suitable for use on the World Wide Web.

Facebook: A social-networking Web site. Visitors can choose to join one or more participating networks, such as colleges and universities, place of employment, or geographic region.

Flowchart: A diagram or visual mapping that shows a step-by-step progression of a plan. It can be a simple (or more complex) drawing that maps out the way your portfolio will be navigated.

Flush mounting: A method of placing art on a page by gluing it directly on the page with no extra protection (such as a mat). The drawback is that the art is not fully protected (unless it is placed inside a sleeve as well).

Font: A complete assortment of letters, numbers, and symbols of a specific size and design—for example, Times Roman Bold Italic 12 point.

Force-justified: Refers to type that is stretched to fill the entire text block in relation to the page margins. Force-justifying can make text difficult to work with and cause awkward rivers of white on the page.

Freelance (independent contractor or consultant): A self-employed person who pursues his or her profession (frequently in the arts) under no long-term contractual commitments to any one employer or company. Many people enjoy the freedom, flexibility, and satisfaction of working for themselves. Although they do not receive company benefits, freelancers can negotiate their own terms and compensation for their work.

Freeware: Software that is usually written by programmers for fun or eventual profit. It is generally distributed via the Internet.

FTP (file transfer protocol): A method for transferring files between computers over a network.

Functional résumé: See Résumé.

Gigabyte: A unit of measurement for either information or memory. It refers to 1 billion bytes of information. Used to describe storage capacity.

Global design: A design system in which links or categories appear on every page of an interface.

Glossy paper: Paper that has a shiny coating, such as that typically used to print photographs. It is excellent for high-resolution digital images.

Graphic interchange format (GIF): One of two popular file formats for graphics on the Internet (the other is JPEG). GIF files have a limit of 256 colors and provide sharper black-and-white images than JPEGs. GIF is popular because it reduces image file size without losing any information in the process. There are three different GIF types: (1) Animated GIF (GIF89a) allows storage and playback of a sequence of still images to create the illusion of animation. (2) Transparent GIF enables a designer to designate a color (usually the background) of an image to be transparent. Only GIFs can accomplish this. (3) Interlaced GIF enables progressive rendering of images, meaning that the focus slowly sharpens to reveal the entire picture. Interlacing indicates to the viewer that the image is loading.

Graphical Interface (or user interface): An interface based on graphics instead of text. A typical interface relies on a series of icons and pictures and uses a keyboard and mouse as input devices.

Headline: The title of an article or a story; words used to introduce or categorize.

Hierarchical design: A design system in which large amounts of information are grouped into major sections or under major headings.

Highlight color: A color chosen to emphasize a particular section of a design. It is usually a color selected to contrast with the primary and secondary colors.

Hit: Request of a file from a Web server. A request for a Web page counts as a hit, but so does a request for a graphic on a Web page.

Home page: The top-level, or main, page of an electronic interface. This is the starting place for an individual or a subject area.

Hue: The name of a distinct color of the spectrum— red, green, yellow, orange, blue, and so on. Hue refers to the main attribute of a color that distinguishes it from other colors.

Hypertext markup language (HTML): A set of tags and rules used to design hypertext documents for the World Wide Web.

Hypertext Preprocessor (also known as PHP): A scripting language used to create dynamic Web pages such as shopping carts.

Icon: A stylized graphic symbol designed to represent something, such as a file, program, Web page, or command.

Image file formats: The common graphics file formats. GIF and JPEG are the formats used in Web design. TIFF and EPS are the most common file formats used in publishing.

Image map: A graphic that contains several "hot spots," or invisible buttons that link to other pages. For example, an image map of the world might contain links to Europe, Asia, South America, and the United States.

Image optimization: The process of making your images suitable for the Web. The main factors that influence the display of graphics for the Web are the size, physical dimensions, and bit depth of the image.

Index color: A color system that minimizes the number of colors and file size of a graphic image to 8 bits or less. Used primarily for Web design.

Interframe: A compression method. Inter means "between two," so compression occurs between consecutive video frames.

Internet: A vast collection of interconnected computers linked together through a series of networks throughout the world.

Internet protocol (IP) address: The numbers that are translated into a domain name. The address is a string of four groups of numbers separated by periods (such as 111.22.3.444) used to represent a computer or other device on the Internet.

Intraframe: A compression method. Intra means "within," so compression is done within a single video frame.

Italic: The slanted version of a typeface.

JavaScript: A programming language for use in Web pages that allows for user interaction. An example is filling out a form to get more information about a product or service.

Jewel cases: Small, hinged plastic cases used to store CDs. They come in a variety of colors and sizes.

Job application: A form used to document an applicant's qualifications for a job. Although many of the questions on a typical application may seem to request information that duplicates what appears on your résumé, the form is required by most company human resources departments.

Job board: A place where positions are listed. It might be within a particular company or in a general area such as at the job placement office of the local college. Jobs are generally sorted by profession. A job board may also be posted at a specific organization's Web site.

Job interviewing: The process of presenting an applicant's credentials and qualifications for a particular position. The idea is to make the best possible match between the employer and the employee. There are many different styles of interviews, but they all give you a chance to present yourself and your work for consideration.

Job skills: Your capabilities, knowledge, and talents that add up to your ability to do the job.

Joint Photographic Experts Group (JPEG): The standard for storing images in compressed form. JPEGs can contain up to 24 bits of color information (16.7 million colors), making them more desirable (but larger) than GIF files. However, most computer monitors are capable of displaying only 8-bit color.

Kbps (kilobits per second): Used as a rating of relatively slow transmission speed.

Kerning: The fine-tuning or adjustment of the space between individual characters in a line of type. Kerning is especially important with large display type. Without these adjustments, many letter combinations can be poorly spaced.

Key accomplishments: A summary list on your résumé of your most significant activities and achievements. This is an important section of your résumé, as it highlights the work you have done for past employers.

KHz (kilohertz): One thousand cycles per second. A unit of measure for signal bandwidth.

Kilobyte: A kilobyte is 1,024 bytes of data. Most users refer to the term as a "K," as in the disc holds 1K of information.

Leading: The vertical space between lines of type. It is measured from baseline to baseline. Generally, the leading is at least the size of the type, although it is usually more generous. For example, 12-point type would be matched with 15-point leading. Type with a generous amount of space between lines is said to have "open leading," and type with relatively little space between lines is said to have "tight leading."

Letter of acceptance: A document you provide that states in writing that you approve of a job offer. It's very important that you answer a job offer in writing, to restate the dates, conditions, and salary structure of the offer.

Letter of agreement: A document provided by the employer offering you a job. It details the dates, conditions, and salary structure of the offer.

Letter of recommendation: A document written on your behalf in support of your statement of job skills and work ethic. It is usually written by a former professor, boss, coworker, or friend.

Line length: The width of a typeset line, typically the area between the left and right margins. Longer line lengths are thought to be more difficult to read.

Lingo: An object-oriented animation scripting language developed by Macromedia (now Adobe) for use in its Director authoring animation program. Lingo is designed to work most effectively with vector-based graphics, but it can also work with raster-based files.

Link: An association established between two Web pages, also called a hypertext link. A graphical icon is usually used to show that a connection is available. An accepted way to navigate digital interfaces.

Local design: A hybrid of the hierarchical and global design systems. It groups a lot of information into broader categories.

Logos and trademarks: Symbols, usually composed of letters and/or shapes, that identify companies, organizations, products, and so on. Logos are crucial for name recognition and branding.

Margin: The white space that surrounds text blocks on all four sides of a page: top and bottom, left and right.

Marker: A prompt created to act as a position holder for moving within an authoring program. Markers are created to assist in programming.

Master file: An original file. A master file should never be altered in any way.

Matte paper: Paper that has a soft, lusterless surface, used to print images with a more subdued feeling.

Matting (or mat boards): A mounting process whereby an image is slipped between two thin boards. A "window" is cut in the top board so that the art may be viewed. The art is well protected. This is the traditional way to present portfolio work if you don't want to use page sleeves in a binder.

Megabyte: A unit of measure equal to 1 million (1,048,576) bytes. Generally refers to the amount of memory a computer or a hard drive has available.

Mentor: A person who offers counsel within your profession or organization. Some companies have formal mentoring systems, but most mentoring relationships are informal.

Metaphor: A symbol. An object, activity, or idea treated as a metaphor, such as a small picture of a house to represent the home page of a digital interface.

Meta tag: Special words that will help search engines locate a Web site. These tags are embedded in Web page coding.

Modern type: More contemporary style of typography in which the letters contain fine hairlines and the axis is vertical. Examples of Modern type include Didone and Bodoni.

Monochromatic: Colors made from tints and shades of the same hue.

MPEG: Moving Pictures Experts Group. Group of industry professionals involved in developing a standardized video compression system.

Multimedia authoring program: A software program that has been designed to help in the creation of digital interactive files. Director and Flash are examples of multimedia authoring programs.

MySpace: A social-networking Web site. The site features a group area to share common files, instant messaging, a video-sharing space, the ability to use the site while on a mobile phone, and a classified ads section. It is estimated that more than 200 million people are currently registered at the site.

Navigation bar: A list of options from which users can choose in order to move through the pages of a digital portfolio or Web site. A navigation bar is usually organized by topics, allowing users to jump to major areas of interest.

Negative space: The white space around type or an image. When a page contains a great deal of type, negative space creates a resting area for the eye.

Newsgroups: Areas on the Net where you can get in touch with people who share the same interests or find out about a particular subject.

Nondirective (or unstructured) interview: Interview that consists of probing open-ended questions to encourage the job candidate to do most of the talking.

Normalize: In the context of audio, to equalize sound files. Most audio editors have a "normalize" command, which prevents audio throughout from being too loud or too soft in certain areas by creating a steady, stable signal.

Occupational Outlook Handbook: Guide created to assist individuals in making decisions about their careers. It provides job descriptions and lists the training and education needed, earnings, and expected job prospects for a wide range of occupations. This guide is published by the U.S. Department of Labor, Bureau of Labor Statistics, and can be accessed at the following Web site: www.bls.gov/oco.

Openware: A type of software that features completely open code that can be modified as needed. One example would be osCommerce.

Optimize: To reduce the size of a file to allow for faster loading. Graphics files are typically optimized through a number of different techniques, such as reducing physical dimensions and dpi and fine-tuning color information.

Path: The direction to a file on a computer. For example, MyHardDrive>MyNewWebsite>picture.jpg means that the file picture.jpg can be reached via the path MyHardDrive>MyNewWebsite.

Point-of-purchase displays: Three-dimensional displays seen in public locations such as supermarkets. They generally feature seasonal products such as candy for Halloween or Easter.

Portfolio: A collection of materials that provides a way to visually show your qualifications. It includes your résumé, artwork, certifications, and any additional materials that document or demonstrate your expertise.

Portfolio case: The binder, case, or folder used to hold images and other items of information.

Primary color: A pure hue that cannot be reproduced by mixing other colors. The primary colors are red, yellow, and blue.

Print shops: Also known as prepress houses (such as Kinko's), these stores offer a variety of printing services. Print shops also often provide computer rental and design services.

Pull quote: A phrase, sentence, or paragraph typically taken from text that serves to generate interest and draw attention to a specific piece of information. It is often used to emphasize a significant statistic or remark from the text.

Raster-based graphics: Also known as bitmapped graphics, raster-based graphics are images created pixel by pixel within a grid of pixels or points of light. Raster images have a fixed resolution that is defined as the dpi (dots per inch).

Recruiters: Professionals (also known as "headhunters" or "executive search firms") whose job it is to identify and prequalify candidates for specific positions. They usually specialize in specific industries or geographic regions, work for corporations, and typically are paid on a commission basis for successfully placing the applicant in the job.

References: A select group of people who have agreed to praise your character and work habits to potential employers. They may be friends, coworkers, professors, or former employers and are usually selected because they will improve your chances of winning a relevant job. This list of names should be given only when requested.

Resignation: A formal letter declaring that you will be leaving your present job within a specified period of time (usually two weeks). It's very important to leave any job under the best of terms. You never know when you might need the contacts you made there.

Résumé: A short descriptive summary of your educational and work history. It lists your primary skills and strengths. A résumé can use either a chronological or a functional format. Your résumé and portfolio are your most important job-hunting tools.

RGB: The primary colors—red, green, and blue—which are used on most computer monitors to display images.

Salary: Typically, a fixed and agreed-on amount of compensation paid to an employee over a specified period of time, usually annually. Salary may also include additional monies in the form of overtime, bonuses, and other benefits.

Salary history: Documentation of the compensation you have received at each of your previous jobs. This information is never revealed to a prospective employer unless absolutely necessary. If you admit to making too little, you may not be offered what you are currently worth. If you made too much, the new company may not feel that it can afford you. This issue is best skirted, if possible.

Salary negotiation: The process of discussing salary in order to arrive at a satisfactory result for both the employer and the employee. The goal is to obtain the best possible salary for your skills and years of experience. However, salary is often based to some degree on industry standards, which can vary from region to region.

Sans serif type: Type that does not use serifs. Examples include Helvetica, Avant Garde, Arial, and Geneva. According to most studies, sans serif fonts are more difficult to read. For this reason, they are used most often for short text components such as headlines, captions, or pull quotes.

Saturation: The amount of purity in a color, also called chroma. Saturation is usually coupled with hue and intensity to describe the physical sensitivity of a color.

Screen resolution: The width and height of pixels on a computer screen. Typical values are 1024 × 768, 800 × 600, or 640 × 480.

Scrim: Fabric that serves as a background. It looks opaque when lit from the front but is actually semi-transparent when lit from behind.

Secondary color: A color produced by mixing two of the primary colors from the color wheel. Red and yellow make orange. Blue and yellow make green. Blue and red make violet.

Secure Sockets Layer (SSL): A protocol developed by Netscape for transmitting private documents via the Internet. SSL employs a cryptographic system that uses two keys to encrypt data—a public key known to everyone and a private or secret key known only to the recipient of the message.

Serif type: Typefaces whose letters have short lines that stem from and at an angle to the upper and lower ends of the strokes of the letters. Examples include Times, Baskerville, and Palatino.

Shareware: A type of copyrighted software usually made available at no initial cost by the author/programmer, who then expects a small fee for continued use of the product.

Sketchbook: A collection of doodles, quick ideas, and drawings that show how an artist thinks and processes concepts and ideas. Also known as a rough book or concept journal.

Split complementary: A color system that combines a color with the colors on either side of its complement. Red and green are complements, so red, blue-green, and yellow-green form a split-complementary combination.

Spray mount: A type of glue that comes in a spray bottle or can. A light coat can be applied to paper to help it adhere to another surface. It is generally used for flush mounting.

Stand-alone presentation: An interface that is created to be device-independent. A stand-alone presentation does not require the original program in order to run.

Storyboard (or flowchart): A diagram or visual device that shows a step-by-step progression. It can be a simple drawing that maps out the way your production will be shot and edited.

Streaming audio: Audio files that are not embedded in the final production but are referenced via programming scripts.

Subhead: A line of type subordinate to a headline, also used to break up long sections of type or to guide the reader as to content.

Tag: A command that describes an instruction that a Web browser interprets in order to display information. Example: `<font size: -1>`

Tear sheet: A page torn from a publication. Used as proof by the publisher or the advertising agency that an ad or article appeared in a specific issue; used by the artist to display printed work.

Temping: Working part-time for a specified period. Some companies use temp jobs to prequalify people for full-time employment. Occasionally, companies just need extra help on a big job or to fill in for permanent employees who are on vacation or leave. Many temp workers enjoy moving from position to position because the changing work environments offer new challenges, flexibility, and variety. Numerous agencies specialize in placing people in part-time or short-term positions.

Tertiary color: A color created by mixing one primary and one secondary color. Tertiary colors are also named for the two colors they are made from, with the primary color coming first, such as blue-green or yellow-green.

Testing: An in-house exercise designed to test your abilities and skills for a given position. Although job tests may be nerve-racking, they can be useful to the employer. They prove that you really can perform as stated on your résumé. You may, for example, be asked to create something on the spot, under timed conditions. Another form of testing is for drugs.

Text editor: A utility program to help create and modify text files. It can refer to an HTML editor or a word-processing program.

Thank-you letter: A follow-up note written to express thanks for the opportunity to interview with a prospective employer. A thank-you letter is considered a common courtesy and should always be sent after an interview. Only a small percentage of job seekers actually complete this task, and by doing so, you separate yourself positively from the crowd.

Thumbnail: A small version of an image. When the user clicks on a thumbnail included on a Web page, a full-sized version of the image appears. This saves file space and download time.

Time code: A signal that contains a chronological record of the absolute time in a recording. Most video cameras have a time-code feature, which should be turned off before beginning a shoot.

Tripod: A three-legged stand used to steady a camera or video camera.

TrueType fonts: Fonts that use a single font file for each font. TrueType fonts are fully scalable and generate bitmaps (screen versions) as the user creates text in a layout or drawing program.

Typeface: All type of a single design. In contrast, a font is an implementation of a typeface.

Typography: The style, arrangement, or appearance of typeset material. The primary function of typography is to present a page that is visually engaging and easy to read.

USB flash drive: Flash memory data storage device. A flash drive is typically small, lightweight, removable, and rewritable.

Value: The relative lightness or darkness of a color, also known as brightness.

Vector-based graphics: A system of design that uses math to describe the points or shapes that make up an image.

Videographer: A person who engages in the profession of video production.

Web host: A company responsible for keeping its clients' Web sites up and running.

Weblog, or blog: A Web page made up of usually short, frequently updated posts that are arranged chronologically—like a what's-new page or a journal.

Web-safe colors: The set of 216 colors common to most browsers. When used, Web-safe colors offer reliable results on different platforms and with different browsers.

Wipe: The transition from one video shot to another. One shot appears to "push" the other shot off the page. Wipes can appear from the left, right, top, or bottom of the screen.

World Wide Web Consortium (W3C): A group of people and companies that work together to define the commerce, communication, and language standards for the Internet.

WYSIWYG (what you see is what you get): A type of visual editor that writes code in the background while you drag in the elements that make up a Web page.

x-height: The height of a lowercase character, minus any ascenders or descenders. The designation derives from the height of the letter x.

home

bibliography

Baron, Cynthia L. *Designing a Digital Portfolio.*
  California: Peachpit Press, 2003.

Berryman, Gregg. *Designing Creative Portfolios.*
  California: Crisp Publications, Inc., 1994.

Hungerland, Buff. *Marketing Your Creative Portfolio.*
  New Jersey: Prentice Hall, 2003.

Linton, Harold. *Portfolio Design, 3rd Edition.*
  New York: W.W. Norton & Company, 2004.

Marquand, Ed. *How to Prepare Your Portfolio,
  3rd Edition.*
  New York: Art Direction Book Company, 1995.

McKenna, Anne T. *Digital Portfolio: 26 Design
  Portfolios Unzipped.*
  Massachusetts: Rockport Publishers, 2000.

Metzdorf, Martha. *The Ultimate Portfolio.*
  Ohio: North Light Books, 1991.

Romaniello, Stephen. *The Perfect Digital Portfolio.*
  New York: Sterling Publishing Company, 2003.

Scher, Paula. *The Graphic Design Portfolio.*
  New York: Watson-Guptill Publications, 1992.

Supon Design Group. *The Right Portfolio for the
  Right Job.*
  New York: Madison Square Press, 1999.

Tain, Linda. *Portfolio Presentation for Fashion Designers.*
  New York: Fairchild Publications, 1998.

Williams, Anna Graf. *Creating Your Career Portfolio,
  3rd Edition.*
  New Jersey: Prentice Hall, 2004.

appendix: internet resources

Creative Pro. 2008. Where Creatives Go to Know. Available from World Wide Web: (http://www.creativepro.com/article/typetalk-a-new-column-creativeprocom)

Drost, Herman. 2002. How to Prepare Images for Your Web Site—Part 2. Available from World Wide Web: (http://www.isitebuild.com/imageoptimization2.htm)

EzineArticles. 2008. 40 Ways to Drive Visitors to Your Web Site. Available from World Wide Web: (http://ezinearticles.com/?40-Ways-to-Drive-Visitors-to-your-Web-Site-and-Keep-Them-Coming-Back!&id=450327)

Holzschlag, Molly. 2000. Color My World. Available from World Wide Web: (http://www.molly.com/articles/webdesign/2000-09-colormyworld.php)

ICANN. 2004. Building a Website. Available from World Wide Web: (http://www.icann.org/new.html)

Jaques, Clare. Interview Stuff. 2008. Available from World Wide Web: (http://www.interviewstuff.com/)

Johansson, Donald. 2007. Colors on the Web. Available from World Wide Web: (http://www.colorsontheweb.com/)

Kimball, Trevor. 2003. My Design Studio. Available from World Wide Web: (http://www.mydesignprimer.com/index.html)

Lerner, Michael. 2004. Building a Website. Available from World Wide Web: (http://www.learnthenet.com/english/html/51server.htm)

Litt, Judy. 2004. Graphic Design. Available from World Wide Web: (http://graphicdesign.about.com/)

Lynch and Horton. 2002. Web Style Guide, 2nd Edition. Available from World Wide Web: (http://www.webstyleguide.com/)

Monster Interview Center. 2004. Available from World Wide Web: (http://interview.monster.com/archives/attheinterview/)

Morton, J. L. 2008. Color Matters. Available from World Wide Web: (http://www.colormatters.com/colortheory.html)

Psychology of Color. 2004. Available from World Wide Web: (http://www.tamingthebeast.net/articles/colour.htm)

Refsnes Data. 2004. W3 Schools. Available from World Wide Web: (http://www.w3schools.com/)

Rutter, Richard. 2004. The Elements of Typographic Style Applied to the Web. Available from World Wide Web: (http://webtypography.net/)

So You Wanna Design Your Own Web Page? 2000. Available from World Wide Web: (http://www.soyouwanna.com/site/syws/designpage/designpage.html)

Timberlake, Sean. 2008. The Basics of Navigation. Available from World Wide Web: (http://www.efuse.com/Design/navigation.html)

index